The economy of Sri Lankan beach seine fishermen appears wildly irrational. Although twenty beach seines, each costing a household's annual income, would be sufficient for continuous fishing, members of the community own 108 nets and the average net is launched only seven times each year. Because of seasonal fish movements, some nets make tremendous profits, but more than half do not recover their operating costs. Dr Alexander demonstrates that these inequalities are the product of the impact of capitalist relations of production on a semi-subsistence economy. In the period up to 1940, when most of the catch was consumed in the immediate area, sophisticated tenure provisions which incorporated a system of share-ownership and rules of access to the water, were an equitable and efficient framework for the management of the resource. But as the village became linked to the national economy, beach seines became an object of capital accumulation. During the past two decades economic and political entrepreneurs have gained control of the shares, impoverishing the fishermen and creating violent factional conflicts.

In the course of his meticulous analysis of both fieldwork and historical data, Dr Alexander discusses many theoretical issues of current concern. His accounts of the nature of common property resources; of the conflict between individual and community goals; and, particularly the relationship between the development of capitalism and the rise of factional conflict, are especially interesting. In addition to anthropologists interested in Sri Lanka, maritime societies and political economy, the work should be of considerable interest to fisheries economists and development experts.

Paul Alexander, who teaches anthropology at the University of Sydney, has had extensive field experience in both Sri Lanka and Indonesia and has published numerous articles on political and economic topics.

VANESSA

Australian National University Monographs on South Asia

No 1
The Congress in Tamilnad
Nationalist politics in South India 1919-1937

David Arnold
ISBN 0 908070 00 4

No 2
Political change in an Indian State
Mysore 1917-1955

James Manor
ISBN 0 908070 01 2

No 3
Businessmen and Politics
Rising nationalism and a modernising economy in Bombay, 1918-1933

A D D Gordon
ISBN 0 908070 02 0

No 4
From Sangha to Laity
Nationalist movements of Burma, 1920-1940

U Maung Maung
ISBN 0 908070 03 9

No 5
Unions in conflict
A comparative study of four South Indian textile centres, 1918-1939

Eamon Murphy
ISBN 0 908070 05 5

No 6
Workers and Unions in Bombay, 1918-1929
A study of organisation in the cotton mills

Richard Newman
ISBN 0 908070 04 7

No 7
Sri Lankan Fishermen
Rural capitalism and peasant society

Paul Alexander
ISBN 0 908070 06 3

No 8
Women in India and Nepal
Michael Allen & S N Mukherjee (eds.)

ISBN 0 908070 07 1

No 9
Peasant Movements in Colonial India
North Bihar 1917-1942

Stephen Henningham
ISBN 0 908070 08 X

No 10
The Making of a Colonial Mind
A quantitative study of the bhadralok in Calcutta, 1857-1885

John McGuire
ISBN 0 908070 09 8

Sri Lankan Fishermen

Rural Capitalism and Peasant Society

Australian National University
Monographs on South Asia No. 7

Sri Lankan Fishermen

Rural Capitalism and Peasant Society

Paul Alexander

ANU

First Published in Australia 1982
Printed in Canberra by ANU Printing for the South Asian History Section of The Australian National University, Canberra

National Library of Australia
Cataloguing-in-Publication entry

Alexander, Paul
Sri Lankan Fishermen.

(Australian National University Monographs on South Asia; No. 7)
Includes index
Bibliography
ISBN 0 908070 06 3
1. Village communities — Sri Lanka. 2. Fishing villages — Sri Lanka.
3. Sri Lanka — Social conditions. I Title. (Series)

307.7'2'095493

PREFACE

This study is based on field research in Sri Lanka between February 1970 and August 1971 which was supported by a Research Scholarship from the Australian National University. Gananath Obeyesekere gave me considerable assistance in Sri Lanka and my dissertation benefited greatly from conversations with Scarlett Epstein, Raymond Firth, Derek Freeman and, especially, Don Tuzin and my supervisor Gehan Wijeyewardene. Although based on the dissertation, this study has been extensively rewritten and I would like to thank Michael Allen, Sharon Bell, Jim Fox, Alfred Gell, Peter Hinton and Michael Roberts for their comments and advice.

I received help and encouragement from many individuals and institutions in Sri Lanka. Officers of the Ceylon Fisheries Corporation; the Sri Lanka Fisheries Department, and Lands and Survey Department; and the Ministry of Planning and Employment provided me with important information, as did the Librarians at the Colombo Museum and the University of Sri Lanka (Peradeniya). The Tangalla District Revenue Officer, District Lands Officer, and District Judge made records available for copying. Roy Mutuwady was a very competent research assistant, while the hospitality of our friends Verna and Vohara de Silva and Devaka and Sunitha Rodrigo made us eagerly await our occasional trips to Colombo.

Although I do not share the view that social anthropology is inherently exploitative, memories of the beauty of Gahavälla and the generosity of the people who live there remind me that anthropologists inevitably receive more than they can reciprocate. During my stay Gahavälla was split by factional competition but this did not carry over to relationships with my family. People were often bored with my questions, but there was very little hostility. If nothing else, living in Gahavälla and the friendship of the three men I have named David Mahattea, Sunil Mudalali and Danny Wijenaike, taught me the difference between analytical and moral judgements.

Jenny and Lanei shared the fieldwork and helped me write the book.

PAUL ALEXANDER

Sydney
July, 1980

CONTENTS

MAPS

LIST OF TABLES

APPENDICES

FIGURES

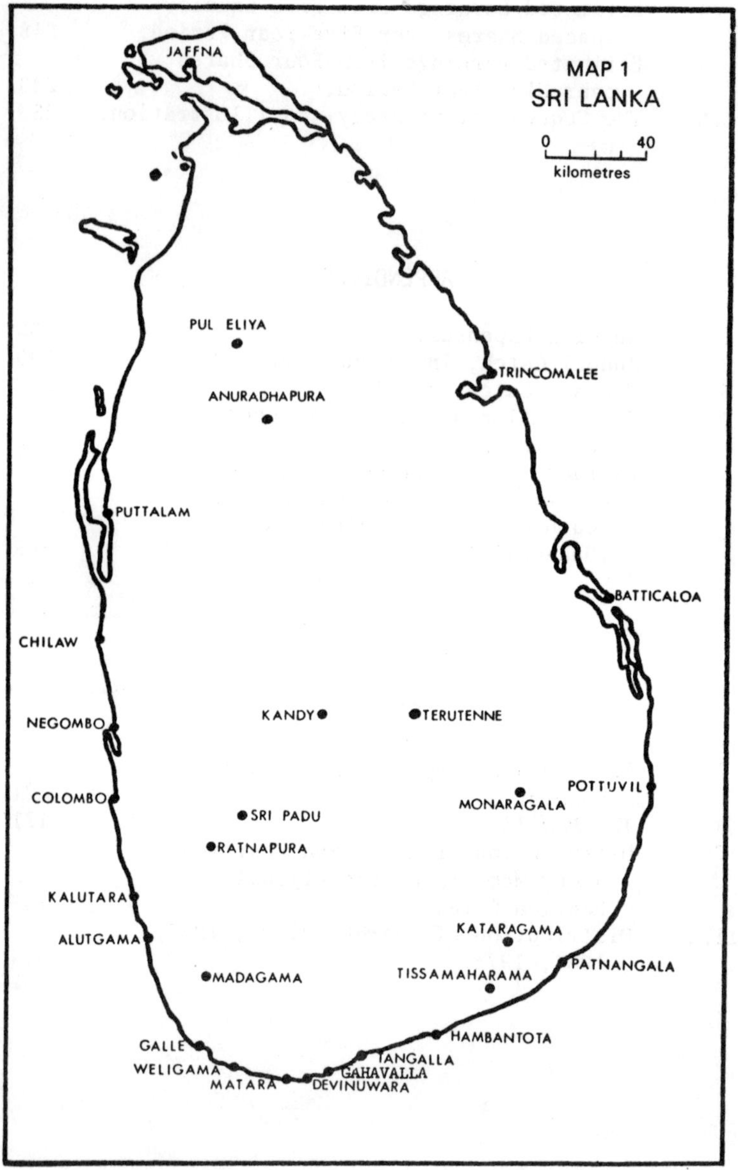
MAP 1
SRI LANKA
0
40
kilometres
JAFFNA
PUL ELIYA
ANURADHAPURA
TRINCOMALEE
PUTTALAM
BATTICALOA
CHILAW
NEGOMBO
KANDY
TERUTENNE
COLOMBO
POTTUVIL
MONARAGALA
SRI PADU
RATNAPURA
KALUTARA
ALUTGAMA
KATARAGAMA
PATNANGALA
MADAGAMA
TISSAMAHARAMA
HAMBANTOTA
GALLE
TANGALLA
WELIGAMA
GAHAVALLA
MATARA
DEVINUWARA

CHAPTER 1

INTRODUCTION

During the past decade most accounts of peasant societies have centred analyses of rural economies on changes in the forces of production. This was probably an inevitable reaction to the mentalistic explanations in terms of peasant irrationalism or conservatism which characterised the preceding period – as well as to the burgeoning growth of international development agencies – but it has severely distorted our understanding of social change. While the introduction of new strains of rice, chemical fertilisers or mechanised fishing craft often does have a considerable impact on peasant societies, to see the subsequent changes as inevitable consequences of the technology is misplaced materialism. Moreover, the single-minded concentration on such highly visible innovations has obscured other, more significant, reasons for the transformation of Asian social structures. Among the most important of these is the emergence of new or modified social institutions which have subordinated localised rural production to the interests of regional, national or international markets. In most cases technological innovations should be regarded as by-products of the new social relationships which have made it possible for extra-village agencies to determine the logic of village production. My fieldsite, 'Gahavälla', is by no means a 'typical Sinhalese village' – it is unusual even among Sinhalese fishing villages – but the development of capitalist relations of production in Gahavälla is a graphic, at times almost grotesque, illustration of a social process occurring throughout Sri Lanka.

Despite an increasing emphasis on over-elaborated methodologies, serendipity retains a critical role in social anthropological fieldwork. I went to Gahavälla to research some of the topics raised in Yalman's fascinating book *Under the Bo Tree*. As the weeks passed, however, I became fascinated by Gahavälla's 'irrational' economy.

Most Gahavälla fishermen are beachseiners using nets half a mile long which take a tonne of fish in a good catch. Beachseines are very expensive by village standards. The average net must be completely renewed within a five year period and costs about three times the average household's annual income, although a system of share-ownership distributes the expenses among several households. There is sufficient space on Gahavälla beach for two nets to be used simultaneously and making a generous estimate of the time required to set, haul and dry the nets, twenty beachseines would permit fishing around the clock.

Yet there are 108 beachseines operating on Gahavälla beach and in 1971 the average net was used only seven times! The excess nets – at least five times the number required to take the maximum catch – have disastrous consequences for the village economy. In addition to tying up scarce finance, they halve the profits from beachseining, cut a fifth from the average household's annual income, produce gross maldistributions of the catch, and destroy any relationship between fishing effort and revenue.

Any temptation to explain this situation in terms of peasant values – as due to a lack of economic understanding perhaps, or to a desire to spread employment as widely as possible – would be quickly dispelled by a conversation with the fishermen. Gahavälla fishermen are acutely aware of the consequences of the excess nets, but they feel powerless to reduce the number. They describe themselves as caught on the horns of a dilemma: although the excess nets are strangling them, a reduction would only speed up the process. The ethnographic challenge posed by Gahavälla is not to describe the economic and social organisation of fishing; nor to reconstruct the historical process which produced the contemporary society: both of these tasks are relatively straightforward. The challenge is to convey at least some understanding of why the inhabitants of Gahavälla feel that there is no solution to their predicament.

My attempt to meet this challenge falls into three natural sections. The first, chapters 2 to 5, is a brief ethnography of contemporary Gahavälla. In addition to providing the necessary background for the arguments advanced later, the ethnography may be of some interest in itself for it differs in three significant respects from other monographs on Sri Lankan social structure (Leach 1961; Yalman 1967; Obeyesekere 1967; Robinson 1975). It is concerned with the Karāva caste rather than the Goigama caste; it is set in the low country, where most of the Sinhalese live, rather than the former Kandyan kingdom; and it is orientated towards politics and economics rather than kinship and land tenure. Kinship does not loom large in Gahavälla social structure, which, in contrast to the Kandyan villages, has a strong degree of 'individuation' (Stirrat 1975, 1977). Households are autonomous production and consumption units and the domain of kinship sentiment is a very narrow circle of close kinsmen. Prescriptive/preferential marriage, endogamous micro-castes, and other aspects of Dravidian kinship systems which have come to be regarded as key features of Sri Lankan social structure (Yalman 1967), are not found in Gahavälla. It is possible that kin relationships between households were more significant in the subsistence agricultural and fishing economy of Gahavälla half a century ago, but as the village became increasingly dependent upon fishing the conduct of economic affairs was increasingly determined by market logic. Accompanying the closer links between village and national economies was a tighter integration of village and regional politics. In this context, relatively stable factions serving both political and economic functions became the major form of supra-household social organisation. Three factions have dominated Gahavälla political life for more than a decade and there is a close inter-relationship between factional struggles and the development of capitalist relations of production.

Beachseining has provided the bulk of Gahavälla's cash income for more than a century and during this period there have been only minor changes in the construction of nets and fishing techniques. But although the forces of production were unchanged, the village economy was not static, and the relations of production were radically transformed. The second section, chapters 6 to 8, begins the analysis of these changes by examining the production and marketing of fish in the modern beachseine economy. Chapter 8 is concerned with marketing, particularly with the economic and political circumstances which have allowed one or two fish traders to establish a monopsony in each village. Chapters 6 and 7 describe the organisation of labour and capital for production and trace the economic consequences of this mode of organisation. Some of these consequences are functions of the ecology: compared to agriculturalists fishing communities always have less control over their income, the time of the year when it is received and its distribution among community members. The most deleterious social consequences in Gahavälla, however, follow directly from the structure of the social institutions which govern the allocation of labour and capital. The procedures which regulate such aspects of beachseining as the ownership of nets, access to the fishery and nominal division of revenue between owner and labourer, evolved in a semi-subsistence economy. In their original context, these procedures, which are based on a moral notion of equal opportunity, were an equitable and efficient means of managing the fishery; but in the contemporary economy dominated by market logic they are both inefficient and inequitable. Any social institution is only in part a reflection of traditional rights and obligations; it is also an adaptation to environmental factors, including available resources, economic opportunities, and individual and social aspirations. It is not surprising that the functions of institutions change when the balance between resources, aspirations and opportunities alters.

Around 1850 Gahavälla was a small self-sufficient settlement of farmers and part-time fishermen. Today fishing provides the sole livelihood of almost all villagers and although many men still fish with their own gear, labour has become a commodity and capitalist control of the means of production seems inevitable. The final chapters attempt to reconstruct the economic history of Gahavälla using a variety of sources to trace the development of capitalist relations of production from their beginning in the cottage industries and petty trading at the turn of the century. The social structure of the modern village is the end product of a complex interaction between extra- and intra-village developments: between factors such as colonial legislation, better communications and the post-Independence development of political parties on the one hand; and population growth, changes in social stratification and the ambitions of individuals on the other. The last point is important, for although explanation in terms of general social processes is the aim of any social science, anthropology has a unique opportunity to illustrate these processes in the actions of individuals and groups. Accordingly much of chapters 9 and 10 is concerned with the social origins of the rural capitalists who emerged at several points in Gahavälla's history and with the strategies, both successful and unsuccessful, which they employed in capital accumulation. The final substantive chapter returns to the peasants. It documents the extent to which owner-operators have been displaced from beachseining in the past decade, and describes the tactics which the survivors are using in attempts - almost certainly unsuccessful - to retain the fishing gear on which their livelihood and their dignity depend.

As I mentioned earlier, Gahavälla is unusual among Sinhalese fishing villages, for although a system of share-ownership was once very widespread, most of Sri Lanka's beachseines and the sites on which they are used had become private property well before 1940. Indeed it has been suggested that the high financial costs and heavy labour requirements of beachseining promote capitalist modes of organisation and a capitalist ethos, and thus had an important role in the emergence of the Karāva as an indigenous entrepreneurial elite (Roberts n.d.) In my view this argument is misdirected. I can see nothing intrinsic to beachseining which in itself promotes capitalist ownership rather than peasant share-ownership, and the control of fish marketing would seem a more likely nursery for budding Karāva entrepreneurs. But the converse argument certainly holds. The pre-war Sri Lankan economy provided very limited avenues for profitable investments by rural Sinhalese capitalists and beachseining, with its economies of scale stemming from large catches and potentially high profits, was an obvious target. By contrast, capitalist control of the larger, but more risky, off-shore fishery took the form of marketing monopsonies and the means of production remained in the hands of peasant owner-operators until after the introduction of mechanised craft in the late 1960s.

A final introductory point: while the arguments developed below draw heavily on the emerging marxian tradition in social anthropology, there are few references to this literature and technical terms are limited to concepts such as relations of production which are, or at least should be, as central to anthropological vocabularies as social structure or descent. Both absences reflect a particular view of the utility of the marxian literature for the study of Asian peasant societies. Marx's work is a consummate blend of theoretical insights and rigorous empirical analysis but, with several obvious exceptions, this is not true of marxian studies of non-Western societies. In the Asian context, substantive accounts of rural political economies are very rare; but there is a surfeit of articles in which rigid and restricting categories – arrived at through purely abstract analysis or derived from the study of European history – have been mechanically applied to whatever information is readily available in secondary sources. The results are not illuminating, while the discussions of peasant modes of production which stem from them have already become as futile as the substantivist/formalist debate of an earlier economic anthropology. In my view the major value of the marxian problematic at this early stage is not as an encompassing explanation, and still less as a set of axioms to be manipulated like a mathematical or logical system. Its major value is as a source of significant problems for research and as a guide, both uncertain and partial, to their analysis. This is the way it has been used here and this is the reason why I have been unable to directly acknowledge some of my intellectual debts.

Fieldwork in Gahavälla

I arrived in the Tangalla region in February 1970 with introductory letters to two local doctors, and with their aid visited all the fishing villages in the region. I was looking for a village that was small enough for me to be able eventually to recognise most of the adult population, one that was linked to the main communications network, and using both modern and traditional fishing techniques. Gahavälla was the only village that satisfied all three criteria, the remaining villages were either too large or too isolated. A house was quickly made available and my family and I moved into the village in March. Gahavälla remained my field base until August 1971, although I made numerous trips to other fishing and agricultural villages in the Southern Province, visited a large number of fishing villages on a trip around the island, and spent six weeks in a migrant fishing camp in the Yala game reserve. Both Gahavälla and the names of people mentioned in the text are pseudonyms.

Until the national elections in May, most of my time was spent wandering around the village talking to whomever was available. I did not have an interpreter, but an unemployed youth who spoke a few words of English appointed himself my companion and eventually I paid him a small wage. Once the elections were over I was eager to begin 'systematic data collection' and (prompted by my slow progress in Sinhala and the residual belief from my High School education that it was impossible to learn a foreign language) attempted to hire an interpreter. Luckily, the attempts were unsuccessful: educated men would not treat the fishermen as equals, while the fishermen were wary of outsiders. Eventually I realised I would have to learn Sinhala and by January when my wife's illnesses forced her to leave, I could understand it adequately, although I had a heavy accent and had to speak very slowly for people to understand me: a situation which provoked unflattering comparisons with my five year old daughter. Later I employed a clerk who lived in Tangalla to copy official records and he visited Gahavälla on many occasions to help me with translation problems. Only after leaving Sri Lanka did I appreciate the force of Devereaux's (1967) observation that the rigid methodology implied by 'systematic data collection' is often the means of repressing the anxiety inherent in a genuinely reflexive anthropology.

Although Gahavälla is a very pleasant place to live, fieldwork poses some special problems in a fishing village. During periods of heavy fishing men are either sleeping, fishing, or repairing their nets and while participant observation is easy, sustained conversations are impossible. If fishing is poor men gather in large groups on the beach or in the tea shops and once again only general conversations are possible. Most men sleep between the midday meal and about 3.30 p.m., and the only time for private conversations is early in the morning and late in the afternoon. In the initial stages I persuaded people to visit my house in the evening, although men are reluctant to wander about at night in case they are mistaken for thieves. I had some success for a month or two, but after a man was shot and wounded and another was killed, the practice stopped.

As with fishing villages in most societies, Sri Lankan fishing villages have a reputation for violence. During my stay three local men were murdered and seventeen other assaults resulted in serious injuries, but this had little effect on my fieldwork other than making it difficult to talk to people at night. The government's reaction to the April 1971 'insurrection', however, spread a blanket of terror over the coastal villages. Immediately after the 'insurrection' the government imposed a daily twelve-hour curfew with a twenty-four-hour curfew on holidays, but these were ignored by Gahavälla villagers who had to leave their homes to urinate, fetch water and to fish. The third *Poya* holiday in April was a twenty-four-hour curfew, which as usual the villagers ignored. About three in the afternoon, two jeep-loads of army reservists came to the village and stopped at the cross-roads near the shops. Smashing down the doors of the shops, they took all the goods such as soap, dhal and rice that could be carried away, and destroyed the vegetables; jumping on the bunches of bananas and throwing the rest onto the road. Two youths caught near the shops were severely assaulted. The following morning two men from a neighbouring village were arrested and shot at the bus station in Tangalla, and their bodies were left lying in the dust for most of the day.

Several village youths who were believed to be associated with the proscribed *Janata Vimukti Peramuna* (People's Liberation Front) went into hiding. One went to Tissamaharama and after some soldiers severely assaulted his uncle, a very respected *mudalali* from Gahavälla, he surrendered and was shot by the army. By this time the inhabitants of the fishing communities were very frightened. Even in 'normal' circumstances relations between the villagers and the police are poor, and people felt that the police would take advantage of the situation to settle a few unsolved crimes; an impression that gained strength after the authorities shot two well-known thugs in Tangalla. Many village youths had had some contact with the JVP, if only in attending their rallies, and this would bring arrest if the army was informed. Rival factions prepared numerous petitions to the police and the army, and many Gahavälla houses were searched, but no youths were arrested and none took advantage of the 'amnesty' to surrender. The adjoining village, whose inhabitants were particularly unpopular with the police, was subjected to several full-scale searches by truckloads of armed police and army reserves.

In these circumstances it was impossible to continue with the systematic collection of household information. The laws provided for groups of more than five to be shot on sight, and people were frightened to allow outsiders into their homes in case they should later turn out to be members of the JVP. During the final three months I was content to complete the schedules for a full year's fishing and to observe political events in Tangalla and the surrounding area.

Sources

While most of my information is based on the usual anthropological methods of participant observation, interviews and casual conversations, considerable amounts of systematic data were collected. Soon after arrival I mapped the entire village and established ownership of land. I then visited each household, collecting genealogies and basic demographic information. For both these tasks the official limits of the village were used as the boundary of the study unit. A complete census of all boats and nets was next, using the physical object as the starting point and establishing ownership. This showed that much of the gear was owned by people who lived outside the initial study unit, and the genealogical and census data was therefore extended to encompass the most important of these additional households.

Production figures for fishing were systematically recorded from May 1970. In regard to inshore fishing I recorded all catches for seven craft, initially meeting the crew once a day and later once a week. This was not a random sample: the crews who seemed most likely to co-operate were approached and none refused. Initially all *madella* catches were recorded as they were landed, but once I understood the system, I obtained the information from the 'secretary' of each net and cross-checked it with my own observations. The owners of all privately-owned mechanised craft passed on their accounts from the fish traders as did the Gahavälla Fisheries Co-operative. I also copied records of mechanised boat catches being kept by the Department of Fisheries and the Ceylon Fisheries Corporation.

The most important Gahavälla fish trader made his rather scanty records available and I accompanied him on several occasions from the time he bought the fish on the beach to the time it was sold in the market. The man who was regarded as the most successful bicycle trader kept a diary for six months at my request. My assistant obtained daily prices in the Tangalla fish market from January to June 1971, but as the selling units were not standardised little use had been made of these.

In December three other sets of systematic data were collected. Every shop in the village was visited, and with one exception, gave full data on capital invested, stock, turnover, etc. Similar data was taken from the co-operatives, and some examples of daily sales were recorded. Unfortunately no profit and loss or monthly trading accounts for individual village co-operatives are available because the co-operatives operate on a district basis. A checklist of household spending was compiled and this was completed by twenty-five households on three occasions, two months apart. This was not a random sample, but included representatives from all economic levels in the village.

Towards the end a further schedule was designed to record major items of property, income, savings and credit, as well as systematic sociological data on the costs and frequencies of ceremonies, children's education, frequency of contacts with various categories of relatives, etc., which could be used to cross-check my impressions of these matters. It was intended to include all Gahavälla households as well as several extra-village households, and when the aftermath of the insurrection made further interviews impossible, 159 households had been visited, 75 per cent of Gahavälla's population. I also have information on eighteen households outside Gahavälla but these are not included in the tables.

Extensive use has been made of government records of which three sets are particularly important. With the permission of the District Land Officer, my assistant copied the records of all land transactions since 1869 which totalled 2,617. Each record includes details of the buyer, seller, mortgagor, and the amount received, and some include other information, such as the occupations of the buyers, which is useful in reconstructing the early history. Marriage and birth records between 1869 and 1915 totalling 737 provided similar information. The District Revenue Officer made available the complete shareholders' lists for the beachseines between 1964 and 1971 and a list of all changes in ownership over the period. The permission of the District Judge allowed me to obtain full details of the nineteen partition cases, beginning in 1880, which included numerous genealogies, the plaintiffs' and defendants' plaints, the judgement, and occasionally, records of evidence. Although the evidence presented in these cases is often internally inconsistent, it provided valuable hints which could be followed up by questioning informants. The District Judge also provided access to criminal court records, but with a few notable exceptions, these amounted to little other than the charge, the list of witnesses, and the decision.

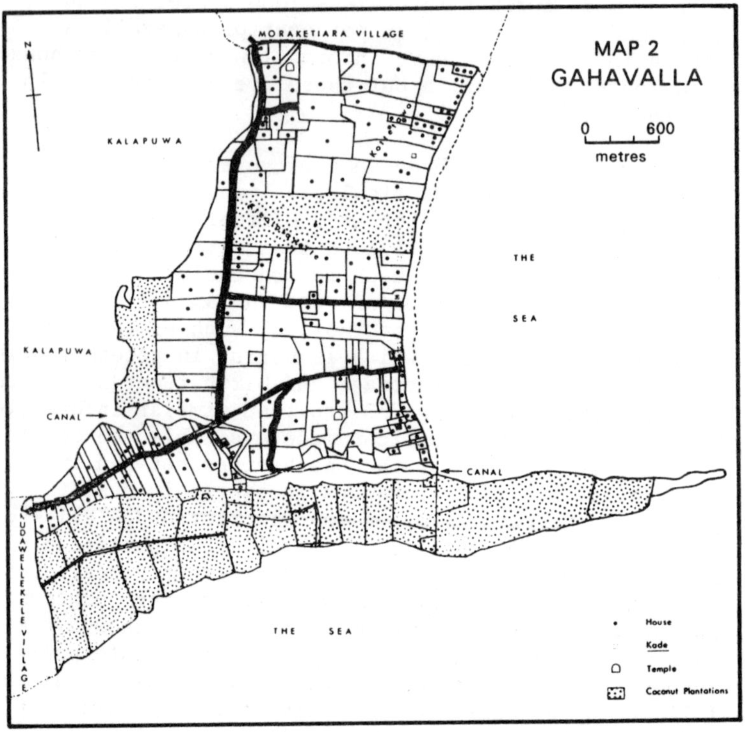
MAP 2
GAHAVALLA
0
600
metres
MORAKETIARA VILLAGE
N
KALAPUWA
KALAPUWA
CANAL
CANAL
THE SEA
THE SEA
House
Kade
Temple
Coconut Plantations

CHAPTER 2

GAHAVÄLLA VILLAGE

Looking down on Gahavälla from the crest of the headland, gives the impression of a deserted tropical beach. Trees hide the houses and all that can be seen is an expanse of multi-shaded green vegetation fringed by the white, shimmering beach. When walking through the village the impression remains. The houses are set well back from the road, shielded by trees, and only in the very heavily populated areas are found the groups of houses huddled in close proximity, which are characteristic of fishing villages further west.

Most household compounds[1] are fenced with coconut fronds tied with coir or with barbed wire, but the larger houses have masonry walls complete with massive ornate masonry gate pillars and, occasionally, wrought iron gates. A few compounds contain more than one house, but normally a man building a new house on occupied land fences off a section. The exceptions are the densely populated areas to the east, in the hamlet named Kottetawa, where groups of five or six wattle and daub houses have been built almost touching each other. These are 'squatter' settlements and the occupants have no legal rights to the land they occupy.

Prior to 1940, all Gahavälla's inhabitants lived in wattle and daub or masonry houses. Even where the masonry houses have collapsed, the foundations are still apparent and it can be inferred that more than three-quarters of the houses prior to 1940 were wattle and daub. These are simple to build and are usually the work of the owner and his friends. Gaps in a timber framework are filled with woven coconut fronds and plastered with mud both inside and out to make a wall about eight inches thick. The thatched roof is supported by a single main beam. This produces a weatherproof house which appears to last for more than twenty years, although the thatch has to be renewed every two or three years. Most houses are single-roomed, with a 'lean-to' for cooking, and the cost of materials in 1970 was less than Rs.200.

The masonry houses were built between 1896 and 1940 and 14 per cent of currently occupied houses are of this type. The walls have a filling of coral, rocks and unfired bricks, covered with a half-inch layer of lime plaster. The floors were originally of similar construction, but have now been replaced with concrete, and the tiled roofs are supported by heavy rafters. Many of these houses are of considerable size, up to six bedrooms, and are ornately decorated with plaster mouldings and heavily carved wooden shutters. Their cost is a minimum of six times that of a wattle and daub house and they could be constructed only by the wealthy.

The brick houses (47 per cent of total) have all been built within the past thirty years, most within the past decade. Most have one bedroom (three have more than five bedrooms) in addition to a main room and cooking is always done in a separate enclosure. These houses are built on a foundation of rubble and concrete, with brick walls plastered with cement and tiled roofs. Most are built in sections as materials become available and the 17 per cent of houses with brick walls and thatched roofs are results of the owners' inability to raise the money to complete them. An indication of the rate of construction is that the average brick house with a thatched roof is more than ten years old. Many of the houses with tiled roofs are also incomplete, some rooms are represented only by the walls and in others the final coating of plaster has yet to be added.

Apart from the houses there are few permanent structures. Seventeen small shops *(kade)*, mainly of wattle and daub, are scattered around the village, but most open irregularly and sell only tea, bread, betel, plantains and cigarettes.[2] The exceptions are a general store which sells most of the village requirements of non-rationed goods, the co-operative store which handles rationed items, and a barber shop.

There are two temples. A small decaying temple on the east is inhabited by an elderly recluse and few villagers worship there. The larger temple in good order near the beach, is the main temple for the village and *Pansil* is held each *poya*. The main temple was re-opened only a few weeks previous to my fieldwork, for the priest had been involved in a dispute with an important faction leader five years earlier and had been forced to leave the village. The priest's efforts to re-establish himself in Gahavälla were not very successful and as only thirty families were regularly sending food to the temple for the priest's sustenance it appeared he would have to leave once again.[3] Most Gahavälla families worship at and give alms to the large temples in nearby villages.

A small one-roomed school opposite the temple provides the only education for most of the children - eighty in the morning and slightly fewer in the evening. Because of the overcrowding, and the teachers' lack of interest, little teaching is carried out. The foundations and walls for a new school were laid seven years earlier and money allocated by the government to complete it, but a land dispute halted work and the foundations are now barely visible through the scrub. Families who can afford it send their older children to the High School at Tangalla and in 1971, thirty-seven children, about one-third of the relevant age group, were attending high school. In addition, six were at university and others were attending post-high school courses, such as the school for co-operative officers. There is no prejudice against female education and in fact girls are over-represented in the upper levels of the education system.[4]

The Beach and the Sea

Gahavälla beach is more than a mile long, but only the section south of the Sinimodera river mouth is used for fishing. Because the northern portion is not sheltered from the surf, the sand is soft and unsuitable for beaching an *orua,* while the submerged rocks close to the northern shore restrict the area where nets can be used. The southern section of the beach, the *varaya* (harbour) is the main working area for the fishermen. The centre section is used to beach the *madella oru* and to store the nets. On either side of the *madella oru*, the 'bible' *oru* are drawn up; those belonging to the Sinimodera, Moraketiara and Kottetawa men on the north, and Gahavälla's to the south. Each group of bible *oru* fish at the mouth of the bay nearest their beaching areas, which means that Gahavälla fishermen have to row only two to three miles each night, compared to four to five miles for the others. Similarly, the mechanised craft owned by the Kottetawa people are usually anchored in the northern, rather than the more sheltered southern, anchorage, although all boats journey to the fishing grounds together to reduce the risk from engine failures.

In addition to the two main fishing areas, for *madella* and 'bible' fishing respectively, marked on Map 3, there are several other ecological niches. The estuary of the Sinimodera River provides mud crabs and river fish such as grey mullet. The rocks along the headland are line fishing sites for rock-fish and crayfish, and provide shell-fish for bait. Handlining from small *oru* is often carried out near the submerged rocks, which although they tear nets, shelter a wide variety of fish.

At the rear of the village is a large lagoon, the *Gahavälli Kalapuwa*, draining through a small channel into the harbour. The tide occasionally flows up the channel, making the water brackish, and while the lagoon swarms with fish, they are too small to eat. Only a few of the very poor families fish in the lagoon, because less than a quarter of the houses have latrines and the banks of the lagoon are a common place for defecation. Pits, dug into the banks of the lagoon, are used to rot coconut husks prior to beating them into coir fibre and these give off a continual nauseating smell.

Climate and Landuse

The Sri Lankan Fisheries Department divides the Sri Lanka coastline into four administrative divisions with the Southern Division covering the coastline from Alutgama in the west to Patnangala in the east. The region west of Tangalla is in the 'wet' climatic zone and subject to the south-west monsoon. Settlement is very heavy, population densities exceed 6,000 per square mile

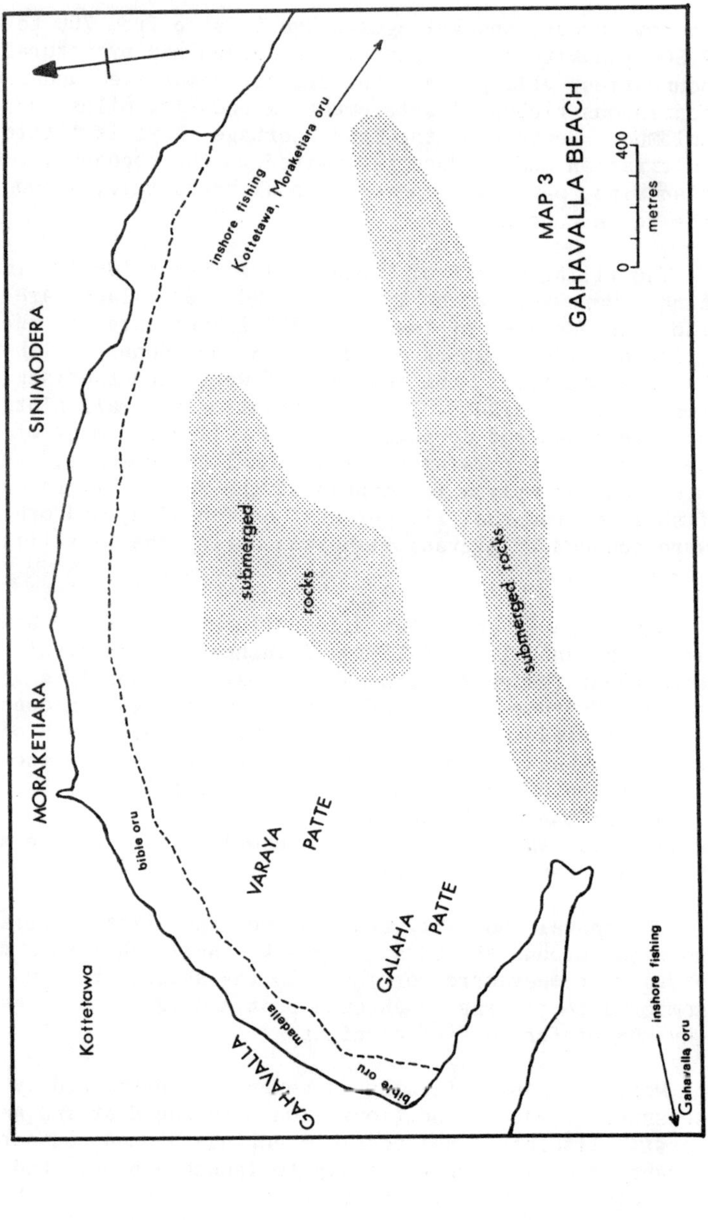
MAP 3
GAHAVALLA BEACH
0
400
metres
SINIMODERA
MORAKETIARA
Kottetawa
GAHAVALLA
bible oru
madella
bible oru
VARAYA PATTE
GALAHA PATTE
submerged rocks
submerged rocks
inshore fishing
Kottetawa, Moraketiara oru
inshore fishing
Gahavalla oru

in some areas, and villages range in size from 700 to 7,500 inhabitants. Except where determined by natural boundaries, villages are not clearly demarcated and a continuous ribbon of settlement extends 120 miles to Colombo. Because of the land shortage there is little cultivation and produce is limited to the coconuts, plantains, papaw and the occasional breadfruit, grown in the house compounds.

The villages east of Tangalla are in the 'dry' climatic zone. Here settlement is sparse and the villages are isolated enclaves of less than 500 inhabitants, in the midst of wide expanses of scrub and sand dunes. Although land is plentiful, the shortage of water and the lack of transport to markets limit cultivation to small plots of vegetables and cereals near the villages. Many of the settlements in this area are seasonal encampments,[5] occupied for only a few months of the year by migratory fishermen from the villages west of Tangalla, and others were founded by migrant fishermen during the last fifty years.

Gahavälla is about ten miles within the wetzone boundary. The annual rainfall is 55 inches, spread evenly throughout the year, although February is usually a dry month. Neither the south-west nor north-east monsoons are reflected in the rainfall. In the middle month of the south-west monsoon, June, the rainfall is 7.4 inches and for the north-east monsoon, the rainfall is 7.5 inches in the middle month, December. Rain falls in short heavy showers and it is unusual to get rain on more than two consecutive days.

The annual and daily temperatures show little variation, hovering around the 80 degree mark. While this is a most pleasant temperature for those in the shade, it is uncomfortable fishing in an open boat and is a major reason why men prefer to fish at night.

Most Sri Lankan fishing is severely constrained by seasonal climatic conditions. On both the East and West Coasts, fishing is not possible during the monsoon periods because the seas are too heavy to launch a boat,[6] and in villages less than five miles west of Gahavälla, fishermen traditionally left home during the south-west monsoon

(April-August) to fish from migratory camps east of Hambantota. But the villages between Gahavälla and Hambantota are not drastically affected by either monsoon, permitting fishing throughout the year.[7] In Gahavälla, the force of the south-west monsoon is further blunted by a 300 foot granite headland at the south-western mouth of the harbour and even when the seas are too heavy to fish outside the bay, fishing is possible within the harbour. For most of the year a steady off-shore breeze begins about 3 a.m. and continues until 6 a.m. The traditional sail-powered craft used this breeze to carry them to the fishing grounds near the edge of the continental shelf, returning on the on-shore breeze which begins around 11 a.m.

Gahavälla soils, like the rest of the southern coastal region, are a mixture of non-laterite loams and sandy soils and although they have a good initial fertility and drain well, the organic content is low (Joachim 1937; Wikramatilike 1963). Today the soil lacks fertility and Gahavälla gardens are limited to tree crops: coconuts, plantains, betel, papaw and a single stand of breadfruit. The south-western headland and the area between the lagoon and the road, were systematically planted with coconut forty years ago, but most coconut was planted in a haphazard manner around the houses. As most trees are more than seventy years old, and planted too close together, the crop no longer meets household requirements. Few households plant vegetables; the soils are infertile and the wandering troops of monkeys extract a heavy tribute. Fifty years ago, however, substantial crops of dry grain, especially millet *(kurakkan)*, were cultivated and provided most of the village's cereal requirements.

An agricultural pattern of tree crops and scattered patches of dry grain and vegetables is characteristic of the coastal region. Some villages have paddy fields, but these amount to only a small percentage of the total land under cultivation. Further, as many landowners now have non-agricultural occupations, there is a tendency for paddy fields to be planted in tree crops which do not require sustained and intensive cultivation. For example, in 1948 Moraketiara had seventeen acres of paddy fields, today all but three acres are planted with coconut or breadfruit.

The Sinimodera River drains into Gahavälla harbour and its muddy waters provide the main bathing facilities for people in Gahavälla and the adjoining villages. Gahavälla, like most of the coastal villages, has a serious water shortage; twenty-eight of the houses have wells, but only four provide water suitable for drinking. While some of the newer houses incorporate roof tanks for collecting rain water, the wells must provide more than three-quarters of the village's drinking water. Several additional wells sunk in the past decade, including two sunk by the Rural Development Society, have proved brackish. One of the most evocative images of the coastal villages, is young girls carrying water in eight-gallon pottery jars balanced on their heads or hips. The girls are a graceful and quite charming sight, but the effort of carrying 80 pounds of water for upwards of a mile, is considerable. Although there was no shortage of water at any time during my stay, in former years the wells have run dry and water has to be carted the three miles from the Sinimodera River. The belief that the wells in the village, although situated on private property, should be open to all, is a strong one, but disputes do occasionally lead to a family being refused access to the well nearest its home.[8]

Demography

A total of 1031 people occupying 204 dwellings live within the official boundaries of Gahavälla.[9] The average dwelling contains five persons with a range of one to twenty-three. The age and sex composition is presented in diagram 2.1. The unusual feature of the age composition is that Gahavälla's population is not as heavily concentrated in the lower age groups as in other Asian societies. The percentage of the population in both the 10-20 and 20-30 age brackets is only slightly lower than the under ten category. Although I was unable to obtain reliable data on birth and death rates, a comparison of the 1970 and 1931 population shows an average population growth of only 0.8 per cent per year over the past forty years. The dependency ratio and the replacement ratio of the 1970 population are also low.

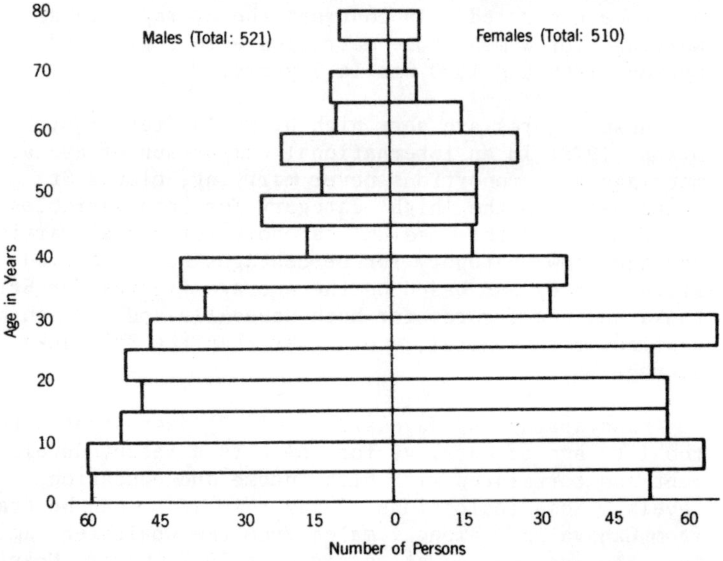

FIG. 2–1: SEX AND AGE COMPOSITION OF GAHAVÄLLA POPULATION

Abahayaratne and Jayewardene's (1967) study of fertility trends in Sri Lanka, concluded that the south-west coast region (within which Gahavälla must be included on both ethnic and socio-economic grounds) has a declining birth rate, which could be ascribed to increasingly late ages of marriage and higher percentages of permanent spinisters and bachelors, rather than increased use of birth control methods. This is in accord with the situation in Gahavälla. The only birth control methods employed regularly are abstinence and a modified form of *coitus interruptus*. But the average age at marriage for women married since 1950, is 24.3 years and for men 31.7 years, while 17 per cent of women over thirty and 13 per cent of men over forty, have never been married. In contrast the average age at marriage for women whose marriages were registered between 1869 and 1900 was 16.7 years.

These figures are very high by world standards. Dixon (1972) in an international comparison of age at marriage and proportions never marrying, places Sri Lanka males in the 'high' category for both variables and females in the 'medium' category for age at marriage and the 'low' category for percentages never married. Dixon's study was based on the average figures for Sri Lanka and the figures for both Gahavälla and the south-west coast in general, are higher than the Sri Lanka average.

Abahayaratne and Jayewardene (1967) demonstrated that the late age of marriage for women is a recent development and correlates with high income and educational levels. Some indications of why this is so can be drawn from Gahavälla. Among females from the wealthier families, the average age at marriage is 29.2 years. Nearly one-third of the women over thirty-five in these families are not married and my impression is that most of these women will never marry. The relatively wealthy rural families place considerable weight on a good education for both sons and daughters. This delays the age of marriage (the Higher School Certificate Examination is seldom passed before twenty-one), and simultaneously both absorbs a large amount of money that would otherwise go towards the dowry and raises the girl's aspirations. The father of the well-educated girl is faced with the alternative of finding a man of similar status who will take the girl without a dowry (which is difficult unless the girl is one of the very few with a job) or saving the dowry over a period of several years and thus postponing the marriage. The position of the younger daughters is particularly acute, for their father will be over sixty when they reach marriageable age. They must depend upon their brothers, or married sisters, for their dowries and other marriage expenses, at a time when their siblings are themselves struggling to establish their households. It is not surprising that most never married women are younger daughters of wealthier households.[10]

The late age of marriage and the high proportion of permanent spinsters is at variance with the community's values which emphasise marriage as the desirable goal for women. Women who do not marry wear the blouse and skirt of the adolescent rather than the cloth and jacket of the married women, appear to be lonely and unhappy and are often cruelly teased by the children. Most of the ritual healing ceremonies I witnessed had an unmarried middle-aged woman as their focus.

Occasionally, a wealthy man takes the younger sister of his wife to live with them. In some cases he has intercourse with both women, in others, only with the younger. Polygyny, or more accurately sexual access to several women, is a mark of high status among men and appears to be tolerated by the legal wife because the sister does most of the work, leaving her free for visiting and other activities. Four Gahavälla households include 'co-wives'.

Leach (1961:85-93), describing marriage in Pul Eliya, indicates that premarital chastity is rare, marriage is almost universal, is frequently not registered, occurs soon after puberty and multiple marriages are common. A similar situation is found in other Kandyan villages (Yalman 1967:xx) but not one of these points is true of Gahavälla. Premarital chastity is the expressed norm and is probably also adhered to in most cases;[11] the major exception is when a couple elopes and uses the fact of intercourse to persuade the parents to agree to the marriage. While there are substantial differences in the ceremonies associated with marriage, registration is an inevitable accompaniment and only one person in Gahavälla, a woman, has been married more than once. However, separation, often including a return of all or part of the dowry, but without the legal actions that accompany a divorce, is common. Nine married women were living apart from their husbands in 1970.

Gahavälla's population will probably increase more rapidly in the future. Although the marriage patterns have held birth rates at comparatively low levels, the main reason for the low population growth rate over the past twenty years is emigration. In the past decade, however, the possibilities of emigration have decreased. There are few opportunities to take up agriculture and it is no longer possible to establish businesses in areas, like Tissamaharama, within forty miles of home. Future emigration will require much longer journeys, to the yet to be developed agricultural colonies of the dry zone and given the government's emphasis on State Trading Corporations, opportunities to establish businesses in the new colonies will be limited.

Hamlet Composition

Many of the Sinhalese villages described in earlier monographs were 'multi-caste villages'[12] (Yalman 1967; Tambiah 1965; Robinson 1968). The relevant social unit in discussions of social structure was, for most purposes, not the village, but the hamlet occupied by a separate caste or 'caste section'. Although this pattern is general throughout Sinhalese-speaking Sri Lanka, and is particularly apparent in the region immediately behind the coastal strip, it is not true of the coastal villages themselves. Without exception, the people in these villages regard themselves as belonging to the *Karāva* caste[13] and social differentiation is based on economic and political considerations, not on caste or caste-section membership. Although the coastal villages are divided into hamlets, these have little social significance and in most cases population growth has obscured hamlet boundaries. In folk geography it is house-sites and compounds, rather than hamlets, which are used as reference points.

Having made this point, it should be noted that one Gahavälla hamlet, Kottetawa, is set apart from the rest and until recently there was no inter-marriage between members of this hamlet and other villagers. The reason for this is not difficult to discover. Traditionally fishing is a despised occupation in Sri Lanka. Not only is it contrary to Buddhist ethics concerning killing, but it provided a very poor and uncertain income for the men engaged in it. The traditional avenue of social mobility among the *Karāva* was to leave the fishing industry, either by becoming agriculturalists or traders. (see Roberts 1968; n.d.; Ryan 1956). Consequently, among the *Karāva* of the southern coast,[14] two status levels are apparent; the landlords and traders, and the fishermen.

Within the fishing community, further status distinctions are drawn. The most prestigious method of fishing is beachseining, which not only requires greater investment and gives larger profits, but the fish are taken alive and are not killed by the fishermen. The least prestigious method of fishing is inshore or lagoon fishing,[15] where the fishermen kill fish for bait and receive very small incomes. Deep-sea fishing ranks somewhere between the two.

The considerable differences in the finance required inhibited mobility between the types of fishing and in some cases this economic barrier was re-enforced by marriage prohibitions and the adoption of honorific surnames. Consequently most fishing villages are split into two status levels. In Kottegoda (see Yalman 1967: 271-81) the distinction is between the elite of deep-sea fishermen and the inshore fishermen, in Gahavälla between the beachseine fishermen of Gahavälla proper and the inshore and lagoon fishermen of Kottetawa. In the poorer villages the status distinction had few consequences and in Kudawellekele, the most heavily populated and until recently the least economically differentiated village along the coast, it is not recognised at all. But in Gahavälla, the distinction has added significance because the men engaged in beachseining originally settled in Gahavälla as agriculturalists, and because the beachseine fishermen wished to prevent others from constructing beachseines to use in the restricted fishing area (see Chapter 7).

Although some marriages between Kottetawa men and Gahavälla women have recently occurred, and because of their greater access to the mechanised craft the Kottetawa people are now among the wealthiest in Gahavälla,[16] strong social barriers still exist. Few men from Gahavälla regularly visit Kottetawa, none would drink tea in a Kottetawa boutique and only the poorest of Gahavälla families would give or accept a bride from Kottetawa.

Intervillage Relations

In local legends the inhabitants of Tangalla and the fishing villages nearby are descendants of *Karāva* fishermen from Negombo. Forced out of their home village by population pressure, a large group of *Karāva* moved southwards down the coast, resolving to settle in the first bay in which they caught more than 100 fish in a single day. Over a period of several years, they covered the entire length of the western and southern coasts until they reached Tangalla (Gahavälla in the Gahavälla version), where the requisite catch was made. At this time Tangalla was the stronghold of the *Salāgama* (cinnamon peeler) caste, who resented the *Karāva* intrusion. A major battle ensued leading to the massacre of the *Salāgama* who were buried in a mass grave which is now marked by a temple.

Today the fishing population of the southern coast is culturally homogeneous. Except for a small number of Muslims near Galle, Muslims and Malays in Hambantota and Kirinda, and a few *Salāgama* near Alutgama, all fishermen are Sinhalese Buddhists of the *Karāva* caste. The people of the fishing villages regard themselves as one caste, one blood *(eka lē)* and relatives *(näyo)*.

Conflicts between *Karāva* and *Salāgama*, and the *Goigama* (cultivators), over caste precedence were characteristic of political and economic relations in the past, especially in Colombo, but today are of little importance. Direct contacts between the fishermen and the inhabitants of the multicaste agricultural villages further inland are rare, most meetings between the *Karāva* fishermen and other castes take place in the relatively neutral setting of the small towns. *Karāva* who have left fishing have established their own agricultural settlements and there are few villages with a *Karāva* minority.[17] *Bereva* (drummer) and *Hena* (washerman) men come often to Gahavälla to conduct ceremonies, but rules of caste deference are not strongly enforced outside the ritual context, although most villagers still retain strong feelings against marriage outside the caste. Electoral boundaries throughout the area ensure a *Goigama* majority, but this has not resulted in the formation of a *Karāva* political party, and *Karāva* are well represented in all political parties. As far as I am aware, the only regular conflicts between castes occur in the Tangalla schools where both children and teachers group themselves on a caste basis.[18]

But despite assertions of *Karāva* unity, there were marked differences in the status of villages. Villages were ranked in a similar manner to the hamlets described in the preceding section.[19] Although it would be difficult to construct an ordinal ranking acceptable to all informants, it is clear that village status was socially significant in the past and remains an important constraint on some social relationships, especially marriage. The criterion for village rank is the distinction between villages with an economy based on agriculture or beach-seines,[20] and the villages with an economy based on deep-sea fishing.

Differences in the living standards of the two types of villages are readily apparent.[21] The deep-sea fishing villages have a single economic base, were settled earlier, have low per capita incomes with little intra-village economic differentiation and many of the male inhabitants are migratory fishermen for at least part of the year. Before mechanised craft, production per head was low and the fishing equipment was owned by men who lived outside the village. The poverty of the villages was reflected in their social customs: intra-village marriage without dowries, burial grounds with unmarked graves, a lack of honorific surnames, and low levels of education.

By contrast, the beachseine and agricultural villages had a more diversified economic base. A substantial proportion of the village income derived from agriculture (especially tree crops) and trading (especially dried fish and coconut products). Internal stratification was sharper and most villages were dominated by a landowning elite, but intra-village social mobility through the acquisition of land, the cessation of fishing and the adoption of honorific surnames, was also common. Moreover, the income of even the poorest households compared favourably with the average incomes of the deep-sea communities. Even in these villages most of pre-war marriages were within the village and dowries were usually very small, but inter-village marriages with large dowries had been common among the elite since the turn of the century. The well educated elite of the beachseine villages provided nearly all the recruits to government service after 1940 and before this date dominated inter-village business enterprises.

The extent to which the social status of villages affected the social relationships of their members can be illustrated by examining Gahavälla's contacts with its neighbours. The present population of Gahavälla, Moraketiara and Sinimodera, are mainly descendants of people who arrived in the area around 1860 (see Chapter 9). Most of the people in the latter two villages are now engaged in cultivation and trading, as were formerly many of Gahavälla's inhabitants, and the only fishing prior to 1930 was beachseining.[22] Since 1900 most Gahavälla marriages have been with members of the other two villages; in 82 per cent of extant Gahavälla marriages both spouses were from the three villages. The remaining marriages involved the Gahavälla elite and spouses from more distant areas, especially Tangalla and the ritual centre of Devinuwara, or marriages between Kottetawa people and adjoining deep-sea villages.

Kudawellekele, Gahavälla's other close neighbour, is a heavily populated village (6,000 inhabitants) which until the introduction of mechanised boats was the poorest in the area. Most of its inhabitants were deep-sea fishermen, for although they owned several beachseines, the harbour was too rocky for these to be used efficiently. I was unable to trace any marriages between people from

Gahavälla (excluding Kottetawa) and Kudawellekele before 1960. Informants said some marriages did take place, but the couple always lived in Kudawellekele. On the other hand, the majority of the Kottetawa marriages with people outside Gahavälla, were with Kudawellekele people. This is a function of the ambivalent position of Kottetawa, a deep-sea fishing hamlet in a superior status village. Today, with more than 300 mechanised craft, many of them obtained through illegal sales, Kudawellekele is probably the wealthiest fishing village in Sri Lanka. Marriages between Gahavälla and Kudawellekele families, although still opposed, have become more common in the past decade, but Kudawellekele's inordinate reputation for violence persists. Gahavälla people are still wary of visiting Kudawellekele by day and almost no one will go there at night.

Communications

Gahavälla is equidistant between two reasonably large towns; Dikwella, with a population of 10,000 and Tangalla with a population of about 15,000. While both have numerous small shops and a petrol station, as the District Court and the hospital are in Tangalla, most Gahavälla contacts are with this town.

Before 1940, only a cart track linked Gahavälla to the main Southern Province highway, but in that year a road was built from Moraketiara, through Gahavälla and Kudawellekele and back to the main highway. As well as widening the market area for Gahavälla's fish, the road integrated other aspects of Gahavälla life with the wider community. The Sri Lankan Transport Board runs a two-hourly service, which brings most of the goods for the stores. Disputes between bus drivers and villagers, especially over the carrying of heavy goods, are common, however, and a third of the time the bus does not run. Heavy goods, such as bricks for houses, are still carried by ox-cart. As a general rule the bus does not carry fish which is transported by van or bicycle. Ten years ago small fish traders commonly used the *pingo* (carrying pole), but by 1970 only one *pingo* carrier remained. Although the villages bordering the main road have electricity and some street lighting, these services are unlikely to be extended to Gahavälla or Kudawellekele in the next decade.

The lively interest in external affairs, as evidenced by the number of newspapers bought by the villagers (seventeen daily and forty-eight weekly), is paralleled by the large numbers of trips made by some Gahavälla people outside the village. On most trips the bus has a full load, mainly from the wealthier households. Members of the poorer families seldom leave the village. They cannot afford to attend weddings and festivals of other than their closest kin, their children go to the Gahavälla school, and when they are ill they rely on the *vedda mahataya*[23] (aruyvedic physician) rather than pay the 50 cent bus fare to obtain free medical treatment at the Tangalla Hospital. Many children from middle income households attend school at Moraketiara, walking there each day. The women make frequent trips to the hospital in Tangalla and on most days the early bus carries twenty or so, dressed in cotton sarees and accompanied by young children.

For the women among the village elite, frequent trips are one of the more important demonstrations of their status. Most days two or three of the elite, dressed in nylon sarees, visit friends and relatives or attend one of the private doctors. Many of these women are money-lenders or land owners and make frequent trips to collect money due, or to supervise the harvesting of coconuts. Their children attend schools in Tangalla and it is not unusual for women to visit Tangalla to collect them after school and to shop. The wealthier men also make frequent trips to town. Apart from strictly business trips, men pay frequent visits to their political contacts in Tangalla, wait on their MP every few months, and attend weddings, funerals and gambling parties.

Even the richest families travel mainly by bus. Hire cars are available in Tangalla, but the fares (Rs.8 from Gahavälla to Tangalla) are too expensive for regular travel and the drivers will not leave the main road after nightfall. Most of the hire cars' income comes from weddings, when the poorest family tries to get two or three cars for the main ceremony, and the richer families use cars for all trips between the bride's and groom's residences.

All families in the village endeavour to make at least one pilgrimage during the year. The most popular is a three-day trip to Kataragama and in 1970, three bus-loads made this pilgrimage, about 240 people in all. A further bus-load, most of them from Gahavälla, visited other important religious centres including Sri Padu and Anuradhapura on a week-long journey. The pilgrimages provide Gahavälla people with their knowledge of the rest of Sri Lanka; few adults have ever visited Colombo, but most have been to Sri Padu, some many times.

Local Level Politics and Administration

There can be few peasant societies where the impact of the state on village affairs approaches the situation in Sri Lanka. The 'accomplishments' of the colonial era, notably the large civil service, good communications and an economy in which half the staple food was imported, were the foundations of the expansion of centralised control in the past two decades. By Sri Lankan standards, Gahavälla is a relatively isolated village, yet every inhabitant wastes considerable time in paper chases. They must visit the District Revenue Office to obtain a rice ration book and the Police for a licence to tap toddy. Chits to buy a variety of goods ranging from cement to extra food for a daughter's wedding are issued by the Government Agent. The Fisheries Department controls the sale of fishing gear and engine parts, while a number of consumer staples including rice, condiments, textiles and kerosene are sold through state run co-operative stores. In every case the villager is confronted by a shortage of goods, long slow-moving queues, and supercilious clerks. Yet despite the centralised control of goods and services, government agencies have few direct contacts with the village.

There are two government instrumentalities concerned with fisheries: the Fisheries Department and the Sri Lankan Fisheries Corporation. The former is responsible for most aspects of fishing ranging from basic biological research to the administration of hire purchase schemes for mechanised craft, while the latter is a commercially orientated body which has little contact with the traditional fishing sector. Neither agency takes much interest in Gahavälla. Fisheries Department Inspectors visit the village occasionally, to discuss the operation of the mechanised craft owned by the Gahavälla Co-operative and to persuade owners of other mechanised craft to pay their hire purchase debts. Inshore fishing craft are supposed to be registered, but in practice registration is only completed where an owner has previously arranged a loan. Although the Sri Lankan Fisheries Corporation maintains a small fish buying shed, its purchases are limited to fish from the three mechanised craft owned by the co-operative.

Contacts with other government agencies on the village level are equally sporadic: a postman visits the village twice a week, anti-malarial teams spray the interiors of the houses with a mixture of oil and D.D.T. twice a year, and there are occasional visits from public health officials. The police are more frequent visitors. Motorised patrols travel daily along the main road and about once a month stop to investigate complaints, search houses for arms, and prevent gambling and illegal toddy tapping.

Attempts by the government to establish voluntary organisations within the village have been unsuccessful. A Rural Development Society was established in 1958 and completed several projects. The present one-room school was built with voluntary labour and government-supplied materials, two unsuccessful wells sunk, and the foundations laid for a new school. But in 1962 the President and driving spirit behind the Rural Development Society was severely assaulted during a dispute over the siting of a third well and the Rural Development Society collapsed in disarray.

A fish marketing co-operative was established in 1946 under the sponsorship of the Fish Sales Union in Colombo and succeeded in attracting forty members, most of them from Kottetawa. It was inoperative by 1948 with debts of Rs.2,500, but was revived in 1969 with the intention of obtaining mechanised craft under a government development programme. Three boats were allocated in December 1970, but six months later all were out of commission. Internal dissension over the allocation of jobs on the boats, inefficient book-keeping resulting in too much of the proceeds being distributed to shareholders, and widespread theft of co-operatively owned gear, all played their part. In 1942 a multi-purpose co-operative was established to handle the distribution of rationed goods. Few villagers bought shares, no dividends were ever paid, and nowadays the sole function of the co-operative is the distribution of rationed goods.

One of the reasons for the failure of government-sponsored rural development initiatives and for the lack of direct contacts between the village and the government, is the presence of an alternative, and from the villagers' point of view more effective, political structure. A comprehensive analysis of the interaction between village and regional politics would require a separate monograph; what follows is merely an outline of the way in which the political system rather than the administrative system has become the major conduit of goods and services from the government to the village.

Before Independence, administration within the coastal villages revolved around two posts, the Village Headman and the *Patabändi Arrachi*. The Village Headman *(Vidāna Arrachi)* was appointed from among 'men of property' in the area[24] and did not receive a salary, although he was entitled to fees for a variety of tasks and to monetary rewards for special services.[25] He was intended to be the main link between the villagers and the colonial administration and as such had a multiplicity of duties. The 1935 Commission of Enquiry (Sessional Paper 27, 1935) listed these under twenty-five separate headings, ranging from the collection of money due to the government, including taxes, licence fees and fines; the issuing of licences for toddy tapping and cattle brands; and the collection of basic statistics on crops and demography. Most headmen were responsible for more than one village and, in the Southern Province, were assisted by a number of minor officials such as the Constable *Arrachi* and the Fiscal. The Village Headman was in turn responsible to a superior Headman *(Maha Vidāna)* attached to the lowest level of the colonial service, the District Revenue Office.

The District Revenue Office controlling Gahavälla is at Tangalla. Along with three other districts, the

Tangalla District Revenue Office is under the control of the Government Agent at Hambantota. The colonial administrative system has been retained, although there are now other loci of power including the Police Superintendant, the Army Area Commander, the MP and the local officers of State Corporations.

In many villages the Village Headman system played a critical part in enabling a small elite to acquire control of large areas of land, especially during the 1860-1900 period. Obeyesekere (1967) has documented the process, whereby the acquisition of local level bureaucratic office facilitated the cheap purchase of large areas of land from men unable to meet tax payments. The ownership of large areas of land was in turn a prerequisite for the attainment of higher level offices, which facilitated the acquisition of still more land. The outcome was the formation of what Obeyesekere (1967) calls a *pelantiya;* a status group of landlords, with a common life-style based on a feudal ideology, linked by marriage alliances, and controlling the local level bureaucratic offices and much of the land within a specified area.

Although there were several enquiries into the headman system, effective changes were not instituted prior to Independence. The landlord-tenant relationship in the production arena, remained the basis for the patron-client relationship in the political arena and by 1946, 45 per cent of paddy land was still cultivated on a sharecropping basis (Snodgrass 1966:154). Although land was of lesser importance in the coastal villages and there was not necessarily a connection between economic control and landlordism, the local elite contrived to dominate village political activities and to retain control of local level offices within small kinship groups. In Gahavälla the Village Headmanship remained in the hands of a group of close kinsmen between 1880 and 1937.

In 1965 the office of Village Headman was abolished and his duties were taken over by a transferable salaried civil servant, the *Grama Sevaka*. He performs most of the tasks that were previously carried out by the Village Headman, but as he often comes from a different area and occasionally from another caste, he lacks authority within the village. In addition, his transferable status makes him very vulnerable to the machinations of local faction leaders - if he offends them they can use their political contacts to have him transferred to some undesirable spot. The office of *Grama Sevaka* was of little importance in Gahavälla during my fieldwork. Because two factions among the ruling party could not agree on a candidate, none of the four men appointed to Gahavälla stayed more than a month.

The *Patabändi Arrachi* was recruited on a similar basis to the Village Headman. In Gahavälla he was the nominee of the wealthier beachseine fishermen and held office for long periods, one man was *Patabändi Arrachi* between 1918 and 1933, and another from 1933 to 1957. In theory the *Patabändi Arrachi* is responsible for all aspects of fishing: he must conduct an annual census of fishing craft, register beachseine nets, make recommendations for insurance payments, compensation and loans, and resolve disputes. But as he lacks the requisite authority to settle disputes, the main task of the *Patabändi Arrachi*, nowadays, is to register beachseine nets once a year.

In the colonial period local administrative offices were a valuable and socially recognised goal of village level political competition. The Village Headman exercised considerable power in intra-village affairs, for he alone interpreted villagers' requirements to higher levels of the colonial administration and in turn enforced the government's decision. Pre-Independence politics thus had both a recognised goal and, in the *pelantiya* formation process, accepted procedures for attaining it.

The social context of modern village level politics has changed considerably. No longer is there a single significant goal of competition. Because of the integration of village and district politics, the aspiring village politician's ability to recruit and maintain a following, depends upon his success in interceding with government bodies on his client's behalf. This, in turn, is a function of the strength of his alliances with members of the centrally controlled political and administrative organisations.

Some alliances are more important than others. If the village politician can establish a close relationship with the electorate level organisation of the political party in power, he can ask the MP, or one of his more powerful supporters, to intercede with other organisations on his behalf. His problem, however, is that at the electorate level the party organisation is itself a loose alliance of competing factions; in aligning himself with the members of one intra-party faction, the village leader forfeits the aid of the others. Further, in most cases he is not the only representative of his party in the village and if he becomes too successful in recruiting a local following, members of the party organisation, fearing that he may switch allegiances to their competitors and take his followers with him, will support one of his opponents.

A Colombo-centered view of Sri Lankan politics might well suggest that the major political parties are tightly organised, but in the rural areas at least, the formal structure only encompasses the supra-electorate level. Within the electorate, the party is a temporary coalescence of a series of patron-client relationships and the political process involves a bewildering system of shifting alliances. Village leaders establish relationships with political activists in the small towns and can request aid in return for mustering votes in national elections and providing support in intra-party disputes. The more successful village leaders also have direct links with members of the administration based on common residence, kinship, or straightout bribes. Within the village the faction leader has a group of close supporters, the faction core, with whom he has very close economic and kin relationships (see Chapter 4). He can rely on these allies - his brothers and brothers-in-law and the men who are employed by him in his businesses - for aid in all situations. The rest of his faction comprises a wide network of less constant followers whose support in most cases is limited to voting as he requests. The basis of these men's support is nebulous and easily broken; distant kinship relationships, common residence, past favours, or the hope of future ones. Against him are ranged similarly organised factions of his own and other political parties. The relations between the faction leaders is one of ever-changing alliances and counter-alliances; a coalition formed to gather votes for an election in September, may be split three ways by the end of the year.

In the social and economic conditions of the early seventies this was a very volatile political structure. The fuel of the system is the exchange of patronage for votes and in the context of ever-increasing unemployment, patronage is synonymous with the provision of jobs. Electoral-level leaders form alliances with village leaders on the promise of providing jobs for distribution among their followers, while the hope of obtaining such jobs is an important factor in the relationship between the village leader and many of his supporters. But following the national elections in 1970, few jobs were available for distribution and factions that seemed tightly organised before the elections in May, had collapsed in complete disarray by September.

It is the instability of this political structure which explains why the results of the 1975 election were identical to every major election since Independence: the ruling party which had come to power with an overwhelming majority was reduced to a handful of seats. Extreme oscillations of the two main political groups do not reflect some ideological fickleness of Sinhalese voters but the more prosaic phenomenon that in situations where political competition is conducted by unstable coalitions, present victories make future defeats inevitable.

CHAPTER 3

STRATIFICATION

A visitor to Gahavälla is quickly aware that this is a community with considerable economic differentiation. The houses make the initial impact: cheek by jowl with single-roomed mud huts are large gaily painted modern homes with several spacious rooms full of elaborate furniture. As time passes it becomes apparent that distinctions based on wealth permeate all aspects of social life. In their ceremonies, their meals and their clothing, to mention only the most obvious examples, the life-style of the wealthy elite differs markedly from the majority of villagers.

In conversations among themselves, as well as in answer to anthropologists' questions, Gahavälla people divide their society into three economic levels.[1] At the peak of the economic pyramid are the *pohasath minissu* (wealthy people) who may also be described as the *salli kārayō* (moneyed group) or *mudalali* (traders). Next are the *samanya minissu* (ordinary people), or *mas marana minissu* (flesh killing men - fishermen), and at the bottom of the pile are the *duppath minissu,* the poor (or unfortunate) people. Survey results presented in the course of this chapter will show that these indigenous categories accurately represent the distribution of resources in Gahavälla. For the purpose of the analysis the three categories have been glossed as rich, middle and poor peasants. These terms have been used only because they provide convenient labels and no theoretical claims are implied. In common with Alavi (1972) I believe that the use of this tripartite division as if it constitutes a class analysis of Asian peasant societies is misguided.

The critical feature of rich peasant households is that their incomes are not subject to the vagaries and fluctuations of fishing.[2] Informants often stressed that while many a fisherman had a higher annual income than a government clerk, the clerk received a cheque every month whereas the fisherman was often penniless for months at a time. Many wealthy men own fishing gear and may even derive most of their income from this gear, but all have additional income sources to tide them over poor fishing periods: businesses, landholdings, or a government job. Rich peasants live in large brick houses built on their own land, their children are educated outside the village, they hold elaborate wedding, funeral and almsgiving ceremonies, and they have a large *pirisa* (following).

Middle peasants live by fishing with their own gear. In most years they can meet their expenses and even save a small amount, but protracted illness, a poor year's fishing, or a court case, forces them to mortgage or sell their assets. In their own eyes they are a threatened and diminishing group. Thirty years ago, they claim, most of Gahavälla's inhabitants were middle peasants, and although a few have since become wealthy, most have grown poor. Middle peasants live in either old masonry houses or incomplete brick houses, situated on undivided land. Their children are educated in the local schools and their ceremonies are reduced in scale, but they try to give dowries for their daughters and alms to the temple.

Most men from poor peasant households own some fishing gear, but the return is insufficient for even a subsistence income and they must also work gear owned by others. Many are female-headed households, which would have been placed in the middle peasant category while the husband was alive, but now subsist on gifts and the proceeds from coir manufacturing, vegetable hawking or small retail shops. The poor peasant families live in decaying masonry, or newly built wattle and daub houses, in many cases on others' land. They do not give alms, their daughters marry young without dowries or ceremonies, and many households have to occasionally sell their ration coupons to buy food.

This brief account of indigenous notions of economic stratification embodies a consistent theme. Poor peasant households are regarded as victims of misfortune, while middle peasant families fear that a series of uncontrollable events may cripple them beyond recovery. A major difference between the elite and the remainder of the population is that economic uncertainty does not loom so large in their lives.

Sexual Division of Labour

Gahavälla fishermen have explicit and forthright views on the sexual division of labour: the man's task is to earn sufficient money for the household's needs, the woman's duty is to provide the household's needs from this income. To a very large extent, the sexual division of economic roles accords with the ideology.

Fishing is work for men alone: all tasks from making nets to retailing fish are in the hands of men. Women sometimes use the beach as a path to distant areas of the village, but they do not linger and never carry fish away. While nearly one-fifth of the equipment is owned by women, they take no part in its use, not even in financial management.[3] Most other money-earning enterprises are also run by men: transport, retailing of vegetables and dry goods, and tea shops. Many women have obtained the qualifications necessary for white collar employment, but apart from school teaching, none have obtained jobs. Gahavälla people, however, are not opposed to female employment in white collar jobs.

The only aspect of production which is mainly women's work is coir manufacturing. The dirty and distasteful task of soaking the coconut husks and beating out the fibres, is carried out on a piece-work basis by the poorest women in the village, but all except the wealthiest, twist beaten fibres into twine and plait coconut fronds into *cadjan* mats. Before the war Gahavälla imported considerable amounts of raw material for coir manufacturing, but nowadays it is an intermittent task using only the husks of coconut trees around the houses.[4] Beating the husks provides regular employment for about fifteen women. Later processes are carried out by the owner of the husks and seldom give more than five days' work, four or five times a year. Women beating the husks earn about Rs.2.50 per day, the others about Rs.6 per day including the value of the material.

A few old and very poor widows operate small tea shops or hawk vegetables and curd door to door, but they do so only because they are without any other means of income and have no status to lose. The Rural Development Society has established a small weaving centre in which six girls are employed. A lack of raw materials, however, restricts it to two or three days' work per week.

Despite their small role in the main productive activities, it is women who manage the household's resources. In all but the richest households, wives receive their husbands' earnings intact and plan consumption until further income is received. Apart from loans between patron and client or advances from middlemen to fishermen, credit is also arranged by the women.[5] All the village moneylenders (eight) are women, as are the revolving credit association *(sittuwa)* organisers (four), and men can only participate in these through their wives. Women make the financial arrangements for ceremonies, especially weddings or funerals, and the decisions to invest in land or fishing gear, although actual purchases are arranged by men.

Wealthy men run their businesses independently of their wives, but in these households the wives often have substantial businesses of their own. A dowry is theoretically the property of the couple and controlled by the husband. But, especially with coconut or paddy land, it is commonly the wife who makes the arrangements for cultivation, supervises the collection of the coconuts and the harvesting of paddy. Inherited land which is jointly owned by a woman and her siblings, is always administered in this fashion. Female supervision of family property does not necessarily end with the transmission of the property as a dowry. Yalman (1967:278) quotes a case of a mother-in-law who went to live with her son-in-law, so as to ensure that the property was managed efficiently. This is common, as is the practice of husband and wife establishing separate households in two villages so as to be able to supervise property in both areas.

Firth (1969:31) and other more recent studies have noted that anthropologists probably consistently undervalue the role of women as managers in the economic process. A possible reason is the dependence of male fieldworkers on male informants. This is not a handicap in Gahavälla: men both emphasise the managerial role of women and argue in its favour. Women are responsible for providing food for the household, and it is important that they know how much money is available so as to ration it accordingly. Furthermore, women do not gamble or drink alcohol and are therefore less liable to temptations which may be disastrous for the household economy. On the other hand, women should realise that their husbands have special requirements and provide small sums for tea and cigarettes when fishing is poor, and money for gambling if possible. These statements are not mere homilies, but conflicts occur: men spend their income on arrack or gambling and pawn their wives' jewellery without their knowledge.

The sexual division of labour severely constrains female participation in the production process and, despite the ideology and practice of female management, this in turn restricts female control of the means of production. As we will see in Chapter 7, women who own fishing gear have severe problems in obtaining the revenue to which they are entitled. It would not be useful, however, to conceptualise female roles in terms of a distinction between domestic and public spheres: as far as economic matters are concerned women operate in the public sphere and indeed some aspects, particularly credit arrangements, are almost solely the prerogative of women at the village level.

Occupational Distribution

Table 3.1 which lists the occupations of all Gahavälla male residents emphasises the extent to which the village economy depends upon fishing. Of the 240 employed males, only seventeen do not derive their income from the sea, either directly as fishermen or indirectly in providing services for the fishermen. Except for the salaries of the teachers and government employees, some of the businessmen's profits, and a little revenue from coconuts and coconut products, the livelihood of the village comes from the sea. The estimated Rs.330,000 earned by the fishermen (see Chapter 5) is thus almost the sole income of the 204 Gahavälla households, as well as about fifty households in adjoining villages. Averaged, this is an annual household income of approximately Rs.1,300 which might be compared with the poverty line figure for 1970 calculated by the Ceylon Central Bank: Rs.1,758 (I.L.O. 1972).

The employment of men in fishing and fish marketing is discussed in later chapters.

TABLE 3.1. OCCUPATIONAL DISTRIBUTION, ADULT MALES

Fishermen	179
Mudalali	12
Kade Owners	11
Carpenters	3
Fish Retailers	10
Wage Employees	16
Civil Service	8
Teachers	1
Students	19
No Regular Employment	23
TOTAL:	282

The *mudalali* are a disparate group. Their main economic activities are outside Gahavälla and they differ considerably in the success of their businesses and the contribution they make to the village economy. The businesses of the five wealthiest men (a cinema and bar proprietor, two paddy mill owners and two transport operators) are vulnerable to political developments for the government intends to nationalise these areas of the economy.

All of these men have wives and families in Gahavälla but only one permanently resides in the village or takes a significant role in village affairs (David Mahattea). The remaining seven *mudalali* are considerably less wealthy. Six are fish traders and the other is a vegetable trader. Three of the fish traders have stalls in the retail markets in Tissamaharama, one has a retail stall in Tangalla, and the others buy fish at the temporary fishing camps along the Southeast Coast. Most of these men would like to establish businesses in Gahavälla - three have attempted to do so - but cannot compete with the entrenched wholesaler (see Chapter 8). It should be noted that he is not included in this or any other table because he lives outside the village boundary.

With two exceptions the *kade* owners are poor men: their daily turnover does not exceed Rs.10 and their annual incomes are less than Rs.500. They sell only tea, bread and other small food items and bankruptcy is a constant threat. One of the exceptions owns the largest private store in the village. His prices on items stocked by the co-operative are higher, but he has a steady trade because the co-operative is frequently out of stock and people exhaust their supplies before their next ration is due. He also sells items such as sweets, toys, kerosene and vegetables, not stocked by the co-operative and provides tea and small meals. His stock is worth around Rs.1,000 and he claims a turnover of about Rs.50 per day, with annual profits of about Rs.2,000. My impression is that the turnover figures are accurate, but that his profits are at least twice as high.

The other comparatively wealthy *kade* owner sells black market arrack. Arrack manufacturing is a government monopoly and it can be bought only at officially approved taverns, the nearest of which are at Matara and Hambantota. While it is legal to transport arrack only two bottles can be carried in any vehicle. These regulations provide a considerable income for some men. Fish traders and van operators purchase the liquor for Rs.8.30 and sell it to the *kade* owner for Rs.10.50 to Rs.12 a bottle depending upon the demand. He in turn retails it at Rs.3 per five ounce glass, about Rs.16 per bottle.

In addition to supplying arrack to the *kade* owner, the fish traders also sell directly to the fishermen. I estimate that around 700 bottles of arrack are brought into the village each year, of which 100 are sold directly. This would leave about 600 to the *kade* owner, and an annual profit of about Rs.2,400.

Two of the carpenters are employed on house construction, mainly laying foundations, bricking walls and building rooms, for the remainder of the work is usually done by the house owner.[6] Most of their work is within Gahavälla. The other carpenter, a man of about sixty, was formerly an *orua* builder and now does repair work on the *oru* and the mechanised craft. Carpenter's pay ranges from Rs.6 to Rs.10 per day plus food and the house builders report about 200 days' work per year. All three men own a considerable kit of tools. The *orua* builder learnt his trade from his father, the other two when they were employed as builders' labourers on government contracts during the war.

A category of wage employees is misleading, for wages are only part of the income of these men who are employed by the *mudalali* in their businesses. One is a driver for the Gahavälla fish traders, three work for fish traders in Kudawellekele, one drives a 'hire car' owned by a relative in Tangalla and the others are drivers and conductors on buses and passenger vans owned by the Gahavälla *mudalali*, David Mahattea. Most receive a small monthly wage plus a share of the takings, but a large part of their income is derived from transporting arrack, to Gahavälla and other villages. One van, for example, plies regularly along the Dikwella-Hambantota road, visiting Hambantota about three times a day. On each visit they buy two bottles of arrack (occasionally more if they feel that the police are unlikely to stop and search the van), which is sold at a profit of Rs.1 to Rs.2.50. The twelve rupees per day are split among the driver and conductor and they claim that this accounts for nearly half their income.

The remaining four categories (teachers, civil service, students, unemployed) can be treated together, for they represent four stages of the same process. They are all members of wealthier families who have had at least a full high school education. Thirty-three children from families resident in Gahavälla have reached this educational level since 1960, but only ten have ever been in regular employment; four are working as 'wage employees', two have permanent jobs in government departments, six are recent university graduates working for a nominal wage as administrative trainees and the other is an 'untrained' school teacher.[7] The remaining twenty-three have never been employed, although they completed their education on average more than three years ago. Despite the faint hopes of obtaining jobs commensurate with their qualifications, nineteen Gahavälla children are presently in the last two years of high school education and four are at university.

Several studies of unemployment in Sri Lanka (Richards 1971; I.L.O. 1972) have argued that the high levels of unemployment among educated youth can be traced to an educational system which stresses non-manual work and produces far more potential clerks than the economy requires. In this view, the high rates of unemployment are the result of the youths seeking 'white collar' jobs, refusing to take other employment. While there is some basis to this argument, two *caveats* should be entered. First, it is by no means certain that alternative employment is available. If the presently unemployed youth did take available jobs, it might well be at the expense of other sections of the population. Secondly, refusal of non-clerical employment is often a decision of the youth's parents, rather than the youth himself, and given present wage levels and avenues of employment access, it is a rational decision. The unemployed youth are from the wealthiest families in the rural areas and it is comparatively easy for these families to keep them out of the labour force. While their earnings from fishing would be negligible, it would prevent them making the political contacts which are the sole avenue to white collar jobs. Even if a youth has to remain unemployed for as long as five years, the income differentials between government employment and peasant fishing or agriculture are so great that the lost income is quickly recovered (see Kaplinsky 1971).

The men employed in non-fishing activities all have regular work, but among the 179 men engaged in fishing there is a great degree of under-employment. The average beachseine fisherman owns five shares. Over a year this provides no more than eighteen weeks' regular work and, in some weeks the working hours will total less than twenty. Similarly, 'bible' fishermen average 200 nights' fishing a year but on 70 per cent of the trips do not catch enough fish to sell. With the exception of the mechanised boat operators and a few of the larger beach-seine owners, the fishermen would like occupations with steady employment and a regular income. Nor do they want their children to become fishermen. But there are very few alternative ways of using their labour. The population density is too high and the soil fertility too low, to permit much cultivation, although the suitable areas are fully planted. Most poor men do a little rock fishing, but the catches from this are very small. Fishermen spend many hours waiting on the beach, sleeping on the verandahs of their houses, or gambling for small stakes.

Men are increasingly turning to political contacts as a means of obtaining employment, although few have been successful. In the meantime the mix of an educated, unemployed, highly politicised youth, *mudalali* whom both major political parties would like to eliminate, and an underemployed and increasingly dissatisfied peasantry, is an extremely volatile combination.

Incomes

Many writers dealing with peasant economies have stressed the difficulty of gathering accurate income data (see Epstein 1962; Cancian 1965). These problems are compounded in a fishing economy where daily catch fluctuations make it extremely difficult for informants to give accurate accounts of their weekly, let alone monthly or annual income. One solution is to calculate income on the basis of ownership of the means of production. In an agricultural community, ownership of land can be established, average yields and production costs calculated, and household income estimated from this data. Although this procedure is open to error (yields and incomes vary and crop-sharing or wage labour will complicate the issue) and therefore cannot be used to differentiate individual households, it does provide a more accurate basis for the discussion of gross economic distinctions within the society than direct questioning of informants.

A variation of this procedure was used in this study. At an early stage the owners of all beachseines and inshore craft were recorded and the responses to a property survey six months later were cross-checked against this data. Some possibility of error remains, especially with respect to the equity of individual households in jointly owned 'bible' nets, but the information on the ownership of fishing gear presented in Table 3.3 is essentially accurate. Each household's income from fishing was then calculated directly from the ownership of fishing gear. Each Rs.100 invested in mechanised craft was estimated to give an annual income of Rs.64, in beachseines Rs.21 and in inshore craft Rs.48. Where the gear was hired, two-thirds of the beachseine profits and one-tenth of the inshore fishing profits were assigned to the owners and the remainder to the hired men. Crew members and owners were assumed to share equally in the profits from the mechanised craft. I appreciate that the marked fluctuations in individual catches make this an invalid procedure for estimating individual annual household incomes, but I would argue that the errors are insignificant for the purposes of Table 3.3.

Information on income from sources other than fishing is taken directly from the property survey. In many cases answers could be cross-checked: information on returns from coconut holdings could be reduced to a price per unit and checked against ruling prices. Errors in the data on income from landholdings, tea shops and coir manufacturing are likely to be small, but the return from money-lending and other businesses and the amounts received in gifts probably involve considerable underestimates.

I have concentrated on cash income throughout, ignoring income in kind because of the difficulties in gathering accurate information. My impression is that income in kind follows the same trends as cash income and that richer households receive larger amounts of fish, rice, coconuts and firewood than the poorer households (see Table 3.6). In terms of the percentage of income, however, it is likely that income in kind, especially fish, is most important among the middle and poor peasant households.

The 159 households included in the property survey (see pp. 9 for details) have been divided into three economic levels using criteria derived from the folk classification. The twelve households in the top category (rich peasants) obtain their incomes from businesses, from mechanised craft, or from the ownership of at least ten beachseine shares. The second level (middle peasants) are fishing households which own fishing gear equivalent to at least five beachseine shares; the third level (poor peasants) are households which own fishing gear worth less than five beachseine shares.

TABLE 3.2. CHARACTERISTICS OF PROPERTY SURVEY SAMPLE HOUSEHOLDS

	Total	Rich Peasants	Middle Peasants	Poor Peasants
No. of Households	159	12 (8%)	58 (36%)	89 (56%)
Average Size	5.9	9.1	7.8	4.2
Average No. of Male Wage Earners	1.1	1.8	1.1	1.0
Dependency Ratio[a]	4.1	4.9	7.0	3.5
Average No. of Consumption Units[b]	4.6	7.9	6.5	2.9
Percentage of Female-Headed Households	14%	Nil	10%	19%

[a] Household size divided by the number of male wage earners.

[b] Males and females over 15 equal one and children one-half.

Some of the more important characteristics of the sample households are shown in Table 3.2. More than half the sample fall into the poor peasant category, the elite amounting to less than a tenth. The rich peasant households are the largest but an average of nearly two employed males per household lowers the dependency ratio. Middle peasant households are almost as large and considerable numbers of children produce a very high dependency ratio. One-fifth of the poor peasant households are headed by a female and while this accounts for the low proportion of employed males, the average household is small and the dependency ratio is low.

Six of the rich peasant households receive most of their income from beachseines, two from mechanised craft, two from business and one from government employment. Landholdings provide most of the income of the remaining household. Six others receive more than Rs.500 per year from land, in all cases coconut plantations. Money-lending contributes a sizeable sum to five households, and white collar employment is a secondary source of income for two.

Fishing with their own gear is the primary income source for all fifty-eight middle peasant households. Secondary sources (contributing at least 10 per cent of total income) include: wage labour on beachseines (29), other wage labour (11), inshore fishing (17), landholdings (6), government employment (2), retail shops (2), money-lending (2), coir work (23) and gifts (6).

Poor peasant households have considerably more diverse sources of income. Thirty-one receive most of their income from fishing with their own gear (seven beachseines, twenty-four inshore fishing) and twenty-six from fishing with other's gear. Three are small-fish retailers, three run tea shops and eight depend mainly on gifts. Among female-headed households, thirteen are dependent upon coir manufacturing and four are vegetable hawkers. Fishing with hired gear is a secondary income source for twenty-one households; others sources include coir (39), tea shops (7), and gifts (26).

TABLE 3.3. OWNERSHIP OF FISHING GEAR BY ECONOMIC LEVEL

	Rich Peasants	Middle Peasants	Poor Peasants
Mechanised Craft	20,000	--	--
Beachseines	68,000	161,000	32,000
Inshore Fishing	4,000	19,000	17,000
TOTAL:	92,000	180,000	49,000
Average Per Household	Rs.7,660	Rs.3,100	Rs.550

Source: Property Survey. The values used were: Mechanised craft Rs.30,000; Beachseine shares Rs.400; 'Bible' nets Rs.75 per piece; Inshore *oru* Rs.600. The total for each level is rounded to the nearest Rs.1,000 and the total for each household to the nearest Rs.10. Small personal fishing gear such as lines and throw nets, is not included. The table underestimates the average rich peasant's investment because most of the households owning mechanised craft were not included.

The extent of fishing gear ownership by each economic category is tabulated in Table 3.3. The rich peasant households own an average of Rs.7,660, as opposed to Rs.3,100 for middle peasants and a mere Rs.550 for poor peasants. Although inshore fishing gear accounts for more than a third of the gear owned by poor peasants, most of the inshore gear is owned by the richer families. Sixty per cent of the beachseines are owned by middle peasant households, but the average household owns beachseines worth only Rs.2,775 compared to Rs.5,666 among the rich peasants.

The table makes it clear that a considerable proportion of the means of production are owned by a small elite. The poor peasants who comprise 60 per cent of the sample own less than 20 per cent of the gear, while the 8 per cent of rich peasant households own 30 per cent of the gear.

TABLE 3.4. EXTENT AND SOURCE OF ANNUAL AVERAGE HOUSEHOLD CASH INCOME

	Rich Peasants		Middle Peasants		Poor Peasants	
	Rs.	%	Rs.	%	Rs.	%
Ownership of Fishing Gear	1806	38	-	-	-	-
Fishing using own Gear	610	13	741	63	167	27
Fishing using other's Gear	7	-	80	7	193	32
Landholdings[a]	438	9	41	4	-	-
Coir	-	-	48	4	157	26
Businesses[b]	1333	29	-	-	-	-
Small Businesses[c]	-	-	32	3	12	2
Money-Lending[d]	100	2	8	1	-	-
Wages[e]	410	9	189	16	30	5
Gifts[f]	-	-	23	2	51	8
TOTAL:	4,704	100%	1,162	100%	610	100%

Notes to Table:

[a] Does not include household compounds.

[b] Large retail stores, fish trading and transport.

[c] Tea shops, fish retailing, vegetable hawking.

[d] Estimated.

[e] Includes government employment.

[f] Estimated.

The disparities in ownership of the means of production are parelleled by the disparities in income presented in Table 3.4. The average middle peasant income (Rs.1,162) is almost twice the average poor peasant income (Rs.610) and is in turn less than a quarter of the rich peasant average (Rs.4,704). The basis for the classification eliminates marked income differentials within the bottom two categories (although a quarter of the poor peasants have incomes below Rs.500) but incomes in the top category range from Rs.2,100 to more than Rs.10,000. Because middle peasant households are considerably larger than the poor peasant households and also have a larger percentage of young dependents, average income per consumption unit is actually lower among the middle peasants (Rs.178) than among the poor peasants (Rs.210).

Among rich peasants 60 per cent of the household income is derived from investments. The middle peasants depend upon fishing for their income, 70 per cent of which is directly derived from fishing. Overall, wage labour provides 16 per cent of income, but this is limited to six families. Fishing with their own gear accounts for only a quarter of the poor peasants' incomes; the bulk is from fishing with others' gear and coir manufacturing. In contrast to the top two categories where female earnings are insignificant, women provide 28 per cent of poor peasant incomes. Gifts are also significant, but are limited to thirty-one households of which eight households get more than three-quarters of the total.

Redistribution of income within the village would do little to alleviate Gahavälla's problems: if the total income was equally distributed, the average household income would be only Rs.1,120. This would place it in the poorest third of the Sri Lanka population[8] and Rs.600 below a poverty line income.

Wealth

The most important property, other than the means of production are houses and their household compounds. As the houses are built over long periods and shares in house compounds are held by large numbers of owners, I was unable to obtain satisfactory data on the value of this property. Ownership of the most important items of wealth other than house-property, is shown in Table 3.5. Income differentials are reflected in property-ownership although the distinctions are not as sharp as might be expected. The rich peasants are wealthier, but most of the differences among the three levels stem from spending on three items: sarees, jewellery, and almirahs (free-standing, often elaborately carved, wardrobes used to store valuables). Sarees and 22 carat gold jewellery are an important avenue of saving as well as a means of expressing status and all rich peasant households have heavy investments in these items. Although the average middle peasant investment in these items is nearly Rs.400, most items are owned by households with newly married or soon-to-be-married women, and some women own little other than ear studs and a saree for special occasions. Nearly two-thirds of the poor peasant households have no jewellery at all. A notable point is the absence of saleable items (including radios, pressure lamps, sewing machines, as well as sarees and jewellery) among most of the poor and middle peasant households. Many claimed that they had been forced to sell these items over the past few years.

Expenditure

Accurate data on household expenditure are probably even more difficult to gather than income data, but some indication of spending patterns within the society can be gained from Table 3.6. Special attention should be drawn to four points which emerge from the information.

1) The table includes most of the items necessary for a subsistence living and other essential items such as clothes (made from rationed cloth), household repairs, etc. would add less than Rs.2.50 to the poor peasant total. Other expenses such as ceremonies, litigation, construction of new houses and medical expenses are not included in the table because they can be more easily deferred until money is available.

TABLE 3.5. OWNERSHIP OF SELECTED HOUSEHOLD CHATTELS BY ECONOMIC LEVEL

	Rich Peasants		Middle Peasants		Poor Peasants	
	No.of Households with Item N=12	Average Value per Household Rs.	No.of Households with Item N=58	Average Value per Household Rs.	No.of Households with Item N=89	Average Value per Household Rs.
Chairs	12	182	58	108	79	65
Tables	12	133	58	84	76	46
Beds	12	114	51	71	74	50
Couches	3	22	3	2	4	1
Almirahs	12	325	28	135	21	79
Pressure Lamps	12	47	21	16	12	14
Bicycles	3	60	4	9	4	7
Radios	5	173	10	48	4	15
Sewing Machines	7	158	9	86	7	52
Sarees	12	159	43	56	36	44
Jewellery	12	847	54	391	37	149
TOTAL:		Rs.2,220		Rs.1,006		Rs.522

Source: Property survey. Respondents were asked for the sale value of each item and in most cases this was accepted. Where the respondent's estimate seemed unreasonable, the item was normally inspected and a value fixed after discussion.

Litigation is a heavy burden on peasant incomes and enables the urban elite to extract considerable sums. In the six months following September 1970, Gahavälla inhabitants were involved in eight court cases: two partition cases and six criminal cases. Each party to a partition case can expect to pay more than Rs.500 in legal fees and the legal costs in a serious criminal case are often as high as Rs.3,500, in addition to the loss of earnings while on remand. I estimate that nearly 10 per cent of the total profits of fishing were used for legal expenses during the period, and while this is unusually high it is clear that legal expenses are a heavy drain on the community's resources. Some indication of the profitability of the legal profession is that there are sixteen lawyers practising in the local district courts.

2) While 53 per cent of total food expenditure is on items provided by the state co-operatives at controlled prices, few middle or poor peasant households fully utilise their rations. There is a free rice ration of 2.2 pounds per person per week and a second ration at a price about 60 per cent below the market price. Less than a third of the poor peasant and half of the middle peasant households consistently buy the second ration, selling the coupons to rich peasants instead. This suggests that the rice rationing scheme does not redistribute income in the ways which were intended.

3) The percentage of the total food expenditure spent on various items is reasonably consistent among all three levels. Most of the differences stem from differences in rice consumption, with the poor and middle peasants substituting the cheaper flour, millet, sweet potatoes, manioc or breadfruit, for rice.

4) There is very little difference in the monthly expenditure of poor and middle peasant households. The differences stem from higher middle peasant spending on rice, milk and vegetables, which is due to the higher proportion of young children in these families. Comparing income with expenditure suggests that the average middle peasant household has an annual deficit of Rs.200. While the data is not adequate for firm conclusions, it does suggest that both poor and middle households are living at minimal levels and have few opportunities for saving or spending on non-essential items.

TABLE 3.6. AVERAGE MONTHLY FOOD EXPENDITURE PER CONSUMPTION UNIT

Item	Rich Peasants Rs.	%	Middle Peasants Rs.	%	Poor Peasants Rs.	%
Rice	5/60	23.1	3/02	19.4	1/89	15.1
Flour, Millet	-/60	0.2	-/30	1.9	-/33	2.6
Bread	-/91	3.8	-/68	4.3	-/67	5.3
Sugar	1/24	5.1	-/71	4.6	-/75	5.9
Tea	-/71	2.9	-/26	1.7	-/17	1.3
Milk, Coffee, Eggs	-/28	1.1	1/09	7.0	-/20	1.6
Condiments	2/75	11.4	1/27	8.2	1/31	10.5
Biscuits, etc.	-/86	3.5	-/35	2.2	-/33	2.6
Barley, Sago	-/21	0.9	-/18	1.1	-/09	0.7
Onions	-/47	1.9	-/35	2.2	-/22	1.7
Coconuts	-/54	2.2	-/18	1.1	-/43	3.4
Coconut Oil	-/27	1.1	-/10	0.6	-/12	1.0
Preserved Fish	-/55	2.3	-/26	1.7	-/31	2.5
Fresh Fish	Nil	Nil	-/21	1.3	-/06	0.5
Pulses	-/64	2.6	-/45	2.9	-/24	2.0
Potatoes, Manioc	-/51	2.1	-/20	1.3	-/67	5.3
Other Vegetables	1/02	4.2	1/32	8.5	-/72	5.7
Breadfruit	-/16	0.7	-/07	0.4	-/24	1.9
Fruit	1/74	7.2	1/16	7.5	-/26	2.1
Curd, *Kitul* Honey	-/71	2.9	-/67	4.3	-/35	2.8
Soap, Tooth Powder	1/25	5.2	-/65	4.2	-/54	4.3
Beedi, Betel	1/44	5.9	-/55	3.5	-/79	6.3
Cigarettes, Cigars	-/65	2.7	-/64	4.1	-/72	5.7
Firewood	-/07	0.3	-/23	1.5	-/07	0.6
Kerosene, Cooking Utensils, etc.	1/56	6.4	-/64	4.1	-/92	7.3
TOTAL:	24/20	99.9%	15/54	99.9%	12/52	99.9%

Notes: The 25 items in the table are condensed from an 83 item questionnaire administered to a non-random selection of 25 households; 5 rich peasants, 8 middle peasants and 12 poor peasants. Each household completed the questionnaire 3 times at approximately two-month intervals. Informants were asked to state the volume, price and source of all purchases and were encouraged to choose their own time intervals which were later converted to a monthly period.

Access to Credit

Credit in any society has the vital role of levelling out peaks and valleys in income. In a fishing community where the peaks are sharper and the valleys deeper, and where most householdings are living at the subsistence margin, access to short and long-term credit is necessary for the household's survival. Poor and middle peasants in Gahavälla have three sorts of credit requirements:

1) Sums of less than Rs.10 for day to day consumption purposes.
2) Sums of up to Rs.200 for longer term consumption purposes, medical expenses, and repairs and maintenance of fishing gear.
3) Larger sums, Rs.200 and above, for major purchases of equipment, legal expenses, weddings, and other ceremonies.[9]

While men may obtain small loans from the fish traders and faction leaders, these are usually for their own use and women do most of the borrowing for household expenses. The major source of small loans is close kinsmen, but there are other sources. Many women, both the recognised money-lenders and others, will make small loans without security at an accepted interest rate of 10 per cent per month.[10] Because of the lack of security, women will lend only to those they trust completely and few households could raise Rs.40 this way. The owner of the main retail shop allows about Rs.10 worth of credit. No interest is charged and prices are not increased to indebted households, but the credit limit is strictly applied.

Medium sized loans, up to Rs.200, are the province of the money-lender. There are eight money-lenders in Gahavälla, all but one (a widow) the wives of *mudalali* or richer fishermen. The richest has about Rs.6,500 for lending, the poorest about Rs.100. In most cases their initial capital was their dowry, jewellery pawned with the larger money-lenders in Tangalla. Loans from these money-lenders require security. Jewellery is most favoured, but other small saleable items such as sarees, sewing machines and radios are accepted. About half the value of the security can be borrowed at an interest rate of 3 per cent per month. If the loan is not quickly repaid, the security is stored with a money-lender in Tangalla for about 5 per cent of its value per annum.

Loans are occasionally sought for long-term consumption purposes or for emergency expenses, but the usual purpose is repair and maintenance costs of fishing gear, especially beachseine nets. Most of the smaller beachseine owners have established relationships, through their wives, with particular money-lenders. If repairs cannot be met from incomes, an item of jewellery is pawned and redeemed three or four months later when fishing improves. Increasingly the security does not change hands: the borrower merely signs a promissory note to provide the item if the loan is not repaid within a certain period.

Interest rates on medium loans are not as high as on the small loans, and far more money could be lent if security was not required. But money-lenders see this as against their interests. At present they lend their capital stock for about six months of the year at about 12 per cent annual interest without risk. Because borrowers who cannot provide security probably could not repay the loan, higher interest is irrelevant. Nor is it sensible to use fishing catches as security; the size of the catch cannot be predicted and it would be difficult for a woman to enforce repayment.[11]

Four of the money-lenders also organise revolving credit associations *(sittu)*.[12] All *sittu* are run by women and all participants are women. The longest established *sittuwa,* which has been in continuous operation since 1953, is organised by an aged widow, Gallapati Babinona. Babinona's *sittuwa* has twenty shares, each presently costing Rs.25 per month. Eleven shares are jointly owned (one by five households) and there are thirty-five participant households in all. Two women, one of them Babinona, hold two shares apiece.

Each *sittuwa* runs for twenty months before being reformed and each shareholder takes the pool once. The first month's collection of Rs.500 goes to Babinona. In the second month an auction is held. The minimum bid is distributed among all contributors including the successful bidder. In the tenth month the minimum bid drops to

Rs.75, and in the fifteenth month to Rs.50. The records of the past decade indicate that the average successful bid in the second month was Rs.130, the tenth month Rs.80, and the fifteenth month Rs.64.

Sittu give very large profits. The organiser receives the first month's contributions without an auction and when this is invested, the interest pays her monthly contribution. In addition she can expect to recover at least 17 per cent of her contribution from the distribution of the bids. On the other hand it is her responsibility to ensure that monthly contributions are collected and that members do not drop out after a successful bid. Careful selection of members is the main way of ensuring this, but Babinona also formalises the procedure by having a regular meeting at her home, serving betel and tea, and making all successful bidders sign a receipt. No member of her *sittuwa* has ever defaulted. Other organisers have been less successful, however, and one large *sittuwa* failed during my fieldwork.

Large loans in the Rs.200 to Rs.2,000 range are usually obtained from money-lenders in Tangalla. Most are short-term loans for wedding and funeral expenses and they are usually secured by land, although the title deeds may be borrowed. Interest rates range from 3 to 5 per cent per month. In all these loans the land is mortgaged and a legal transfer document is prepared, but if the loan is repaid within a month the deed is not registered and legal fees are avoided. If the loans are not repaid within a year or so, the loan plus the interest payment is likely to be greater than the value of the land. The money-lender is well aware that his costs of foreclosing the mortgage are likely to be more than the land is worth and the pledge of land appears to have a symbolic rather than an economic function.[13] Money-lenders protect themselves by carefully investigating the purposes of the loan and the possibilities of repayment, rather than by the value of the security.

Credit from these sources is not usually available for the purchase of major items of fishing gear. While many of the early 'bible' nets were financed in this way catches were low and few of the loans were repaid. Nowadays, only faction leaders give credit for the purchase of beachseine shares, and only close associates of the faction leaders can use credit to improve their economic position. The function of credit in Gahavälla is limited to ameliorating short-term fluctuations in income and temporary misfortunes. Most fishing households have a series of dyadic relationships which can be used to even out differences in day-to-day incomes, while the money-lenders alleviate the planning problem of matching seasonal incomes with continuing expenditure.

Class Polarisation

This chapter has described economic stratification as reflected in statistics on wealth and income gathered in 1971, but attention should be drawn to the dynamic implications. The economic data presented in this chapter suggests that the community is rapidly polarising into two opposed classes: a small capitalist elite and a large mass of poor peasants. Middle peasants, men making a living by fishing with their own gear, are rapidly becoming impoverished.

There are both structural and developmental reasons for the impoverishment of the middle peasants. In recent years the resources available to the community as a whole have not increased. It is difficult to essay new ventures outside the village and established businesses are threatened by government policies. Most of the land is now occupied by houses, so that agricultural products or industries based on these products make insignificant contributions to the village economy. Improved communications have linked Gahavälla more tightly to the national economy, but while this has raised fish prices, it has also made it possible for capitalists, both within and without the village, to exploit the fishermen. One of the two technological innovations in fishing, the 'bible', redistributed the catch without increasing it, and although the mechanised boats did increase the catch, the middle peasants received few benefits. Gahavälla is now more dependent upon its fisheries than at any time in its history (see Chapters 9 and 10), but fisheries production is increasingly controlled by non-fishermen.

Although Gahavälla's population growth rate is not high in comparison with other Asian peasantries, it is growing significantly, and most of the increase is among middle peasants. Despite their greater incomes, the standard of living of middle peasant households is barely higher than the poor peasants, and resources sufficient for a household's maintenance in one generation will not provide a reasonable living for the widow and her children. It is not surprising that female-headed households are common among the poor peasants. Even those households with average incomes sufficient to maintain their autonomy are vulnerable to the income fluctuations characteristic of maritime economies. As few can save large sums and the high costs of credit limit its use to the short term,households hit by misfortune - an illness, a poor season, or a court case - may have to relinquish control of the fishing gear on which their livelihood depends.

Later chapters analyse the historical development of capitalist relations of production in Gahavälla; at this point it is sufficient to note that by 1970 class polarisation was decimating the middle peasants.

CHAPTER 4

AUTONOMOUS HOUSEHOLDS AND FACTION FORMATION

A recurring theme in accounts of peasant societies is the importance of kinship in structuring economic activities. Many aspects of the economy can be conceptualised as the product of a belief that economic transactions among kinsmen should embody moral considerations which are not applicable to dealings with outsiders. While this notion has a place in the analysis of Gahavälla social organisation, in Gahavälla the domain of kinship sentiment is restricted to a small circle of 'close kin'. As a result of the household's autonomy in the economic process and the limited domain of extra-household kin relationships, issue-orientated alliances and relatively stable factions are the major form of supra-household organisation.

The Household

The most concise and accurate way of defining the Gahavälla household is 'the occupants of a single dwelling'. In all but four cases[1] the occupants of a dwelling are a single consumption unit, for although the wife of a married man living in his parents' home may cook his meals, food is purchased in common with her mother-in-law. The usual term for household is *pavula,* a multi-connotative term usually translated as family (see Leach 1961; Yalman 1967). Where a more specific and accurate reference is required, *ge minissu* (house people) is used.[2]

Household composition in Gahavälla is tabulated in Table 4.1. Most of the households are nuclear families and the others represent different stages in a single developmental cycle. A notable point is the high proportion of female-headed households. Women head 14 per cent of households and the majority of extended families are a product of widows returning to their parents' home. No household includes non-kinsmen, but in earlier times several of the wealthier households had servants.

TABLE 4.1. HOUSEHOLD COMPOSITION

Type		No.	Percentage
Nuclear Family		124	61%
Truncated Nuclear Family		31	15%
Mother and children	25		
Father and children	2		
Widows living alone	4		
Extended Families		49	24%
Nuclear families plus:			
Wife's sister	4		
Daughter-in-law & children	27		
Son-in-law & children	4		
Daughter's children	9		
Other relatives	5		
	TOTAL:	204	100%

Marriage is a convenient point to begin a discussion of the development cycle of the household.[3] As in other areas of Sri Lanka (Yalman 1967) the number and scale of marriage ceremonies, the area from which the spouses are drawn and the size of the dowry, differ with the wealth and status of the families concerned. Among wealthy families marriages are arranged by a broker, normally a professional, but occasionally a relative. The initiative may come from either party and although the broker, who is rewarded with gifts of rice, clothing and money from both parties, has the responsibility of ensuring that the match is suitable, both parties make extensive enquiries through other channels. Nowadays people do not conceive of marriages as establishing alliances between large bodies of kin and post-marital contacts are limited to the immediate households involved.

The most important criterion governing the choice of a husband is a steady job, preferably outside the fishing industry. Contrary to Yalman (1967:277) there is no notion of ritual hypergamy, although there is a marked preference for hypergamy in terms of wealth. Most families use a disproportionate amount of their wealth for the dowry of their eldest daughter so she can marry into a richer family than would otherwise be possible. She is expected to reciprocate with large gifts at her younger sisters' weddings.

If the preliminary enquiries are satisfactory, a series of elaborate formal visits follow during which the horoscopes of the bride and groom are compared and the details of the dowry and other settlements negotiated. The formal visits make it possible for both bride and groom to be consulted over the choice of spouse and often three or four prospects are canvassed before a match is arranged.

The dowry is the responsibility of the bride's father, but if he is old or deceased, the bride's brothers and married sisters may give large contributions. Most of the dowry is given directly to the bride in the form of jewellery, sarees, furniture and a sewing machine. Cash, and less often land or fishing equipment, is presented to the couple. The groom's parents also present gifts to the bride: usually a sovereign set in a necklace, or other gold jewellery. Elaborate arranged marriages normally lead to virilocal or neolocal residence, and during the pre-marriage negotiations the groom's parents will be pressed to provide a house-site and to guarantee the construction costs.

The bride's family finance the major wedding ceremonies. The costs include the construction of a marriage altar (*poruwa*) and sheds for cooking and eating; the hire of lights, public address system and a generator; new clothes for the family; repairs to the house; and an elaborate feast lasting two or three days. Among rich peasants the dowry is around Rs.5,000 to Rs.6,000, with a slightly greater sum for the other marriage expenses.[4]

While the dowry is normally met from savings, the remaining wedding expenses are commonly financed by a short-term, low interest,[5] loan, using land as a security. This loan is repaid by contributions from the guests whom the bride's father invites to the ceremony. These gifts, which are recorded in a book and announced over loudspeakers, should be repaid and preferably increased, on later ceremonial occasions including puberty ceremonies, healing ceremonies and 'house-warmings',[6] as well as weddings. Most contributions are between Rs.10 and Rs.15, but close relatives or wealthy *mudalali* may give as much as a thousand rupees. While close relatives are expected to give larger sums than more distant kin, I was unable to discover an ideology of differing contributions based on genealogical distance which Yalman (1967:276) describes.

In addition to the gifts, the host also profits from the gambling that inevitably accompanies ceremonies. Men who have won several hands in succession will give some of their winnings to the host and this might total Rs.500 on each of two nights.

Informants claim that the guests' contributions plus the gambling proceeds normally cover the wedding expenses, for the host can estimate the size of contributions from past transactions. The gambling proceeds are more uncertain, for many gamblers are not invited guests. It should be noted, however, that the bride's father does not make a profit on the wedding ceremony and thus it cannot be used to call in capital for other purposes. Puberty ceremonies on the other hand usually produce a profit and here the decision to hold an elaborate ceremony with invited guests, rather than limit the celebration to close relatives, is often dictated by the father's need for cash. Puberty ceremonies are always on a smaller scale than marriage, however, and the contributions would seldom amount to Rs.1,000.

Following a two or three-day honeymoon at a hotel, the newly married couple return to a home-coming feast at the groom's parents' house. Occasionally, especially the marriage of an eldest son, this compares with the earlier feast in scope and duration. Invited guests are expected to contribute towards the cost but on a diminished scale. The expenses of the groom's family, while less than the bride's, are considerable. In a wedding with a dowry of

Rs.5,000, the cost of the home-coming feast, transport, and gifts for the bride's family, would be about Rs.2,500, with a similar amount in marriage settlements such as construction costs for a house.

Among less wealthy households marriages are arranged informally by the parents, usually on the initiative of the groom's mother.[7] The spouses are drawn from nearby villages and are usually distant cross-cousins.[8] Dowries are small and limited to jewellery, furniture and clothes, with perhaps a share in undivided land and a small amount of cash. Immediate kinsmen and friends of the couple, share a small meal, at which the bride's mother's brother performs the marriage ceremony, and the couple later visit Tangalla to register the marriage. There is no honeymoon and seldom a home-coming feast.

Elopements are common, especially involving cross-cousins. The only marriageable woman a man can visit freely are his cross-cousins and these visits often lead to a desire for marriage. Characteristically such marriages are supported by the bride's mother who will be able to marry off her daughter without a large dowry and opposed by the groom's parents. Eventually the couple elope, often with the covert assistance of the bride's mother, register the marriage, and a week or so later return to the village. Initially the couple may be rejected by most of their kinsmen, but eventually the marriage is accepted.

An example may illustrate the differences in the attitudes of bride's and groom's parents towards cross-cousin marriages.

> Heenhamy is the wife of a rich peasant beachseine fisherman. At the time of the first incident they had four children: a daughter aged 26, two sons, 20, 19, and a daughter of 16. In 1964 the youngest daughter who was still at school, fell in love with her father's sister's son who was fifteen years older and lived in an adjoining village. Heenhamy was sympathetic, but the marriage was opposed by the groom's parents, who thought the age difference was too great and wanted him to marry with a large dowry; and Heenhamy's husband, who felt his eldest

daughter should be the first to marry. Despite the opposition Heenhamy made it possible for the couple to meet in secret and eventually gave her daughter the money to elope. The couple fled to Tissamaharama and three weeks later, after registering the marriage, returned to Gahavälla accompanied by a police escort. A large crowd of kinsmen and non-kinsmen gathered, and in a highly dramatic scene (which she takes pleasure in relating), Heenhamy persuaded her husband and his kinsmen to allow the couple to live in her house. Although the couple now have an independent household, Heenhamy is a constant visitor and brings them frequent gifts of money and food.

Heenhamy's eldest son is a small fish trader and she provided the deposit so that he could buy a small ramshackle van on hire purchase. The son spent much of his time in the house of Heenhamy's brother which was in a village more convenient for his business, and in 1970, he asked Heenhamy to arrange a marriage with the daughter of the house. She refused indignantly, for although she was on good terms with her brother, he was a poor man. Heenhamy claimed that her son was too young to marry (he was 26) and in any case she had already arranged a marriage for him in Tangalla. Heenhamy attempted to stop her son visiting her brother's house and when this failed, had the van repossessed, despite the considerable financial loss this entailed. Eventually the couple married, but none of the groom's relatives attended the ceremonies and even after a child was born, Heenhamy refused to allow her daughter-in-law into her home, although her son slept there two or three nights a week. About nine months after the marriage, the two families were partly reconciled when the bride's brother, of whom Heenhamy was very fond, was murdered. But when I left the bride had not yet visited her mother-in-law's house.

Marriage seldom brings immediate economic independence. Men begin fishing with their father's equipment and while they remain in their parents' households, their mothers receive their earnings, not their wives. Men may be over sixty when their sons marry, but seldom retire if they are capable of working. Unless their father is ill or very old, sons do not attain full control over their earnings until after his death and even then the gear is registered in their mother's name.[9]

Intra-household organisation is characterised by rigid age and sex distinctions. Men play little part in the running of the household: they eat alone and are absent for most of the day. When at home, they spend time on the verandah at the front of the house, while the women and children congregate inside or in the kitchen. At night men sleep on the verandah, women and children inside. Only in the wealthiest households do newly married couples have a room of their own; usually sexual relations between husband and wife are hurried and furtive. A mother has undisputed authority in household affairs. She disciplines the children while they are young, controls the household income, prepares food with the aid of her daughter and daughter-in-law and purchases food, equipment and clothing for all household members.

While the children are very young, relationships between parents and children are close and affectionate. Men often take their 3 or 4 year old sons to the beach and spend hours making them toys or telling them stories. As the children grow older, care increasingly passes to an elder sibling or close relative and relations between father and son become more formal. By the time a boy is 9, he spends most of his time with his peers and at 15 or 16, begins fishing, often with his father's bother. Around 20 he leaves his father's brother's crew and begins fishing with friends of his own age. Nowadays young men turn to inshore fishing or, where possible, the mechanised boats for there is little chance of employment in beachseining.

Girls have few opportunities to leave the house. When they return home from school they must care for their younger siblings, fetch water from the well and help their mother about the house, a pattern which continues until they are married. But relations between mother and daughter are much more affectionate than between father and son, and elder daughters quickly become the main confidante of their mothers and joint organisers of household affairs.

The final stage in the developmental cycle of most households is the female-headed household. The average wife is seven years younger than her husband and many women are relatively young when their husbands die. Among the wealthier households the death of the father does not diminish the authority of the mother. Her husband's property is transferred to her and she continues to make the financial decisions of the household. As she grows older, a daughter or daughter-in-law may arrange most of the day-to-day affairs but she retains control of major decisions until she dies.

Widows have a very difficult life in poor households. Because her children marry earlier, she has little inherited wealth, and her children cannot afford substantial gifts, she must take any employment opportunities that are available: beating coir, hawking vegetables and curd, or running a small tea *kade*. It is these households, widows with their unmarried children, who are at the bottom of the economic pile; in many cases too poor to buy even the second measure of subsidised rice.

Kinship

In the agricultural villages of Sri Lanka, as in many peasant societies, kinship ties are the basis of inter-household relationships (Leach 1961; Yalman 1967; Obeyesekere 1967; Robinson 1975). Kingroups are prominent in agriculture, especially during the periods of peak labour demands such as harvesting; kinsmen are an important source of loans and other assistance in emergencies; and most marriages are between relatives. In these communities even relatively distant kinsmen can assert moral claims, and the kinship system links household production and consumption units into wider circles of co-operation. Kin relationships have a much more limited function in Gahavälla: the domain of kinship claims is restricted to a small circle of close relatives. As Sinhalese kinship has been the subject of several comprehensive studies, this account concentrates on the aspects of Gahavälla kinship which appear to differ from other areas and which have some economic significance.[10]

Gahavälla kinship terminology is Dravidian with similar terms and usages to those tabulated in Yalman (1967: 211). The kinship domain is subdivided into 'close kin' (*langa näyo; ävässa näyo*) and 'distant kin' (*dura näyo*). Individuals are not always classified on genealogical grounds: distant relatives may be included among the close kin because they live nearby. Nevertheless, the distinction does have a clear ego-centred genealogical base. Ego's close kin are his parents and their siblings; his own siblings, their spouses and children; his wife, her siblings and parents; and his children.[11] Among close kin, kinship terms are always used, both in reference and address. Distant kin are addressed by generalised[12] kinship terms or by name, usually the latter. In reference, relative product terms are used. For example, ego's FBS is referred to as *bāppage puta* (father's younger brother's son) not as *aiya* or *malli*, and ego's brother's wife's brother as *mallige massinā* (brother's male affine) rather than *massinā*.

In contrast to the close kin, the distant kin are an unbounded and amorphous category. Most Gahavälla men are capable of tracing exact kinship links to every person in Gahavälla, Sinimodera and Moraketiara and may have relatives in as many as twenty additional villages, but little weight is attached to such relationships and it is only within the close kin that moral notions of kin amity govern behaviour. Individuals may have warm relationships with some of their distant kin and cast these relationships in a kin idiom, but they are invariably based upon other grounds: a joint business, geographical proximity, political allegiance, or friendship.

Because kin relationships are effectively limited to the close kinsmen, the expected behaviour between some kinship dyads sharply contrasts with other areas of Sri Lanka. Some aspects of this contrast can be highlighted by comparison with Pul Eliya.[13] In his account of the kin basis of faction organisation, Leach (1961:126) emphasises differences in expected behaviour between siblings and parallel cousins on the one hand, and cross-cousins and brothers-in-law on the other. He describes the relationship between siblings and parallel cousins as one of marked respect tending to avoidance and says 'that the *aiya/malli* relationship between full brothers is often a cloak for strain and jealousy'. (1961:127) Relations between *massinā* (cross-cousins or brothers-in-law) are described as 'familiar' and it is these relationships that are the basis of political factions.

In Gahavälla the division is along different lines; siblings and brothers-in-law are close kin, parallel and cross-cousins are distant kin. In other words a distinction is drawn between two types of *massinā*: brother's-in-law and cross-cousins. Brothers co-operate in many activities and it is often a very affectionate relationship. Unless the age gap is large, the hierarchy implied by the terminology is not readily apparent, and the spokesman and dominant figure in a group of brothers is not necessarily the eldest. There are occasional disputes between brothers, but co-operation, cemented by numerous small loans and gifts, is more common. Tambiah (1965) argues that the very close ties between brothers-in-law should be seen as extensions of the ties between brother and sister. This encapsulates the situation in Gahavälla, where the marriage was often arranged by the bride's brother who was already on good terms with his prospective brother-in-law. Brothers-in-law who live in different villages do not co-operate closely in day to day affairs, but they attend ceremonies in each others' homes, visit regularly, and give aid in emergencies. Financial aid may be arranged between brother and sister without her husband's knowledge, but ideally a man should not object to such arrangements and should help support his wife's family if necessary.

My informants say that a man should not differentiate his behaviour towards male cross and parallel cousins. Male cross-cousins are addressed by the parallel terms (*aiya/malli*) rather than *massinā*, although informants noted the latter was in theory the correct term. Female cross-cousins, however, are never addressed by the parallel term and the conceptual distinction between cross and parallel cousins is clearly apparent in cross sex relationships. While they are young, male cousins regularly visit each others' houses in company with their parents and as they grow older relationships remain cordial, but without close affection on either side. A slight tendency towards closer relationships between cross-cousins and strained relationships between parallel cousins can be discerned and the reasons for this are both demographic and economic. Parallel cousins are more likely to live in the same village, often in adjoining houses, and are potential claimants to the same property: cross-cousins more often live outside the village and are less likely to enforce inheritance claims. Cousins of opposite sex, however, are likely to maintain close and affectionate relationships throughout their lives.

The other important kin relationships are with the father's brother and the mother's brother.[14] Ideologically there should be considerable differences between the two. The mother's brother/sister's son relationship should be very close and affectionate. The mother's brother plays a prominent role in all life crisis ceremonies, especially wedding and puberty ceremonies, and the sister's son reciprocates at the mother's brother's funeral. In addition the mother's brother is the father of a prospective spouse and while special marriage claims between cross-cousins are not acknowledged, it is accepted that such unions often occur. The father's brother plays a far sterner role in the ideology; he is 'like a father' and should be shown great respect.

The ideology is to a large extent reflected in behaviour. A man's mother's brother often lives outside Gahavälla and his visits are semi-formal occasions with gifts on both sides. As he is less embroiled in the disputes that characterise village life, he can act as mediator, especially in disputes between siblings, and contentions among siblings are often resolved by his intervention. If the role of the mother's brother is one of the 'kind uncle', that of the father's brother, especially a younger brother, is closer to 'teacher'. The fishermen believe that the ever-present possibility of accidents makes it undesirable for members of a nuclear family to fish together,[15] so most fishermen learn their trade in their father's brother's craft.

There is less consistency in relations with the wife's father which vary with individual economic and political circumstances. One should pay even greater respect to the wife's father than to one's own father and the usual form of address and reference for father-in-law (*māmandi*), is an honorific form of *māma* (mother's brother). In some cases, especially where the spouses come from distant villages and social contacts are limited, the relationship does meet the ideal, but more commonly it involves considerable strain: disputes over the payment of dowries, the management of dowry property and ill-treatment of the wife. The relationship is particularly tense where the marriage was arranged with the covert support of the bride's parents against the wishes of the groom's parents. In such situations the husband is forced to rely on his father-in-law for support and as he grows older resents it.

Kinship relations between individuals are the template for relations between households, especially households headed by male siblings. Brothers seldom fish together and even when jointly engaged in businesses divide responsibilities as much as possible, but they cooperate in all other activities. As we will see, a group of brothers is at the heart of most factions, it is the brother's responsibility to remove a man who is drunk and causing trouble, and if a fight does start, brothers should come to each others' aid irrespective of the cause of the fight. Gifts of food, especially fish, and small sums of money are freely given between siblings' households, and there is no attempt to establish balanced reciprocity. Larger sums are usually spoken of as loans, but lack the paraphernalia of receipts or promissory notes that usually accompany loans, are usually interest free, and are without fixed periods of repayment. Loans among the close kin tend to be repaid when the lender requires the money. Money borrowed for a child's education, for example, may be returned many years later after the child has obtained a job.

Where there is marked economic differentiation among the close kin, there is a regular flow of gifts from the richer households to the poorer. Sometimes these gifts are not limited to clothing or special foods on festive occasions and are a major source of income. Fifteen per cent of the households in the property survey, reported that a quarter of their income was gifts from close re-relatives. Most of the recipients were households of aging parents and unmarried children receiving help from their children. Others were female siblings being helped because their husbands had died.

Occasionally a man borrows money from a relative to finance a wedding or puberty ceremony, but usually loans for these purposes are sought from outsiders and the relatives' contributions are limited to ceremonial gifts. These should be larger than those of outsiders and need not be increased when reciprocated. The only economic context in which the siblings participate as a group is the funeral of their parents. The funeral costs are divided equally among all siblings and each has a serious moral obligation to meet his own share, although he may receive a loan from the others.

To some extent the boundary of economic and political aid between kinsmen is a function of economic status. All families, irrespective of wealth, attempt to help within the limits outlined above, but wealthy families may extend help to cousins and even more distant relatives. In most cases these extensions are selective; only a few of the possible households are selected for aid, either because of a political tie or because the recipient family is very poor.[16]

The Pelapata

In his account of *Karāva* social structure Yalman (1967:271-8) places considerable emphasis on the *pelapata*. He describes it as a non-exogamous patriline 'kept up for the purpose of tracing ritual status in the complex conditions of the low country and their rank is expressed by hypergamous marriages between them.' (1967:229). The description of the *pelapata* is an important part of Yalman's argument that *Karāva* social organisation tends towards patrilineality, but, in my view, his account is misleading.

The *pelapat kattiya* (genealogy group) is a category of kinsmen bearing the same patronymic (*pelapat nama*). Ideally the name is transmitted by patrifiliation, but matrifiliation and adoption are recognised. Although informants claim that the patronymics were conferred by the Sinhalese kings, the Portuguese or the Dutch, the origins of most Gahavälla *pelapata* can be traced to the 1860-1910 period when the adoption of an honorific surname was one of the concomitants of social mobility through *peläntiya* formation. The honorifics were drawn from a variety of sources, including the names of villages, traditional Sinhalese titles, and the names of prominent families in the area,[17] and more than one *pelapata* may bear the same patronymic. People with the same patronymic are not necessarily regarded as kinsmen, except in the sense that the entire *Karāva* caste are kin.

As all members of a *pelapata* are patri-parallel kin, marriage within the *pelapata* is prohibited. Yalman's description of the *pelapata* as non-exogamous stems from his failure to appreciate, that although marriage within the *pelapata* is prohibited, people with the same patronymic are not necessarily members of the same *pelapata* and in these cases marriages are permitted. The *pelapata* is not important in regard to marriage choices. Prohibited relatives are calculated on the basis of direct genealogical links, not *pelapata* membership, and the two parties to the marriage are described in terms of close kin, not *pelapata*. Informants denied that marriages between *pelapata* were hypergamous and the genealogical data support this view: all pairs of *pelapata* with more than four marriages between them, show women marrying in both directions.

In the situation of rapid social mobility that characterised Gahavälla's history at the end of the century, the *pelapata* name was probably an important status marker differentiating socially mobile families from their less successful kinsmen, but nowadays it has little social significance. With the exception of families engaged in land litigation, few men are capable of tracing descent past the grandfather's generation and most have reduced the complex *pelapata* names to a single name or series of initials.[18] In many cases men are unaware of the meaning of the initials of *pelapata* other than their own.

The Kattiya[19]

In Gahavälla the household is an autonomous production and consumption unit. Fishing does not foster extra-household cooperation and there are few contexts, other than weddings or funerals, where kinship links are used to muster non-household labour. Some forms of inter-household cooperation are based on kinship sentiments and have the critical economic functions of providing short term credit and supplementing the income of poor widows, but kin amity has little moral or emotional force outside the 'close kin'. Nevertheless, there are numerous economic and political situations in which a household needs allies other than the 'close kin', and in the absence of corporate kin groups, these requirements are met by factions.

In its widest sense the term *kattiya* (pl. *katti*), which I gloss as faction, means simply group. In common parlance it is always combined with an adjective as in *dell kattiya* (net group), *pavul kattiya* (family group) or *pelapat kattiya* (genealogy group). When used in the sense of faction, it is preceded by the faction leader's name: *Sunil Mudalalige kattiya*, Sunil Mudalali's faction. Other terms occasionally used for faction include *patte* (side) and the English term 'party', but *kattiya* is the most common.

This usage emphasises one characteristic of Gahavälla factions; in both ideology and practice they are leader-centred groups, recruited through his efforts, acting in accordance with his instructions, towards objectives which he decides. As the nucleus of a faction is often a group of close kinsmen and the faction leader is seldom the senior member in kinship terms, he may defer to kinsmen in some contexts, but there is no suggestion of a leadership clique in Mayer's (1966:116) sense. All important decisions are taken by the faction leader: his close kinsmen, like other faction members, both regard themselves and are regarded by others as his subordinates.

My informants consistently described contemporary Gahavälla politics in terms of three *katti*, led by Danny Wijenaike, M.A. David (David Mahattea) and J.A. Sunil (Sunil Mudalali), respectively. Throughout this book I have followed their lead and analysed village politics in terms of competition among the three groups. This, of course, involves some simplification. The Wijenaike faction, for instance, might more accurately be described as an unusually stable alliance among three faction leaders who are also brothers-in-law, for although the three leaders do not compete against each other, some disputes have involved only one, while the others remained neutral. Moreover, less than a third of the Gahavälla households[20] are associated with any of these three factions, and the remaining households contain several groupings, to which the label might be applied.

Nevertheless there are good reasons for limiting the term faction to the three major groupings. First, the factions are much larger than the other groupings and their members are linked by multiple ties; David Mahattea's faction core (see pp.84) has 27 members, and there are 18 and 17 in the other two. In contrast, the largest non-faction group has only six members, four of whom are brothers. Secondly, the three faction leaders are among the wealthiest men in the village and have numerous contacts with extra-village political and governmental institutions. In addition to providing economic services such as loans, gifts and jobs, they alone are in a position to distribute political patronage and to act as brokers between the village and the outside world. Thirdly, the three factions have achieved some degree of stability: despite their origins as issue-orientated alliances, all have survived for more than ten years. At least two other comparable-sized groupings emerged momentarily during the past decade,[21] but they were short-lived.

The catalyst for faction formation is the personal qualities of the leader, particularly his economic success. All three leaders are entrepreneurs: David, is a transport operator, Sunil is the largest fish wholesaler, and Danny, although he now obtains most of his income from the beachseines, introduced the 'bible' net to Gahavälla. All are young men, under forty-five, and their wealth was obtained through their own efforts. Their fathers were among the wealthiest fishermen of their time, however, and a relatively good education and family resources were crucial factors in their early economic successes. All have lived outside Gahavälla and contacts made during this time remain an important source of loans, patronage and information. All three have close relationships with electoral-level party leaders: David and Sunil with the Sri Lanka Freedom Party and Danny with the United National Party, although Sunil's alliances seem intended to preserve his economic position rather than satisfy political ambitions. Finally all have justifiable reputations as very violent men: only Sunil has been convicted, but all three have been charged on several occasions and are believed to have personally killed rivals.

Although David's and Sunil's incomes are among the five largest in the village and Danny's is also well above average, their expenses (especially legal expenses) in maintaining their political position are also very high. David's annual income is around Rs.10,000 and he is about the fifth wealthiest man in the village. Sunil's income is even larger (see Chapter 8), but he has spent a lot on court cases in the past decade and he is not among the twenty wealthiest men.[22] Sunil still lives in his father's substantial, but old, masonry house and has been unable to complete the house he began building five years ago. Danny's income is much lower, perhaps Rs.5,000, but he spends much less on maintaining his following and his living conditions are similar to Sunil's. All three factions own large numbers of beachseine shares but of the three leaders, only Danny is dependent upon the beachseines for his income. The four wealthiest men in the village play little part in faction politics. All but one are aging men who made their wealth soon after the war and are now in semi-retirement.

The Faction Core

In analysing relations between faction leaders and their followers, a useful distinction can be drawn between two types of supporters; the clients and close kinsmen who make up the faction core, and the followers. This distinction between clients[23] and followers is based on three grounds: the stability of the relationship; its context, and the type of actions taken in support of the leader. Clients and followers should be seen as points on a continuum rather than polar types and must also be viewed in a dynamic context for followers may eventually become clients. But at any particular time it is not difficult to distinguish the two and informants showed remarkable unanimity in listing the close associates of the faction leaders.

The relationship between the leader and his clients appears to be the only area of stability in village politics. The relationship may have begun as a temporary issue-centred alliance, but in time it has developed into what Pitt Rivers (1954:140) aptly described as 'lop-sided friendship'. While the faction leader is clearly the dominant partner in economic, political and social terms, there is a substantial basis of friendship and trust which underwrites the promises of future mutual support. If the client is also a close kinsman, the trust is a product of childhood experiences, in other cases, the friendship has been created by joint participation in disputes over a long period. Although most of the leader's support in any particular dispute is based on unstable issue-centred alliances, the successful faction leaders have a core of followers whose actions are not determined by immediate self-interest.

An analysis of the cores of the three factions indicates the interplay of two principles: close kinship[24] and economic dependence. At the heart of Danny's and Sunil's factions are their brothers, six and seven respectively. David has only one male sibling living in the village, but his wife's brothers and her sisters' husbands are prominent among his supporters. While there is no doubt that the strong bonds of affection created during early childhood play an important part in maintaining cohesion among such members of a faction core, a large body of close kin is neither a necessary nor a sufficient condition for faction formation. Several equally large groups of close kinsmen have not developed into factions and several of David's close affines only joined at a relatively late stage of the faction's development.

Complementing and extending the kinship links are ties of economic dependence: faction leaders turn their kinsmen into supporters and recruit other clients by providing employment. The 'hired man'[25] position on the beachseines has an important role in this process and all three leaders use it extensively. The Wijenaike faction recruit all their clients through the beachseines, but Sunil obtains additional supporters from among the small-fish traders by guaranteeing a regular supply of fish (see Chapter 8) and David recruits men through jobs on his transport enterprises. David also allows one of his clients to organise the gambling among his faction and to take the 'house cut', but other leaders reserve this privilege for themselves.[26]

Accumulating clients by providing employment poses many difficult decisions for the faction leaders. These difficulties are least apparent in David Mahattea's case. He regards the beachseines almost solely as a means of obtaining clients: giving the 'hired men' full control of the nets, taking little of the proceeds (except with very large catches) and treating the cost of the net as the price of a close supporter. As David receives a sizeable income from his transport business, the lost revenue from the beachseines is unimportant. Similarly Sunil in recruiting supporters from among the small bicycle traders receives both monetary and political benefits. The Wijenaike family, on the other hand, obtains most of its relatively small income from beach-seining and could work all the shares it owns. In allowing non-kinsmen to work some of the nets, the Wijenaikes forego employment and income which they themselves need. Further, some of the Wijenaike brothers are relatively poor men and there is a strong moral obligation to provide them with employment before outsiders. Danny Wijenaike is therefore forced to trade off economic losses against potential political gains to a far greater degree than the other faction leaders.[27]

Employment is the most important economic service which the patron provides his clients but he also maintains a constant flow of small gifts and loans throughout the year. These reach a peak in the New Year *gannu-dennu* (take-give) institution when token gifts from the clients are reciprocated with food, tobacco, liquor and clothing. These prestations further emphasise the dominance of the leader and the extent to which the faction depends upon his economic success. New Year's Day in 1971 was a special case because the 'insurrection' and the curfew which followed strictly limited celebrations, but David Mahattea's gifts to his clients on this occasion included Rs.25 in cash and a sarong worth about Rs.10 to each man. He also provided ten bottles of arrack (Rs.100), five cartons of cigarettes (Rs.65), and large quantities of cigars and betel to be distributed among other supporters.

The third distinction between clients and followers lies in the sort of actions they are prepared to undertake at the leader's behest; one indication is that clients are often referred to as *chandiyo* (thugs). Clients should support their leader without reservation: assaulting his rivals, burning their nets and *kade*, persuading fellow members of net crews to accept lower prices for their fish, and giving false evidence in court cases. Secrecy and intrigue are an essential part of faction competition and in many disputes the faction leader retains an appearance of neutrality, leaving the overt acts of aggression to his clients. In elections clients are expected to seek voters for the candidate supported by their leader; canvassing men in their houses, in the tea shops and on the beach, and making the early speeches at political meetings before the major politicians arrive.[28]

Membership of a faction core is a product of demonstrated loyalty rather than constant affirmations of membership and some men eschew public demonstrations of support so are able to work more efficiently behind the scenes. Nevertheless, faction members have numerous opportunities to demonstrate their membership: gambling together, attending ceremonies in each other's houses and drinking tea at a particular tea shop.

David Mahattea's Faction Core

A description of the composition of David Mahattea's faction core should put some flesh on the dry bones of the preceding analysis. David's was selected because it is the largest and is based on a greater variety of links than the other two.[29] The Wijenaike faction core is predominantly kin based, while Sunil's is a combination of kin and small-trader/wholesaler relationships.

On first acquaintance, David is an expansive, openhanded individual. Taller than average, solidly built with a chubby face, he has a perpetual smile and a delight in boisterous horseplay and salacious jokes which sets him apart from most Sinhalese men. Quickwitted, intelligent, cheerfully combative, he loves gambling, but after several hours' concentration is apt to throw away his winnings with an outrageous bet. The cheerful visage, however, masks a moody and violent personality: very minor incidents can provoke destructive rages. Most people are afraid of David and even close friends are unable to explain some of his actions.

David's father, Don Charlis, is among the largest net owners and wealthiest men in the village. All of his sons were well educated and with the exception of David and the youngest, entered government service. After finishing high school, David began a trading business along the Hambantota-Batticaloa road, initially using hired transport but later acquiring a lorry of his own. In 1961, when he was 36, increasing competition made the business unprofitable, and David sold his lorries and purchased two vans with the intention of entering the Gahavälla small-fish trade, which at this time was controlled by Sunil Mudalali and his brothers.

Kinsmen of David in the M.A. *pelapata* owned shares in more than forty nets, but because of a series of disputes with David and his immediate family, they were unwilling to sell fish to him on credit. There were several reasons for the bad feeling: a land case which pitted David's father against his brothers; David's assault on two men, W.A. Peter and W.A. Dawith (see Chapter 8), who were married to distant kinsmen in the M.A. *pelapata;* an assault by David and some of his followers on the president of the Rural Development Society which was a contributing factor to the halting of construction of the new school; and David's sexual relations with two daughters of W.G. Sammiappu, a twice convicted criminal. Cut off from the fish of the M.A. owned nets, as well as the fish from the nets which Sunil's faction controlled, David formed an alliance with the Wijenaike faction which resulted in the introduction of twenty-five new nets (see Chapter 10).

The combination of the new nets, the alliance with Danny Wijenaike, the capital saved from earlier ventures and the jailing of Sunil Mudalali after a police jeep was fire-bombed, ensured David's success and after six months he appeared to be taking control of both fish wholesaling at Gahavälla beach and some of the mechanised boats. But the alliance with Danny did not survive the 1965 election campaign, two mechanised craft whose owners were heavily in debt to David sank during a storm, and after Sunil returned from jail a series of increasingly violent incidents culminated in the death of David's mother-in-law. Frightened for his own life, David converted his fish vans into passenger vehicles and started a local bus route. Later he purchased a larger bus suitable for tours and pilgrimages and began several ventures in partnership with his sister's husband who owned a cinema and bar at Beliatta.

Although he joined the Sri Lanka Freedom Party in 1959 and had used his political contacts to obtain route licences for his buses, David played little part in party politics until he returned to live in Gahavälla following his marriage in 1962. In 1965 he was the main election organiser for the SLFP in Gahavälla and in the 1970 election his responsibilities encompassed neighbouring villages as well. Along with Danny Wijenaike, he has definite long-term political ambitions. My impression is that this is unusual among village-faction leaders, for most appear to have become involved in national politics for motives similar to Ratna's: to preserve their economic position and to retain political control within a small circumscribed area, rather than widen their influence.

The members of the core of David Mahattea's faction are tabulated below. The comments are very selective and are designed to show only the most important relationships between leader and client. The reader should bear in mind that many of the men have been associated with David for more than ten years and it is the close friendship created during this period, rather than the original basis for recruitment, that is now the most important factor promoting faction cohesion.

1. W.G. Sammiappu

   The owner of 14 beachseine shares, he was earlier in conflict with David over his marriage (David is married to one of Sammiappu's daughters and has another as co-wife) and the introduction of the new nets (see Chapter 10), but was reconciled when his wife was murdered in a dispute over David's fish vans. A bad-tempered and violent man with two convictions for assault, he controls fish sales from most of the nets in which David owns shares.

2. A.H. Clement

   A close friend since childhood who has been David's accomplice in many escapades including several assaults on members of other factions. Occasionally employed as a driver on David's vans, he obtains most of his income from organising gambling for faction members.

3. W.G. Dasa

   Wife's brother. He was a van driver for David until 1970 when David arranged a job with the Sri Lankan Transport Board. Earlier David lent him the money to purchase three beachseine shares which are now worked by his brother (4).

4. W.G. Heensingho

   Wife's brother. Works four of David's shares and three of his brother's shares. Owns one share which David gave him as a wedding present.

5. W.G. Adwin

   Wife's brother. Works three shares owned by David. Was severely assaulted in the dispute in which David's mother-in-law was killed.

6. D.V. Arisena)
7. D.V. Suganapala)
8. D.V. Sugathadasa)

   D.V. Arisena is married to David's wife's sister. All three brothers own shares bought with loans from David. Suganapala and Sugathadasa were acquitted of the attempted murder of one of the Wijenaike faction, an attack which David is generally believed to have instigated.

9. T.M. Heensingho)
10. T.M. David)

   Heensingho is David's wife's sister's husband and both brothers work on David's vans.

11. G.A.P. Wimal

An inshore fishing partner of No.6. He was earlier closely associated with the Wijenaike faction (he is married to Danny Wijenaike's brother's wife's sister) but badly injured one of the Wijenaike brothers in a fight. David paid his legal costs in the case.

12. M.A. Heensingho

Younger brother; a fish trader operating in a very small village about ten miles away. In 1968 David provided money for the deposit on a van, but Heensingho was afraid to compete with Sunil and the van was repossessed. He is now employed by David's brother-in-law.

13. M.A. John Singho

Father's brother's son; he assisted David in his marital problems despite the opposition of the rest of the consanguineal kin. David lent him money to buy six beachseine shares and he now owns eleven.

14. M.A. James

Father's brother's son, about ten years older than David and a close friend for many years. David arranged a job for James' eldest son at the Fisheries Corporation and has also helped with the education expenses of the other children.

15. M.A. James

Father's brother's son of both David and No.14. The owner of a mechanised boat and a *vedda mahataya* (aryuvedic physician), he stood for the Village Council in 1970 as David's nominee but was defeated.

16. A.G. Martin

Father's sister's son; driver on David's vans.

17. U.H. Punchisingho

Works on David's vans.

18. P.M. James)
19. P.M. Harold)

Father and son. David lent them the money to buy a 'bible' net and gave them work on three beachseine shares owned by his mother's sister.

20. A.P. Adwin

Works two of David's shares and owns three of his own. Was jailed for three months for burning some of Sunil's faction's nets, supposedly at David's behest.

21. A.G. Charlis)
22. A.G. John)

Both were close associates of Nicholas Ediriweera who was killed by Sunil Mudalali. Along with members of the Wijenaike faction they were charged with the attempted murder of Sunil Mudalali's father but were acquitted. In 1969 they became involved in a land dispute with their father's brother, A.G. Mendis, who is Danny Wijenaike's father-in-law. David lent them the money to contest the partition case.

23. H.P. David

Worked for David when he attempted to enter the fish trade. Now owns six beachseine shares, some of which were purchased with loans from David.

24. H.P. James

Not related to H.P. David. A close companion of David during his trading ventures along the East Coast, he acts as David's agent for the six nets in which they both own shares, but does not receive any money from these nets.

25. M.M. Puniyadasa)
26. M.M. Peyaseena)
27. M.M. Charlis)

Three brothers who are close neighbours of David's father-in-law. All three are inshore fishermen who receive regular gifts of food and clothing from David. Known as the M.M. *chandiyo* (thugs), they are reputed to obtain most of their income from stealing nets and

> dynamiting fish. All three were crucial witnesses in the conviction of two of the Wijenaike faction and one of Sunil's brothers for the murder of David's mother-in-law. In 1971 Charlis was killed by one of Sunil's faction in a dispute over fish prices.

The Followers

There are three broad reasons why faction leaders acquire supporters other than the faction core. Common to all leaders is a desire to acquire prestige through demonstrations of esteem by the *pirisa* (following). In Kenny's words 'the client has a strong sense of loyalty to his patron and voices this abroad. By doing so he constantly stimulates the channels of loyalty, creates good will, adds to the name and fame of his patron and ensures him a species of immortality.' (1962:136). The usual contexts for such demonstrations of esteem are ceremonies at the faction leader's home and it is not unusual for more than 300 adults to attend a wedding and for 2,000 to attend a funeral. Events as disparate as the dedication of a new temple and a large political meeting, are situations in which the presence of a large body of supporters, both kin and non-kinsmen, demonstrate that the faction leader is a man to be respected.

A striking example was the building of a large statue at a Dikwella temple. Each *poya* day the incomplete statue was lit by a series of lights, flags were raised, and recorded music was played. Men acquired the right to perform various tasks, such as turning on the lights, by offering a donation ranging from Rs.250 for turning on the main lights to Rs.5 for raising a minor flag. The men who would perform such tasks were listed on a notice board three weeks ahead and were fulsomely praised over the loudspeakers on the night. Prominent local leaders attempted to muster sufficient supporters, about forty, to perform all the tasks on a given night and the group was described as 'so-and-so and his *pirisa*'. (cf Obeyesekere 1967:215-33).

A second reason why faction leaders enlist followers is to obtain increased influence in the political party organisations by demonstrating their ability to control votes. From the faction leader's point of view it is important not only that men vote for his party's candidate, but that they are seen to do so because of his influence. Leaders therefore recruit large bodies of supporters to accompany them to electoral meetings and attempt to persuade voters to attend the polling booths as members of their following. It is the size of the leader's *pirisa* which determines his standing within the party, and the favours he can exact in return for his support. My impression is that in the 1970 national elections, the policy of the parties, especially the record of the governing party, was the most important determinant of individual votes and that faction competition was primarily intra-party competition.[30] From the faction leader's point of view, however, the demonstrations of support are the major objective and the actual votes are a secondary consideration.

Intra-party faction competition is more obvious in the Village Council elections, for although the candidates run under party labels, they are selected by local faction leaders. This is one of the reasons why despite the overwhelmingly SLFP victory in the local elections in May, the Village Council elections in September were won by the U.N.P. In the Gahavälla ward both David and Sunil nominated candidates under the SLFP banner, but received only 637 and 605 votes respectively, as opposed to 653 for Danny Wijenaike the UNP candidate.

Individual leaders also have additional reasons for recruiting followers. Danny is interested in attracting as many men as possible to the gambling run by his brothers; while for Sunil Mudalali, a large body of followers, even if they are unlikely to give physical support, deters potential assaults by fishermen and acts as a claque in bargaining over fish prices.

Although men have diverse motives for joining factions,[31] most can be grouped under three headings: economic, brokerage, and protection. The hope of obtaining a job, either within the leader's own enterprises or through his political contacts is a powerful motive for faction membership. Ten years ago such aspirations were often satisfied, but today there are few jobs available and men recruited on the promise of future employment are very unreliable supporters. Leaders provide other economic services for their followers, however, small cash loans for daily consumption purposes, larger cash loans and transport, furniture and cooking utensils for ceremonies, and token gifts on festive occasions.[32]

Faction leaders are the brokers between the villagers and the central political, social and economic organisations. They act as spokesmen for villagers presenting petitions to the District Revenue Officer; introduce villagers to the M.P. and other party leaders; arrange lawyers for partition and criminal cases; intercede with the authorities to obtain permits and licences; and indicate the people who will make limited goods available on the payment of a small present.[33] Protection, against both government agencies and fellow villagers, is a powerful motive for joining a faction. Any serious assault is fertile soil for petitions and counter-petitions and villagers believe that any arrested man will be assaulted by the police to extract a confession. In their view such assaults can only be avoided through the intervention of a prominent man who can use his prestige, his political contacts and strategic presents, to ameliorate the situation. Within the village, a man without numerous siblings who is not associated with a major faction is in a vulnerable position in contentious situations and, as is described in Chapter 8, gets a lower price for his fish.

This discussion of motives for joining factions, to some extent implies the recruitment mechanisms. Promises of jobs, loans, intervention with extra-village agencies and protection, are important in obtaining supporters, but the decision to join one faction rather than another mainly depends on pre-existing relationships. One of these is kinship, for although all men in the village are related, kin ties are usually closer to one leader than another. Another is residence; David Mahattea lives in Gahavälla proper, Danny in Moraketiara and Sunil in Kottetawa, and men tend to support leaders from their own area. In David's and Danny's factions, neighbourhood support is often mixed with instrumental factors such as the desire to have a new road or a new school in their village rather than another, but the Kottetawa people have a very strong sense of identity arising out of their history as a 'pariah' hamlet.

'Faction membership' means different things to different people. At one extreme are followers who are almost indistinguishable from clients and will eventually merge into the faction core; at the other are men whose 'membership' consists of attending ceremonies at a faction leader's house or gambling with faction members. For most of the followers, faction membership is limited to a particular dispute in which they have an interest; a particular action, such as joining an election *pirisa*; or a particular sphere, such as beachseine fishing.

Social Disintegration?

Gahavälla citizens are apt to assert that the factions are a recent development, and that their traditional, kin-based social structure has disintegrated under contemporary pressures. Chapter 9 presents information against which these claims might be evaluated, and my inclination is to regard them as an overly romantic view of the past. It is probably true that around the turn of the century, when the village was closer to self-sufficiency and isolated from political events in the capital, kinship was more important in inter-household relationships than it is today. But the difference is one of degree, not kind, and 'traditional' is not an appropriate adjective for Gahavälla during this period. As the historical analysis in Chapter 9 indicates, the ancestors of most of Gahavälla's population were immigrants who took advantage of colonial legislation to displace the original inhabitants. A century ago, Gahavälla politics pitted the beachseiners and agriculturalists of Gahavälla against the fishermen of Kottetawa: the modern inhabitants are the descendents of the victors.

Romanticising the past is one way of expressing dissatisfaction with the present, and many Gahavälla people dislike the society in which they live. Economic uncertainty is a constant threat to a household's survival, while the integration of national, regional and district politics has made village factions a vital link in the distribution of goods and services. Men who are not prepared to give at least token allegiance to a faction cut themselves off from the most accessible source of the products on which their livelihood depends. Moreover

Gahavälla is a violent society and it is difficult to avoid becoming involved in inter-faction competition. The cost of neutrality is not merely the loss of potential gains; it is the danger of being regarded as an enemy by all three factions.

The intention of this chapter was to describe those aspects of modern Gahavälla social structure which promote factionalism, and to describe the ways in which factions are formed. Later chapters analyse the historical process in which factions became the dominant form of supra-household social organisation, and the role of factions in the contemporary mode of production.

CHAPTER 5

THE FISHERIES

The earliest account of Gahavälla fishing is the 'Report on the Working of the Fish Curing Scheme in the Southern and North-Western Provinces' (Sessional Paper 20, 1886), where the Assistant Government Agent from Hambantota reproduces diary extracts of a visit to [Gahavälla] and Kudawellekele.[1] In August 1885, he met fifty prominent men from the two villages who informed him that

> [Gahavälla] has one hundred fishing canoes and cures about 600 cwt. of fish annually, valued at about Rs.2,000. Suriyagahawella has two hundred fishing canoes, and cures and sells 1,200 cwt. of fish on the spot, valued at about Rs.5,000.[2]

The Assistant Government Agent had earlier noted that the fish curers were paying the high price Rs.2.36 a hundredweight for salt in the Tangalla market and recommended that a fish curing yard be established in Gahavälla to supervise the curing of fish and sell salt at 80 cents per hundredweight. The yard established in 1885 proved a failure: only 61 cwt. of dried fish was produced, sales of salt totalled only Rs.25, and the yard closed in 1886. According to the Auditor-General, the main reason for the failure of the yard was the people's fears that the government supervised yard was the first step in a plan to extend fish taxes, paid by fishermen in the towns, to the more isolated villages.

These reports[3] shed considerable light on the fishing industry of the Southern Province during the last decades of the nineteenth century. There were two main fishing methods. Large *oru* carrying up to seven men were used for deep-sea fishing, and smaller *oru*, with a crew of one or two, fished within the bays or close to the shore. If the species of fish cured are a sample of the fish caught, deep-sea fishing was the most productive technique with spanish mackerel, tuna and shark heavily represented. The deep-sea craft used vegetable fibre lines and cotton lures and were mainly engaged in daytime trolling, but occasionally they used a heavy twine net to catch sharks at night. In a few villages, notably Kottegoda, pole and line fishing with live bait for tuna was also important. Smaller craft fishing close to the shore used multiple-hooked handlines baited with cotton lures, small throw nets, and, when fishing at night, torch lures and pole nets for squid. With the exception of a net used in Tangalla in 1886, beachseines are not mentioned.

The reports concentrate on the marketing and distribution systems. In the majority of villages, including Gahavälla and Kudawellekele, the entire catch was distributed among the crew for their household's consumption, retailing in the local area or to be dried for later use. But in the deep-sea fishing villages, such as Gandara, Kottegoda and Devinuwara, where most of the catch was *bäleya* (skipjack tuna), three-quarters of the total catch was salted or cured with *goraka* (a spice resembling tamarind), for sale in interior villages. Most fishing villages had serious marketing problems: much of the fish was not suitable for sun-drying, salt was very expensive, and the lack of ice and transport prevented the sale of fresh fish outside the district. Reports describe fish rotting in heaps on the beach and fishing craft tied up for long periods because of market gluts. The establishment of a fish curing yard at Gandara in 1886 apparently increased landings by 40 per cent in less than eighteen months and

> this has been so far effected without any increase in the number of new boats or men employed, the increase being secured by old boats being less frequently laid up, and the men more busily employed.
> (Administration Report, Government Agent, Matara, 1887).

By 1886 there was a large migratory fishing industry on the south-east coast and all fishing camps used in 1970 are mentioned in the reports. Most of the migrants lived in the deep-sea fishing villages near Matara and visited the camps during the south-west monsoon. Some idea of the scale of migratory fishing can be gained from reports of two fish curing yards at Hambantota and Patnangala (in the Yala game reserve) where more than 330 tons of fresh fish were cured by migrant fishermen in 1887. In Hambantota twenty-five deep-sea craft and forty-five small *oru* landed 67 tons of fish for curing during February and March: nearly a ton of fish per craft in a season of only six weeks!

Traditional Fishing Methods

An examination of accounts of nineteenth century fishing indicates that the technology used in the Southern Province immediately before the introduction of nylon nets and mechanised craft in the 1960s, was unchanged from a century earlier. In 1970, traditional methods were still being used alongside modern gear.

There are three ecological niches in the contemporary Gahavälla fishery and a distinctive type of gear is used in each: first, the *vavaya* section of the bay where beachseines catch anchovies and other shoal fish; secondly, the area of the bay outside the range of the beachseines and extending a couple of miles down the coast, which is fished by small traditional craft using nets and lines. These craft compete with the beachseines but also take rock fish and squid. Thirdly, in the area on the edge of the continental shelf the main catch is tuna. As both inshore and deep sea fishing have been radically altered by technological innovations in the past decade, the traditional methods warrant only a brief mention and the discussion concentrates on the current situation. The account of beachseining is postponed to later chapters.

The deep-sea fishing *orua* is the fishing craft *par excellence* of the Sinhalese fishermen.[4] The 35-foot hull is dug out from the trunk of a large jak or wild breadfruit tree. Wash-boards are attached to the hull with coir binding and resin glue to raise the free-board area, and the hull is strengthened by three sets of cross joists. The outrigger is joined to the hull by arched struts, which provide the flexibility needed to adjust to the shocks and strains of a heavy sea. The craft is powered by a square sail rigged on a single mast and although it can sail reasonably close to the wind, the fishermen normally use the early-morning off-shore winds to reach the fishing grounds and return with the on-shore breezes in the afternoon. The main fishing method used with deep-sea *oru* is trolling. Most craft carry a crew of five, each using a single floating line made of twisted cotton and baited with a cotton lure. If the wind is insufficient for trolling, handlines baited with two hooks, catch rock varieties such as mullet and snapper, or bottom feeders, especially shark. Very occasionally coir nets are set for sharks during the early morning outward journey and pulled up on the return trip.

Prior to 1960 the *orua* was the only deep-sea fishing craft used in the Southern Division. In many villages lacking sheltered beaches, the entire fishing economy was based on deep-sea *oru*, and even villages which were mainly beachseine centres, had a few, but in Gahavälla the only deep-sea *oru* were in the hamlet of Kottetawa. The fishing gear census of 1950 (Administration Report, Director of Fisheries, 1950; MacDonald 1954) reported a total of 476 *oru* engaged in deep-sea fishing in the Southern Division, but by my count less than 100 large *oru* were still afloat in 1970. Few of the remaining craft are currently used for deep-sea fishing. Most are nearing the end of their operating lives and their owners, who are nearly all older men, have dismantled the rigging and use the craft for inshore fishing.[5]

In 1960, immediately before the introduction of nylon nets, Gahavälla had about thirty of the small *oru* used for inshore fishing. Approximately half were owned by men from Kottetawa or the adjoining villages of Moraketiara and Sinimodera, and the rest by Gahavälla men. There were two main methods of inshore fishing. During the day the craft fished just beyond the beach-seines. The most common technique was the use of a handline with about 20 small hooks baited with cotton lures. The fishermen continually jerked the line in the water and if a shoal of fish appeared, often caught ten or so fish in one haul. Other fishermen used the *gahana della* or throw net: a round net which was thrown over a shoal and then pulled slowly out of the water by a cord attached to the centre. Both of these methods produced catches of small fish such as sardines or anchovies and if 1970 figures are a reliable guide, the catch seldom exceeds ten pounds per trip, with the average catch around five pounds.

Fishing at night, fishermen used a heavier line, with one or two prawn-baited hooks, for rock fish. This method requires considerable skill in distinguishing a bite from the movement of the sinker more than 150 feet below, but it gives larger catches and it is not uncommon for a boat to get more than fifty pounds in a night. During the new moon period a torch lure was, and is, used for squid. The squid, attracted by the lure, feed on a floating bait and are picked up, bait and all, with a pole net. Occasionally larger fish, such as spanish mackerel, take the bait. This is the most profitable 'traditional' method of inshore fishing and in 1970 a crew might catch 800 squid (worth Rs.4 per hundred) a night.

The 'Bible' Net

In Gahavälla today the most important inshore fishing equipment is a half to one inch mesh nylon gill net, which is called the 'bible' because it was adopted from the Catholic fishermen of the west coast. This net is normally used in conjunction with the traditional inshore *orua*, but some of the larger deep-sea *oru* also use the 'bible' in inshore fishing. Although inshore fishermen occasionally used nets in the past, most of the traditional methods were based on handlines and the speed with which the 'bible' was adopted says much for their receptiveness to technological innovations. The first 'bible' net appeared in 1962 and by 1964, there were about thirty-five fully equipped *oru*. In 1970, all of the thirty-seven inshore *oru* in good repair had 'bible' nets, and there was sufficient netting to equip another ten craft.

Initially, the 'bible' net was used in the daytime within the harbour, directly competing with the beach-seines. Waiting until they sighted a shoal, the crew laid the net across its path. The two men who introduced the 'bible' employed this technique and in less than six months made more than Rs.15,000 each. Not surprisingly, the beachseine fishermen protested vigorously and there were several fights. When the District Revenue Officer prohibited 'bible' fishing within the bay in 1963, this practise had already been abandoned and pressure from the beachseiners prevented daytime use of the 'bible' even outside the beachseine sites.

Encouraged by the big profits, most of the inshore fishermen bought 'bible' nets and began using them as drift nets during the night. The *oru* leave just before dark and row a little more than a mile offshore and one or two miles down the coast. The nets are cast and allowed to drift with the current, while the three crew members[6] sleep or fish with a handline. The nets are pulled in a little after midnight and the crew returns to the beach to sleep. At dawn the fish are sold, mainly to local men seeking fish for home consumption and small bicycle traders.

The fishermen soon realised that they had been too quick to invest in 'bible' nets, for the fishery is too small for the number of craft involved. The area in which the nets can be laid is limited by several constraints; the lack of propulsion other than oars restricts the craft to four or five miles off the beach;[7] the nets and craft drift with the current and tide and run the risk of drifting onto the shore rocks; and some areas of the harbour have concealed rocks close to the surface which tear the nets. Consequently the fleet fishes in two sections, one on each side of the mouth of the bay, and incoming shoals are confronted by a series of parallel lines of nets. Most of a shoal is entrapped by one or two nets. Because each fisherman wants his net to be first in line, the fleet fishes further down the coast than conditions require.

Although there are thirty-seven *oru* equipped with 'bible' nets, for ten months of the year only eleven of these craft fish regularly.[8] The thirty-three men manning these craft derive very little income from other sources[9] and fish on every occasion, irrespective of the chances of a good catch, in order to obtain fish for their households' consumption. The average operating results for seven of these craft are presented in Table 5.1.

TABLE 5.1. OPERATING RESULTS: AVERAGE INSHORE CRAFT

Number of Craft	7	Production Expenses	
Number of Days Fished	244		
Squid Only	37	Net Replacement	Rs.330[a]
Drift Nets	207	Repairs	Rs. 60
Days Without Sales	92		
Average Sale	Rs. 5.01		
Total Cash Receipts	Rs.761.52	Total Expenses	Rs.399

[a] Assuming net life of three years. The nets carried by boats varies considerably; among the sample craft it ranged from 12 to 37 pieces. In general, the boats used by the younger men are larger and carry more nets and this further increases their effectiveness.

The men regularly employed on the 'bible' nets caught sufficient fish to sell on only 72 per cent of their trips and only 11 per cent of the trips resulted in cash sales of more than Rs.2.50. The average annual cash return per crew member was only Rs.292, although Rs.162 should be added as the value of fish consumed. If the production costs are calculated on a basis which includes the replacement of gear and interest on the money invested, the profit per fisherman (including the value of fish consumed) is only Rs.302. In the present situation, however, no attempt is made to replace damaged gear and if nets are damaged beyond repair, new nets can be borrowed for a token payment. There is little point therefore in deducting production costs when looking at the living standards of inshore fishermen.

As with the beachseines a large proportion of the inshore catch is taken during a four to six week flush season. At this time all thirty-seven craft are used on most nights and catches are very heavy; my records show eight nights when the total cash sales exceeded Rs.1,000.[10] But there is also severe maldistribution. On the most successful night (according to the fish trader's figures), the three most successful craft took Rs.600 each, and twenty-four craft shared less than Rs.400.

The sixty-odd men who fish only during the flush period fall into two groups. About twenty-five are beachseine fishermen using 'bible' nets to supplement their incomes. The remainder are young single men without regular employment. Because these marginal workers are younger and fitter, they fish further down the coast and take the greater share of the catch.

TABLE 5.2. ESTIMATED ECONOMIC CONSEQUENCES OF REDUCTION IN INSHORE CRAFT

	At Present Rs.	Twelve Craft Rs.
Cost of Gear	48,100	15,600
Total Catch	39,000[a]	37,000[b]
Production Expenses	15,873	5,148
Nett Catch	23,127	31,852
Number of Men	81	36
Return Per Man	286	885

[a] Assuming that the average annual catch of the men who participate only during the flush period is the same as that of the regular fishermen. My impression is that the cash sales are probably higher, but that this is balanced by the larger percentage of the annual catch used for home consumption by the regular fishermen.

[b] The slight reduction in the total output is to account for the reduction in the fish caught with handlines. It is doubtful that there would be any reduction at all in the catch from the nets.

While it is clear that the same catch could be taken with many fewer craft, it is difficult to estimate the optimum number. If there were eight craft, incoming shoals would be confronted by two lines of nets, each two miles long, and the vast majority of the shoals would probably be trapped. The fish trader's records show that on nights when the total catch exceeded Rs.200, 70 per cent was taken by the top three craft.

Allowing a 50 per cent margin for error, the consequences of a reduction of the 'bible' fleet to twelve craft are set out in Table 5.2. The cost of gear and annual production costs would be lowered by 68 per cent and profits would increase by Rs.9,000. Distributed among the crews of the twelve craft, this would give a return per man of Rs.885. Even if distributed among all eighty-one men who are presently engaged in 'bible' fishing, it would increase their annual incomes by 40 per cent.

I mentioned earlier that Gahavälla fishermen are aware that there are too many 'bible' nets, but it remains to be explained why the situation arose and why new craft are continually being added. To some extent the reasons for the excess effort in bible fishing are the same as with beachseining (see Chapters 9 and 10) but there are additional considerations. It should be stressed that the initial thirty-odd nets were purchased in a very short period. The innovators made very large profits, mainly because they could fish in the optimum positions, and others were eager to emulate them. The 'bible' was relatively cheap and men were prepared to incur debts to equip their otherwise unemployed sons. While the profits never met expectations, the initial assumption was that this was due to unfamiliarity with the new methods or merely a poor season.

There are several reasons why the fleet has not diminished. First, although the average catch is very low, there is also a considerable range. The most successful crew was not included in the sample, but the fish trader records show sales of more than Rs.250 on six occasions. Secondly, many of the 'bible' fishermen are young, about a quarter are under twenty-five, and have no other source of income. For these youths, 'bible' fishing for thirty to forty nights in the year provides relief from a boring existence and even small catches bring money for cigarettes or the cinema. Thirdly, there are few barriers to the marginal participant. A beachseiner can use the 'bible' at night and gear can be hired for one-tenth of the catch or less. Finally, some men have no option but to continue 'bible' fishing. Lacking other employment they must fish every night despite poor catches. Most of the regular 'bible' fishermen are older men and for ten months seldom catch enough to sell. When the flush period arrives, catches increase, but the bulk of the catch at this time goes to the younger men who are prepared to row well down the coast to intercept approaching shoals.

In a technical sense the 'bible' is far more efficient than the methods it displaced, but it is difficult to see this innovation as benefitting the community. While the catch of the inshore craft has tripled, it is reasonable to suppose that a major part of this increase was at the expense of the beachseines.[11] Production costs have doubled and, unlike the earlier gear produced within the village from locally available raw materials, are paid to the extra village sources who import nylon from Japan. The most deleterious social effects stem from the distribution of the catch: whereas earlier methods provided subsistence incomes for many, the 'bible' gives high incomes to the few. In Gahavälla, as in the other Southern Province villages, the introduction of a more efficient fishing method without a concomitant increase in the area of the fishery, has further impoverished the fishermen.

The Mechanised Craft

The reason for the demise of the deep-sea *orua* was the introduction of mechanised craft under government sponsorship. Gahavälla received its first mechanised craft in 1960 and by 1968, twenty-three had been issued to Gahavälla fishermen. Thirteen were still afloat in 1970, although only six (including three owned by the Co-operative) used Gahavälla as a fishing base. The programme has been very successful in increasing fish production in the Southern Division: landings doubled to an average annual catch of 7,400 tons in the 1960-64 period, and tripled to 21,400 tons in 1969. But the social welfare and financial aspects of the programme have been far less successful.

The 28-foot, three and one-half ton mechanised craft were introduced in 1958, and by September 1969, 1,946 had been issued to fishermen under the fisheries department hire-purchase scheme. It is not known how many of these craft are still afloat, but 75% is probably a generous estimate. The early craft were powered by a 9 to 11 horsepower motor and were designed for the same type of fishing as the sailing *orua* they were intended to replace; pole and line fishing or trolling for surface-feeding varieties and handlining for bottom-feeders. It was hoped that once the fishermen became accustomed to the new craft, multiple-hooked long lines, of both the bottom and floating varieties, could be developed as the main fishing technique.

Catches during the first few years were not impressive,[12] and the fisheries department decided that the craft were underpowered for trolling or pole and line fishing. Accordingly, a 22 to 23 horsepower motor was substituted without substantial design changes to the craft. Multiple-hooked long lines did not prove popular and today the bulk of the catch results from driftnetting; though both pole and line and trolling are important during the short seasons when schools of feeding tuna are sighted.

The government appreciated that the high capital cost of the craft (Rs.17,500 in 1960, Rs.30,000 in 1970) would place them beyond the reach of the genuine fishermen and a hire-purchase scheme was introduced. The owners, who were selected by ballot from qualified applicants, had to provide a deposit of Rs.1,000 and the government loan of Rs.15,000 was repayable over five years. Although the loan scheme was well-intentioned it had several technical defects. The provision for a Rs.1,000 deposit and the fact that the loan covered only the cost of the hull and engine, not the gear,[13] meant that the fishermen had to borrow money from private sources before taking over the boat. Because the men lacked experience in the operation of mechanised craft, breakdowns were frequent in the early operating period,[14] and as no provision was made for financing repairs the boat operators had to have access to private capital for this purpose also. But the most important defect was that the loan repayment was not related to the value of the catch and had to be met by a fixed monthly payment. Because the catch was sold through private traders there was no alternative to this system, although it meant that the loan repayments in the case of the unsuccessful operator would amount to a high proportion of his yearly income, and even the most successful fisherman was faced with months in the off-season when the loan repayment was greater than his income.

TABLE 5.3. ESTIMATED ANNUAL OPERATING COSTS, MECHANISED CRAFT

	Rs.	Rs.
Capital Costs	27,000	
Depreciation		5,334
Running Costs:		
(a) Fuel, Bait		5,000
(b) Maintenance & Repairs		4,900
Capital Repayment		5,400
Crew's Wages		9,600
Total Expenses		30,234
Catch	30,000	
Loss for Year		Rs.234

Source: Administration Report, Director of Fisheries 1968-69 (Appendix E).

The estimated operating costs of the 28-foot mechanised craft (on the basis of which the Ceylon Fisheries Department advocated more craft) with the addition of crew's wages at Rs.200 per man per month and loan repayments over five years, are given in Table 5.3. The capital cost of the hull and engine is Rs.22,000 and the gear Rs.5,000. Depreciation (calculated over a six-year period for the hull and engine and three years for the gear) amounts to Rs.5,334, and running costs to Rs.9,900. Assuming that the craft is in use for 200 days per year, with an average catch of Rs.150 per day, the yearly income will be Rs.30,000 and after provision for capital repayment, depreciation, and crew's wages, this leaves a small loss for the year.

These estimates were based on very small numbers of craft operating over short periods of time, but the main defect is that they were prepared in a cultural vacuum; no consideration was given to the social milieu in which the craft operate. It was assumed that the values and institutions governing the craft will be those of an urban mercantile community and that the boat owners will be able to make full use of facilities available in urban communities. Among the implicit assumptions used in the preparations of the estimates which are crucial to the successful operation of the scheme, are: (1) that the man to whom the craft is issued will continue to fish in the craft and will be content to earn approximately the same as the other crew members; (2) that overheads, such as loan repayments and depreciation, will be the first charge on the boat earnings and that crew members will be content to share the nett proceeds after these expenses have been met, or alternatively, that the boat operator will be able to recruit labour on a wage basis; (3) that the boat operator will be able to calculate depreciation and that facilities exist for him to save income in a readily convertible form for the time when he has to replace the boat; (4) that repairs can be financed from current earnings and that if need be the boat operator can borrow from banks or other finance houses.

In reality all of these assumptions are false. Most boat operators cease to fish after the first three or four years. Local tradition decrees that the crew members should receive 50 per cent of the catch after fuel and bait costs are deducted, so that the crew's share of a Rs.30,000 catch is approximately Rs.14,000, not Rs.9,600 as provided for in the estimates. While it is possible to slightly vary the percentage the crew receives, it would be very difficult to recruit crew members on a wage basis.[15] The boat operators lack the security required to obtain bank loans. Neither the boat nor the potential catch is accepted as security for bank loans, which must be secured by a clear title to land. In any case loans from agencies such as the Rural Bank are very slow in forthcoming and the boat operators cannot afford to have their boats beached for long periods.

Actual operating results for ten Gahavälla craft during the year April 1970 to March 1971 are given in Table 5.4.[16] The results are broadly commensurate with the estimates. The catch per trip and the price per pound are both higher, but the utilisation rate (the number of trips as a percentage of the total days in the year) is lower. As a result, the value of the catch is Rs.2,400 less than estimated. Running costs are also lower, with nothing being spent on bait and less than Rs.2,500 on fuel.

The table shows that the money available to the owner does not meet the overheads. The income of the average Gahavälla craft was Rs.4,709 short of the requirements, and the most successful was Rs.1,515 short. With the most competent management, it is still not possible for the owner to provide for repayment of the government loan and eventual replacement of the boat, even if he fishes himself and limits his consumption spending to the income he receives as a crew member.

Management of Mechanised Craft

The mechanised craft pose management problems which did not occur in the traditional methods of fishing. They are a high cost technology with a short operating life: approximately five years for the engine, eight years for the hull, and three years for the nets. Although the ratio of the operating costs to the value of the catch is similar to that of the traditional craft, the amount of money that is involved is very much greater and there is little flexibility in making payments. Fuel costs and repayment of the government loans should be met each month, irrespective of the size of the catch.

The expensive engine and nets introduced new uncertainties into fishing operations. In the traditional form of fishing operations owners are unlikely to be faced with

TABLE 5.4. ANNUAL OPERATING RESULTS
AVERAGE GAHAVALLA MECHANISED CRAFT: APRIL 1970-MARCH 1971

Number of Boats	10	
Catch - Pounds	35,368	
- Rupees	Rs.27,701	
Catch per Trip - Pounds	285	
- Rupees	Rs. 223	
Boat Utilisation Rate	31.7%	
Fuel Costs	Rs. 2,494	
Income per Crew Member	Rs. 3,164	
'Boat's' Share	Rs.12,658	
Overheads		
Repairs & Replacement of Lost Gear		Rs. 4,900
Depreciation - Hull & Engine (6 years)		Rs. 3,667
Gear (3 years)		Rs. 2,750
Repayments (5 years)		Rs. 6,050
Total:	Rs.12,658	Rs.17,367

expensive repairs; unless a craft is caught in very rough weather, repairs are limited to replacement of worn sections of the gear or *orua*. But with the new boats, fishermen are often faced with the theft or total destruction of a set of nets worth more than Rs.7,000 and engine repairs costing in excess of Rs.4,000. As both the labour and the materials for repairs come from outside the village, repair costs have to be met immediately upon completion and are too high to be paid out of current income. The high cost of the new boats makes it imperative that the time lost through repairs be minimised; the structure of the new economy makes delays inevitable.

The high costs and short operating life of the new craft mean that the owner has to make provision for the eventual replacement of the boat out of each year's income, and he can no longer rely on his income at the time, plus a series of small loans for this purpose. But the fishermen lack the concept of depreciation and even in the case of the cooperatively owned boats, operated under a management system devised by the fisheries department, no provision is made for eventual replacement of the craft. The system of management used for agricultural cooperatives, based on an asset (land) which appreciates over time, has been applied unaltered to the fishing cooperatives. Although the introduction of the mechanised craft has led to increased incomes for the crew members, the return on the owner's capital is less than was the case with the traditional gear: 4 per cent for the mechanised craft, as opposed to 8 per cent for the sailing *orua* and 6 per cent for the beachseines, (see p.116). The main reason for this is that the percentage of the catch received by the owner has not been adjusted to cover the increased capital investment required.

The mechanised craft give one big management advantage to their owners. Because of the large annual catches of high value fish, an individual boat owner is in a strong bargaining position vis-à-vis the *mudalali* (fish buyers). In return for the sole rights to the catch, the owner can demand higher prices for his fish, or, more likely, the credit facilities that are necessary for him to operate the craft.

In the Southern Division the bulk of the catch of the mechanised craft is sold through a system of 'tied' boats, in which the owner makes an agreement to sell all of his fish to a particular *mudalali*. The *mudalali* or his agent meets the craft when it returns and the fish are weighed. Each week the owner receives an itemised account in which the weight of the catch, the price per pound, and any deductions are recorded. Fisheries administrators commonly look on 'tied-boat' arrangements as a device for the exploitation of the fishermen by the middlemen but one should be wary of such stereotyping. From the fisherman's point of view, the system has several advantages. Firstly, it ensures that the catch can be speedily marketed before decomposition sets in, an important point when the driftnetting catch is often damaged in the water and only small numbers of craft are based on some harbours. Secondly, the *mudalali* serves both a short- and a long-term credit function. The short-term loans should be regarded as advance payments for the catch and are usually small, but the latter amount to sizeable sums, and are the fishermen's main source of credit. The loans are provided for both consumption, especially weddings and funerals, and production purposes. In addition, the *mudalali* is expected to make outright gifts on festival occasions and to lend equipment such as transport, chairs, and crockery. The loans, including advances for migratory fishing, are commonly free of interest and are repaid out of the catch.

All of the Gahavälla 'tied' boats are in debt to their *mudalali* for sums ranging from Rs.2,000 to Rs.8,000. The more successful of the fishermen could operate their craft without becoming indebted to the *mudalali* but they see it in their own interest to incur such debts. On the one hand it means that they can devote all their income to other purposes and rely on the interest free loans to finance repairs; on the other hand the possibility of repudiating the debts gives them a sanction if the *mudalali* treats them unfairly.

The *mudalali* system is based on an implicit contract with both sides having sanctions if the contract is broken. Competition for 'tied' boats is fierce and the fisherman can transfer to a new *mudalali* if he is dissatisfied. The new *mudalali* may then repay the fisherman's debts. The fisherman can also unload part of a large catch to another boat at sea and recover the money later. The *mudalali* has the ultimate sanction of violence; it is not unknown for boats to be dynamited, nets slashed, and owners assaulted or killed. But it should be stressed that the system operates within a framework of generally accepted customs and a *mudalali* or fisherman who consistently breaks these customs is likely to become isolated from the community. Fishermen often grumble about the generally low prices they receive for their fish, but the *mudalali*-fisherman relationship is generally a stable one. Indeed it is common to hear a fisherman finish an account of how rapacious *mudalali* are with the remark that his is an exception. This should not occasion surprise; unlike other areas, the Southern Division *mudalali* come from fishing stock and the patron-client relationship is founded on ties of caste, residence, kinship, and custom.

Fisheries administrators in Sri Lanka often argue that the main advantage accruing to the *mudalali* from this system is that he pays lower prices for the fish, but in my experience this is not correct. The price paid to 'tied' boats is much the same as the ruling rate in the area. The profits made by the *mudalali* (usually 60-90 per cent) are such that he maximizes his return by ensuring as large and as regular a supply of fish as possible. Clipping the price to the fishermen would militate against this while adding only marginally to his profits.[17] The other advantage of this system for the *mudalali* is that he does not have to pay for his purchases immediately. Thus, he can purchase very large amounts of fish with only a relatively small amount of cash. *Mudalali* are generally aware of these advantages and can see that it is not in their own interests to cut prices. In practice most *mudalali* operate on an implicit fixed price system which, in the case of migratory fishing, is made explicit to the fisherman at the start of the season.

Given the rather stringent management requirements of the mechanised craft, and the lack of any training to meet these requirements, it is not surprising that the management systems used by the fishermen differ from those envisaged by the planners. The boats are allocated by the government to individual fishermen who are solely responsible to the government for the loan repayments. Because the loans are not sufficient to fully equip the craft, the new owner borrows from a *mudalali* in return for the sole rights to the catch. Loan repayments are deducted at an annual rate of about 40 per cent of the owner's share of the catch (i.e., 17 per cent of the gross catch), but no interest is charged. The procedure for loan repayments is very flexible. During the months when the fishing is poor the *mudalali* may deduct nothing at all for the loan, while in good months the deduction may be as high as 80 per cent in the case of fishermen who are heavily indebted. Because of this flexibility in loan repayments, as well as the speed with which loans can be arranged, the fishermen see the credit facilities provided by the *mudalali* as superior to those offered by government agencies. Loans for small repairs are deducted from the catch as a whole, but larger loans are a charge on the 'boat's' share only.

Payment for the catch is made at weekly intervals, or at the end of the season in the case of migratory fishing, and the system of catch distribution is based on traditional methods. First the cost of fuel and any other goods (including small consumption loans given to the crew as a whole) supplied by the *mudalali* are deducted and the remainder is paid to the skipper. This is divided as follows: if the owner supplies both craft and nets, the owner's or 'boat's' share is 50 per cent; if the crew supply the nets, or if the craft is line fishing (in which case the individual crew members usually supply their own gear), the owner's share is a third. The crew's share is equally divided among the crew members without special payments to the skipper. In the early years of operation at least, the owner is usually also the skipper and receives a share as a crew member as well as the 'boat's' share.

Later developments depend on the skill, or the luck, of the initial owner. If the owner is unlucky, he is faced with heavy repair and gear replacement costs during the first two or three years' operation, and consequently will become indebted to the *mudalali* for sums ranging from Rs.5,000 to Rs.10,000. Despite the debt, the owner's income during these years is likely to be high (Rs.3,000 to Rs.6,500), because the debt is repayable at a rate of only 40 per cent of the 'boat's' share of the catch and the owner will not be repaying the government loan. In many cases the owner responds to this apparently high income by ceasing to fish and by giving the craft to a close relative to skipper. Much of the income is spent for consumption purposes, but most boat owners invest money in building a house on land in which they have inherited an undivided share.[18]

If the total debt exceeds Rs.5,000 at the end of the third main fishing season, the *mudalali* is unwilling to advance any further money. When another breakdown occurs, the owner is unable to raise the money for the repairs and is forced to sell the craft, with the money going to the *mudalali* to repay the debt. Because of the uncertainty of title, the prices for second-hand craft are very low: a three-year old craft in reasonable condition but needing repairs and without gear, is unlikely to bring more than Rs.2,500. The craft that are sold are bought by other fishermen, not *mudalali*, although the latter may advance the money. At the end of the three-year period, the unsuccessful boat owner has lost his boat and his means of livelihood, although he is still responsible for the government loan repayments, and is indebted to the *mudalali* for Rs.1,500 to Rs.5,000. On the other hand he often has a new, if uncompleted, house.

The sequence in the case of a skilful, or lucky, owner is rather different. If the repair and gear replacement costs are low during the early life of a boat, the owner can limit the extent to which he is indebted to the *mudalali*. Although at some points during the year the debt may exceed Rs.5,000, he is able to reduce it below this point at the end of the main fishing season. Consequently, when boats from less successful owners are sold, he is in a good position to buy them, either from his current income or with the aid of a loan from a *mudalali*. The new boat is given to a close relative to operate but the 'boat's' share goes to the owner. Once the owner has acquired two or three boats he can manage them in a manner derived from the traditional system. In some cases the craft are operated under this system from the beginning as when two or three brothers are allocated boats. In this case the transference of funds from one boat to another may be technically a loan, but the same principles apply.

With the income and the credit facilities of all three boats at the owner's disposal, repair and gear replacement costs can be met immediately they fall due, and as less time is lost through repairs the income from the craft is higher than average. When one of the boats is beyond repair, the owner can easily purchase, repair and re-equip a second-hand craft to replace it, or in a few cases, finance the purchase of a new craft. As owners make only nominal payments toward the government loan and have no need to make provision for depreciation, their nett income from the 'boat's' share is high, and may exceed Rs.10,000 per annum. Compared with the single boat owners, a large percentage of the income is available for investment so it is possible for the owner to purchase the sole rights to land and complete a house on it. This in turn increases his ability to raise money in an emergency.

A prerequisite for the successful operation of boats under this system is complete trust between the owner of the boats and the skipper. As the boats are often fishing away from the home village, the skipper is in a good position to defraud the owner. The owner usually appoints a close relative as skipper and this limits the number of boats that can be collectively managed to three or four. The key to success of this system is the collective management; the 'boat's' share of the catch is treated as a single unit and is not devoted to each boat individually. Thus, a run of bad luck by a single boat will not put it out of commission for long periods of time, as is the case with the individually managed boats, be they co-operatively or privately owned.

It is difficult to provide a conclusive account of the extent to which mechanised boats are operated under this system. Because the sale of boats is illegal many owners are unwilling to admit that they have bought craft, while others may claim ownership of the craft they operate so as to boost their status. But it is possible to gather information by indirect means and only three of the Gahavälla boats are individually owned and operated.

One of the intentions of the programme was to increase employment among the villages and in this it failed completely. Up to September 1969 a total of 803 boats had been issued to fishermen residing in the Southern Division. Assuming that 75 per cent are still afloat and that each provides employment for four men, this would give a total of 2,408 men engaged full-time in deep-sea fishing. It is very doubtful that this is any more than were employed full-time in 1958,[19] and it is certainly true that employment opportunities have not kept pace with the increase in population, even if the baseline is limited to the families engaged in deep-sea fishing prior to the introduction of mechanised craft. Although it is true that any further boats issued will provide new employment opportunities, two points must be emphasised. Firstly, using the population data provided by De Silva (1964:44) and applying medium projections of population growth rates (cf. Selvararatnam 1970:7) it will require an issue of eighty-three boats per year in the Southern Division to provide jobs for the increase in the labour force alone. Thus, the issue of new boats, even at the level of 500 per year for the island as envisaged in the development plan, will do little to alleviate the very high rates of unemployment in the fishing villages. Secondly, working on a mechanised boat gives a relatively high income and jobs are keenly sought; experienced deep-sea fishermen have few difficulties in obtaining jobs, but the inexperienced men tend to be recruited from among the relatives of the owners. Consequently, there are few opportunities for those outside the boat-owning elite to acquire the experience necessary for the allocation of a boat.

In assessing the consequences of the mechanised boat scheme for employment opportunities, attention must also be paid to the impact of the mechanised boats on other fishing technologies. Contrary to the assumptions of the Ministry of Planning and Employment (1970), the deep-sea *oru* have not continued to operate alongside the new craft, the most important reason for this being the diversion of capital previously invested in the deep-sea *oru* to the mechanised craft.

The mechanised craft have also had a marked impact on the beachseines. Many of the harbours which were previously used for beachseining have now been made over as anchorages for the mechanised craft, and in harbours beachseining has ceased. In the absence of reliable figures an accurate account cannot be given of the employment loss, but an optimistic estimate is that only twenty-five per cent of the beachseine sites in use in 1950 were still in production in 1972.

Summary: The Three Technologies

The contribution of each of the three main fishing methods - beachseining, inshore fishing and mechanised craft - to Gahavälla's economy is set out in Table 5.5.

TABLE 5.5. COMPARATIVE OPERATING RESULTS: BEACHSEINES, MECHANISED CRAFT, INSHORE FISHING

	Beachseines Rs.	Mechanised Craft Rs.	Inshore Fishing Rs.
Cost of Equipment	383,625	302,500	48,100
Annual Catch[a]	173,571	279,250	39,000
Production Costs	66,330	74,000[b]	14,430
Nett Catch	107,241	205,250	25,570
No. of Men Employed	274	47	81
Return Per Man	391	4,367	315

[a] Includes fish distributed for consumption without payment.

[b] Includes fuel costs and repairs.

While these mechanised craft produce 57 per cent of the fish caught by Gahavälla fishermen, as opposed to 35 per cent from the beachseines and 8 per cent from inshore fishing, they do not make the largest contribution to the village economy. Production costs for the mechanised craft are high, and much of it goes to extra-village sources: approximately Rs.74,000 is paid for fuel and repairs, and Rs.111,000 goes in wage-payments to crew members living in other areas. As all fish produced by the mechanised craft are sold to *mudalali* from other villages, the total contribution is about Rs.100,000. In contrast, most of the production costs of the beachseines are intra-village and less than Rs.2,000 leaves Gahavälla. Nearly all of the beachseine catch is sold to Gahavälla fish traders and assuming a 25 per cent profit, the contribution (total catch plus marketing profit) of the beachseines to the village economy is nearly Rs.275,000: 70 per cent of all fishing income.

The mechanised craft provide employment[20] for forty-seven men and the average return per participant is Rs.4,173. Two hundred and seventy-four men are employed in beachseining for an average return of Rs.349, and eighty-one in inshore fishing for an average return of Rs.285.

The table also gives some idea of the different economic structures of the three methods. Although the mechanised craft provide the largest gross return on capital (0.92 for the mechanised craft, 0.45 for the beachseines, and 0.81 for the inshore fisheries), and a comparatively high profit excluding labour costs (mechanised craft 0.64, beachseines 0.21, inshore fishing 0.48), the finance required is considerably greater. Overall, Rs.7,500 are invested for each man employed on the mechanised craft, as opposed to Rs.1,400 for the beachseines and Rs.600 for the inshore fishing. Investment on the scale required for mechanised craft is beyond the reach of fishermen and all was provided by the government.

It is often argued that the appropriate way to measure the effectiveness of a fishing technique is in terms of catch per man-hour (Bottemanne 1959). Although the value of such a measure is doubtful in an economy lacking alternative employment and where men fish irrespective of the possibilities of a good catch, it does give some indication of the relative effectiveness of the three methods. The data are summarised in Table 5.6, the first column is the total output per man-hour, the second the profit (i.e. the return after the deduction of production costs excluding labour) per man-hour.

The data in Table 5.6 reflect differences in the degree of subsistence orientation. The beach seines and the mechanised craft are market determined. Men fish only when the probabilities of a reasonable catch are high and the profit per man-hour approaches Rs.2.50. But the output per man-hour in inshore fishing is less than Rs.0.50 and the profit closer to Rs.0.30, for this is a subsistence activity for most of the year. If the figures for the short flush period were excluded the output per man-hour was less than Rs.0.30.

TABLE 5.6. CATCH PER MAN-HOUR

	Total Man-Hours[a]	Output Per Man-Hour Rs.	Profit Per Man-Hour Rs.
Beachseines	42,793	4/06	2/23
Mechanised Boats	55,214	4/99	2/23
Inshore Fishing	79,948	0/49	0/29

[a] The figure for the beachseines is calculated from the data in Table 6.6 multiplied by the number of hauls. Mechanised boats = No. of men (40) average number of trips (115) hours per trip (12). Inshore fishing = No. of men (81) average number of trips (90) hours per trip (8). The data on the mechanised craft include only time at sea and do not include repairs, marketing, collecting bait etc. The beachseine data do not include time 'on call', but do include time maintaining gear. The margin of error for the beachseines and mechanised boats is small, but for the inshore fishing may be as great as 25 per cent.

The comparison of the three methods establishes the paramount position of the beachseines in Gahavälla's economy. Inshore fishing is mainly a subsistence living for men without other employment and even during flush periods most of the catch is sold within the village. The mechanised craft are the only technology where the marginal product of additional labour and capital is not either close to, or equal to, zero; but employment access is limited to men who have boat-owning relatives or good political contacts. Despite the technological innovations of the past decade the beachseines still provide two-thirds of Gahavälla's income and are the major livelihood for nearly 300 households. Any changes in the relations of production in beachseining have far-reaching consequences for the village as a whole.

CHAPTER 6

THE ECONOMICS OF BEACHSEINING

Beachseining is one of the most common fishing techniques used in peasant societies. It has been reported from Africa (Hill 1970), South America (Forman 1971) and Asia (Blake 1970; Fraser 1962) and was formerly widespread in both Europe and North America (Bottemanne 1959). Early references to beachseining in Sri Lanka appear in the 'Report of the Commissioners Appointed to Inquire into the Sea Fisheries of Ceylon' which was convened in 1867 to deal with disputes between Sinhalese fishermen living immediately south of Colombo and migrant Indian fishermen from the Madras coast (Wright 1868). Witnesses appearing before the commission stated that Sinhalese fishermen had been using beachseines, which they called *madella* (*mahadella* - 'big net') for as long as anyone could remember, certainly 'before their grandfathers' time.' These *madell*, less than 200 yards long, were constructed from coconut coir, a relatively cheap material but one which imposed severe limits on the mesh size. The minimum mesh size was about six inches and the nets could take only mature fish, of the 'rock' and small tuna varieties.

In the decade prior to 1865, however, Tamil fishermen, who visited west Sri Lanka to buy logs for their *cattamaran*, began fishing with a new type of net imported from India. Because it was made from a combination of hemp and cotton (hence its name *nuldella*, 'cotton net'), a much smaller mesh was possible, in some cases less than an inch. The *nuldella* was also considerably longer than the *madella*, occasionally exceeding 400 yards on each side, and its high cost (£40 in 1867) put it out of the reach of the Sinhalese fishermen. The local fishermen claimed that *nuldell*, operated solely by labour recruited in India, were destroying their livelihood and asked the government to ban them.[1] The commission did recommend restrictions on the use of the *nuldell*, but these appear to have been ineffective, for the new nets spread rapidly throughout the island and reached the Tangalla region before 1886 (see Administration Report, Government Agent, Hambantota, 1886). Indian fishermen, however, were barred from the fishing grounds south of Colombo and shifted their activities to the north-eastern coast of Sri Lanka.

While the older type of *madella* is found occasionally in the smaller and poorer fishing communities, most beachseines are now of the *nuldella* type, and as this net is called a *madella* in contemporary Sinhalese usage the term is also employed here. *Madella* is the general term for beachseines and sub-types of nets are named after the variety of fish they are designed to catch. The *hāl mässa della* is used for *hāl mässa* (anchovies). But as the differences concern only mesh size and length, the nets described for Gahavälla are typical of the Southern Province.

The Madella

Beachseines consist of a cod-end (*maduwa*), a large body (*punchi kata*, 'small mouth'), the wings (*maha kata*, 'big mouth') and the hauling ropes. In Gahavälla the nets measure approximately 500 yards from the middle of the cod-end to the end of the wings, and weigh about two tons when wet.[2] The cod-end has a mesh size of 0.4 inches and is made from cotton yarn. Laid flat it is trapezoid, fifteen feet long, five feet wide at the mouth and ten feet wide at the enclosed end. It is attached to the net body by lacing ropes, which can be drawn tight to prevent the fish escaping. The normal capacity of the cod-end, about 2,000 pounds, is increased to nearly 4,000 pounds if the entire catch is small fish.

The body is also made of cotton yarn and like the cod-end is dyed dark brown with an extract of mangrove bark. This stain prevents rubbing and chafing of the twine and apparently makes it more difficult for the fish to detect. The body consists of eight, five-foot sections. Its mesh is 0.6 inches at the point where it joins the cod-end, increasing to three inches at the wing end. Laid flat,

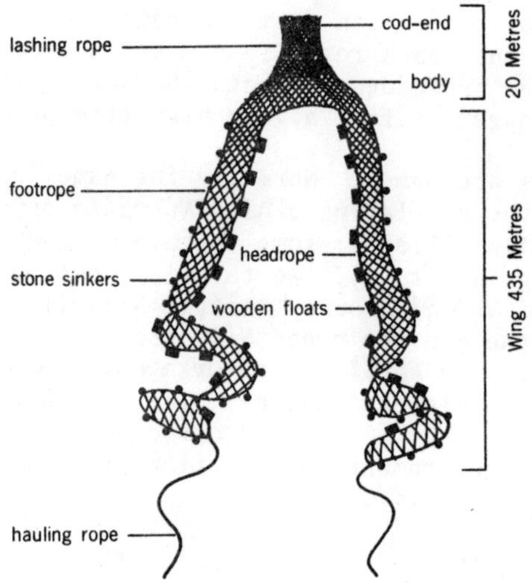

FIG. 6–1: THE MADELLA (not to scale)

the body is a vertical conical section fifty feet across at its widest point adjoining the wings. The wings are made of coconut coir twine, forming a coarse gill net with a mesh that increases gradually from six inches to three feet, and a depth in the water of eight to twelve feet. The headrope along the body and wings has wooden floats at five foot intervals complemented by stone sinkers along the footrope. Additional coir hauling ropes are added if required and sometimes exceed 500 yards.

When the nets are not in use, the cod-end is detached and the remainder of the net is stacked on the beach; one wing on the bottom, followed by the body and then the second wing. The top of the net is tightly plaited to give some protection from the rain and the nets stacked on the beach resemble stooks in a cornfield. This storage procedure protects the nets efficiently and the only danger is from a very high tide or arson.[3]

All nets are named. Normally the names record the origin of the net-laying craft (*Nilvälla orua* an *orua* from Nilvälla village); some feature of the original owners (e.g. *Api tunay*, 'we three', a net built by three men; *Punchi Nilvälla orua*, 'little Nilwella *orua*', a net bought by the men who owned *Nilvälla orua*); or a literary title (e.g. *Gama Periliya*, after a novel by Sri Lankan writer Martin Wickramasinghe). The nets are also linked in a sequence, which nowadays corresponds to their numbers in the government registration list.

Equipment Costs

The cost of a fully equipped *madella* is shown in Table 6.1.

The cod-end and body of the net are purchased in the form of pieces of woven net, thirty feet long, from *Madella* fishermen near Colombo. These are cut into sections about two feet square, which are sewn together two or three deep, to strengthen and add weight to the net. While no nets have been built for seven years, informants estimate that forty large pieces (Rs.43 each) are required, with Rs.55 of nylon yarn for sewing. The wings require 2,000 hanks of village-produced coconut coir

TABLE 6.1. MADELLA COSTS

		Rs.
Net - Cod-End		725
Body		1,050
Wings		1,000
Hauling Ropes[a]		100
Orua[b]		1,000
	Total:	3,875

[a] Assuming that the ropes are shared between ten nets.

[b] Assuming that the net has its own *orua* and allowing Rs.200 for initial repair costs.

twine at Rs.0.50 per forty-yard hank. About a quarter of the net owners use family labour to twist the twine and in these cases about Rs.250 are required to purchase beaten coconut husks. Sufficient coir twine for the hauling ropes cost Rs.0.75 per yard of completed rope, but as the nearest equipment for twisting the eight-strand rope is twelve miles from Gahavälla, transport and hire costs lift the price to about Rs.1,000 for a 1,000-yard rope. Few nets have hauling ropes of their own and the cost is usually shared among ten or so nets.

Government regulations require each *madella* registered to have a separate net-laying craft. In practice this regulation is not enforced because, apart from any other considerations, there is insufficient room on the beach to store 108 *oru*. In the latter part of 1971 there were fifty-eight *oru* for the ninety-nine *madell* in use. The *oru* were not distributed evenly among the nets: whereas forty-three *madell* had their own *oru*, one particular *orua* was used by five nets. The *oru* used for net-laying in Gahavälla are second-hand deep-sea craft, more than thirty-five feet long. More than twenty years old when purchased, they are too dangerous for deep-sea fishing, but informants claim a twenty-five year operational life when used for beachseining. In 1971 two of these craft were purchased. The first cost Rs.875 and a further Rs.150 for repairs; the second, in very poor condition, cost Rs.800 plus an estimated Rs.400 in labour and materials to replace a section of the hull.

The average annual operating costs of the *madella* are given in Table 6.2.

TABLE 6.2. MADELLA, AVERAGE ANNUAL OPERATING COSTS

		Rs.
NET:	Cod-End and Body (Replacement over 10 Years)	172 Rs.
	Wings (Replacement over 3 Years)	330
	Hauling Ropes (Replacement over 3 Years)	33
ORUA:	Repairs	25
	Replacement over 25 Years	40
WAGE:	Dyeing (Twice Yearly)	20
PAYMENTS:	Restacking (3 Times Yearly)	45
	Total:	Rs. 665

The coir sections of the net are replaced in a set sequence over three years, while the *maduwa* and the body are repaired as necessary. The ten year period used in Table 6.2 represents a consensus of informants, my own data give a range of Rs.30 to Rs.280 and an average Rs.164, for 1970-71. Annual repairs to the *orua* are limited to small patches on the hull and replacing the lashings on the washboards and outrigger. Most nets are dyed and restacked by wage labour, but when the catch is poor the latter is carried out by crew members without special payment.

The data provided in Table 6.2 are intended only as a guide to the annual running costs for these are subject to a great deal of fluctuation. There is always the possibility that nets may be washed out to sea by a high tide or damaged by rocks during fishing, leading to well over Rs.1,000 worth of repairs. Poor men owning nets which have a bad season, often postpone repairs and may attempt to borrow an *orua* and *maduwa* from another net. In fact the only cost which cannot be delayed is the replacement of the coir sections of the net, for if this is neglected the net will break under the strain of a heavy catch. But the net owners can twist the coir themselves reducing the costs to about Rs.129. It should be stressed, however,that the running costs cannot be postponed indefinitely. Nets must have their own *maduwa* to be registered and borrowing an *orua* is much easier for men with many nets than poor men with only one. Thus over a three or four year period the average annual running costs will approximate the figures in the table.

Madella Ecology

Beachseining, which still produces about 35 per cent of Sri Lanka's fish, requires an area of approximately 6,000 square yards with a sandy bottom, free from rocks or other obstructions which might rip the net. This restricts operations along the 120 miles of the south-western coast to about twenty sites (*padu*), for in most areas with reasonably sheltered beaches the coral reefs lie close to the shore. The *padu* must also be sufficiently sheltered to permit the launching of the one and a half ton net-laying craft through the surf and most *padu* can only be used for the six months of the non-monsoon period; September to February for the coastline west of Tangalla, and March to August for the area to the east. Most west coast *padu* are further restricted in that even during the non-monsoon period, the sea is sometimes too rough to launch a boat, or a strong current makes it too difficult to haul the net.

Two aspects of Gahavälla beachseining are atypical of the region. First, fishing is possible throughout the year. Gahavälla is not affected by the north-east monsoon and the area of the harbour used for *madella* fishing is protected from the south-west monsoon by a headland. A series of rock shelves, in combination with the action of the surf on the beach, restricts fishing to the southern half mile of the beach, which is subdivided into two fishing stations (*patte*): the *varaya* (harbour), and the *galaha* (rock). The second atypical feature is the type of craft used. In most *padu* the surf is sufficiently strong, even during the non-monsoon period, to make the launching of heavily laden *oru* a difficult and hazardous operation. This has resulted in the construction of thirty-foot, flat-bottomed craft called *pāru*, based on a double keel of two dugout logs. Both ends of the *pāru* slope at an angle of 50 degrees to the water and its flat bottom and great buoyancy, even while fully laden, make launching possible in heavy surf. The *pāru* is an expensive craft, however, and the Gahavälla fishermen use converted deep-sea *oru*, no longer sufficiently sea-worthy for deep-sea fishing, for net-laying. With the cessation of deep-sea *oru* construction following mechanisation, few second-hand craft are now available and Gahavälla fishermen will eventually have to turn to *pāru*, with a consequent increase in production costs.

A complete analysis of the fish varieties caught by the *madell* is beyond my competence, but some observations would not be out of place.[5] The bulk of the catches were identified by informants as *hāl mässa* (anchovies), *sudaya* (sardines), *udässa* (silver biddy), or *katuvälla* (herrings), with the first comprising more than half the catch. Although a few *hāl mässa* are caught throughout the year, the fishermen expect a series of large catches once a year, around September. Two other species of fish, *saleya* (ribbon fish) and *ätavalla* (mackerel tuna), also provide occasional large catches. The most valuable single catch any of my informants could remember was in late 1963, when 3,500 *ätavalla* were sold at Rs.3.25 each and many others given away. The entire catch is used except for poisonous varieties such as blowfish, and occasional turtles, which are always thrown back into the water.[6]

There is no question of beachseining depleting fish stocks. This is an important point in view of the accumulating evidence that the entry of capitalist enterprises to fisheries often results in the destruction of fish stocks (Christy & Scott 1965). The anchovies which comprise the bulk of the beachseine catch are migratory fish and research by the Sri Lankan Fisheries Department suggests that only a small proportion of shoals venture sufficiently close to the shore to be taken by beach-seines, or other peasant fishing techniques (Canagaratnam & Medcof 1956). Using current methods the yields can be sustained indefinitely, although the use of large industrial craft would radically alter the ecology.

Madella Operation

About two weeks before the *madella* is to be used, damaged sections of netting are replaced, floats and weights re-attached and the cod-end redyed. The net-laying craft (*della orua*) is repaired and its outrigger, which is detached to prevent the craft drifting with a high tide, lashed to its mountings with coconut coir. On the evening before use the *madella* is loaded into the *orua*, one wing in the prow, the *maduwa* and body in the centre and the other wing in the stern.

Fishing begins a little before dawn. Two men lift the prow of the *orua* with their backs and the remaining seven crew members push against the outrigger struts. As the fully laden craft weighs nearly two tons, nine men can only move it inches at a time and at low tide it takes half an hour to launch. The dangerpoint is after the *orua* is fully afloat and before the rowers are in position, for an unexpected wave may swing the *orua* sideways, badly injuring anyone in its path.

One end of the hauling rope is attached to a heavy object on the beach or held by one of the crew, and the *orua* is rowed towards the nearest boundary of the *padu* and then out to sea. The usual crew are four oarsmen rowing from the prow, three net-layers who pay the net down the length of the *orua* and over the stern, and the *marrakalai* (skipper) who is also the steersman. If the net is the first for the day, it is set to enclose the maximum area of water as quickly as possible, and as soon as one side has been paid out the *marrakalai* directs the *orua* towards the shore. Later in the day, especially if catches are poor, the *marrakalai* may pause at sea for as long as two hours searching for a shoal, aided by men on the beach and cliffs who wave sarongs to direct him. It is common to see two *della oru* more than a mile off-shore, both watching the same shoal and hoping that it will enter their *padu*.[7] In such cases the net is deliberately set to enclose the shoal, but the normal practice is to seine 'blind'.

The second wing is paid out on the return trip to the beach and as soon as the water is less than four feet deep, all the crew, except the *marrakalai*, jump out and drag the hauling rope up the beach. Occasionally the net will not reach the beach and one of the crew swims out with a rope. The initial task of the shore crew is to bring the two ends of the nets, which at this stage are often more than 100 yards apart, together. Unless there is some danger from rocks, they use the run of the tide for this purpose, holding the net firm as the waves ebb and letting it float as the waves come in. Consequently, the northern side of the net tends to remain in position and the southern side moves to meet it.

Meanwhile the *marrakalai* pulls the *orua* hand over hand towards the cod-end and ties the *orua* to the centre of the net. At this stage the mouth of the *maduwa* is closed by the lacing rope and using a short rope attached to the bottom of the *maduwa*, the *marrakalai* prevents it from dragging on the sea bottom or pulling the top of the net too far below the surface. Then with a series of simple arm signals he directs the shore crew in hauling the net, trying to ensure that the two sides are pulled in at the same rate and the *maduwa* is kept centred. The hauling movement and the action of the waves vibrates the net, scaring the fish towards the centre. As the fish cannot enter the *maduwa* and few become entangled in the body of the net, most are chased towards the beach and for this reason a net with a heavy catch is as easy to haul as an empty net. This point is of some importance, for many observers, noting the large numbers who often participate, have suggested that the labour requirements of beachseining are far greater than is the case (Canagaratnam and Medcof 1956). While it is probably true that the larger nets found near Colombo require bigger crews than the nine men customary in Gahavälla, reports of 50-100 men crews reflect the poverty of these villages, not the demands of the beachseining technique. The last stages of a big catch require a larger than normal crew, but at no time are more than fifteen men required. It is interesting to note that the brief survey of beachseining in several *padu* reported by Canagaratnam and Medcof (1956) shows an inverse relationship between the number of participants and the catch per head.

In the early stages of hauling each crew member walks waist deep into the water, attaches his hauling harness[8] to the net and strains slowly backwards up the beach. About forty feet from the water's edge an old man or young boy coils the net. Once the *maduwa* is approximately thirty yards from the beach, and the two wings are parallel about fifteen yards apart, two crew members take up positions shoulder deep in the water at each side of the net. As the wings are dragged past them, they bring the top and bottom together, vigorously shaking the net to increase the vibration and scare the fish towards the *maduwa*. Simultaneously the *marrakalai* drops the rope holding the *maduwa* off the sea bed, unlaces the mouth of the *maduwa* and unties the *orua*. As soon as the *maduwa* comes within reach of the men in the water, they haul on the lacing rope reclosing the mouth of the *maduwa*.

This is the most critical point in the haul. If the *marrakalai* is too slow to open the *maduwa*, fish will leap over the wings or escape through the interstices of the net. If it is opened too early, fish may escape from the *maduwa* before it is closed because the weight of the fish drags the wings below water level. The *marrakalai's* decision is governed by the speed of the hauling, the skill of the men in the water, and his estimation of the size and species composition of the catch. The last factor is particularly important in the frequent cases when the net contains a shoal of *hāl mässa* (anchovies) being chased by *thora* (spanish mackerel). The *marrakalai* must get the *thora* into the *maduwa* and smothered by the *hāl mässa* before their teeth can wreck havoc among the shore crew's legs.

Once the *maduwa* has been closed, the body of the net is folded inwards and carried up the beach dragging the *maduwa* behind it. At this point a few fish escape and are chased by small boys, using their hands or a small gill net, but contrary to some reports (Canagaratnam and Medcof 1956), the number of fish that escape from a skilfully operated net is very small. Occasionally the catch is so large that the *maduwa* cannot be closed or dragged up the beach. Five or six men then detach the *maduwa* from the body of the net and attempt to hold the mouth above the water, while others use hand nets to remove the fish. The men are continually knocked off their feet by the surf and many fish escape, but most are probably caught by later nets.

Once the *maduwa* has been beached the fish are left to die, and the crew spread the net to dry. If the catch is a good one, small fish caught up in the body of the net may be left for whoever wishes to collect them but usually these are tossed into the *maduwa* for later sale. In the evening the dry net is reloaded into the *orua*, or if the net's cycle (see below) is complete, two men re-stack it until it is used again three months later.

Labour Requirements

As was noted above a *madella* is usually operated by a nine-man crew and, except for the final stage of an exceptionally heavy catch, this crew carries out all tasks associated with the net. The man-hours required for the operation of the average net are set out in Table 6.3.

TABLE 6.3. MADELLA LABOUR INPUTS

	Man-Hours
PER NET CYCLE	
Running Repairs	16
Maintenance (one-third of annual cost)	30
Restacking	6
	52
PER HAUL	
Loading Net in *Orua*	3
Launching, Setting and Hauling	36
	39

MAN-HOURS PER NET CYCLE = 52 + (39 x number of hauls)

Running repairs (including re-attaching the outrigger to the *orua*, shifting the *orua* along the beach to the stacked net and replacing damaged sinkers and floats) take a couple of men a leisurely day. Maintenance (repairing the *orua* and replacing a third of the coir sections of the net) is the task of the entire nine-man crew and the time required depends upon the condition of the *orua*. Thirty-six hours is a minimum assuming that a man can weave 1/24th of the net in eight hours and sixteen hours is sufficient to re-assemble the net. Loading the net into the *orua*, whether from the stack or the drying area, occupies three men for less than an hour. Launching the *orua* takes half an hour, setting and hauling the net about two and a half hours and a further hour is required to sell the fish and spread the net out to dry.

These figures are based on a nine-man crew, although at times as many as fifty men will haul the net. In the vast majority of cases, however, only the permanent crew work the net and even when others join in, the total labour inputs do not markedly increase, for most of the additional men participate only in the final stages of the hauling operation and work for no more than ten minutes each.

On the day of the biggest catches of the year all labour inputs were recorded in half-hour units. In the case of the most labour-intensive net (which also took the biggest catch) three members of the net crew worked for seven hours each and the other six for four hours each.[9]

Three men requested to help worked for two and a half hours and four men for two hours, while thirty-two bystanders participated for less than half an hour apiece. The total man-hours for this net were 76½; which is thirteen hours longer than any other net on the day. The net, which was the sixth for the day and launched at 11 a.m., took only two hours to launch, set and haul; but it took nearly two hours to shift the heavy catch from the *maduwa* to a storage area on the beach and a further three hours before all the fish was sold. With the exception of the data gathered on this day the estimates of labour inputs are based on observation rather than detailed records, and include only the activities that are strictly necessary for the operation of the nets. In practice the fishermen spend a considerable amount of time 'on call' in case their net is used, and it is not uncommon for a man to spend a week on the beach in anticipation of his net being used, only to be disappointed each day.

Although the average net takes three hours to launch, set and haul, during periods of good fishing the period between the landing of successive nets is seldom more than two hours. As only nine daily hauls are possible in each of the two fishing stations, and as the need to dry nets precludes the use of an individual net more than once a day, the optimum number of nets for Gahavälla beach is eighteen. Assuming that an individual could participate in the hauling of three nets per day, the optimum number of nets could be worked by a labor force of fifty-four. In 1970-71 there were ninety-nine nets in use on Gahavälla beach and 274 men were engaged in beachseining, 180 of them full time.

Fish Landings

The value of the fish taken by the ninety-nine Gahavälla beachseines during three complete net cycles is summarized in Table 6.4. The three cycles occupied 317 days between 1 June 1970 and 7 July 1971. Beachseining for the remainder of the year lifted the total catch by only Rs.8,732 and did not increase the earnings of any individual net by more than Rs.300. The table includes only the money received from the main sale of the catch and does not include fish distributed to members of the net crew, although much of this is immediately sold. The total catch, including the value of fish consumed by members of the crew's households is estimated as 10 per cent greater than the cash sales receipts.

The annual cash sales were nearly Rs.160,000. There was a marked fall in the catches during the June-September cycle, but although this coincides with the last months of the south-west monsoon, the reason for the fall in the catch was scarcity of fish, not difficulties in launching the *orua* or setting the net. Returns from inshore fishing were so low during June, July and the first week

TABLE 6.4. BEACHSEINE FISH LANDINGS

	Cycle One (June-Sept.) Rupees	Cycle Two (Sept.-Dec.) Rupees	Cycle Three (Jan.-April) Rupees	All Cycles (June 1970-April 1971) Rupees
VALUE OF CATCH				
Total Catch	11,627	79,021	67,081	157,729
Average Per Haul	124	352	176	225
Average Per Net	113	798	678	1,589
Highest Net	2,064	5,244	5,647	7,762
Lowest Net	Nil	Nil	Nil	38
Catch Per Man-Hour	1.3	5.7	3.3	3.7
HAULS				
Total No. of Hauls	94	225	382	701
Average Per Net	0.9	2.3	3.9	7.1
Highest Net	3	9	8	14
Lowest Net	Nil	Nil	Nil	4

of August, that only thirty-seven beachseine hauls were attempted, of which only seven had a catch worth more than Rs.25. In my opinion, and in the opinion of the fishermen, the *madell* could have been used on every day during this period, if catches were worthwhile.

By contrast, October was a month of very high catches. Eighteen days fishing, between October 5 and 25, produced nearly one-third of the annual catch, with the daily catches averaging Rs.3,500 and two days producing more than Rs.6,500. The other two-thirds of the catch were spread throughout the remaining eight months of the year. Few days fishing produced less than Rs.500, but the catch exceeded Rs.2,500 on only three days. The contrast between the flush period and the rest of the year is normally more marked than Table 6.4 suggests, for the ban on night fishing following the 'insurrection' in April 1971 lifted fish prices by more than 150 per cent. If this price rise had not occurred more than 40 per cent of the annual yield would have been taken during the flush period. (See Appendix Three).

The statistics on the seasonal bias of fish landings agree with accounts gathered during the early stages of fieldwork. Informants claimed that although catches fluctuated from day to day, monthly catches were relatively constant, with the exception of a two month lean period around July (*hēen kāleya*, 'thin time') and a much shorter period of high catches in late September (*salli kāleya*, 'money time'). But they stressed that they were unable to predict the exact months in which the high and low peaks would occur and the general opinion was that the lean period in 1970 was about a month earlier than usual.

It is not possible to provide quantitative data on annual catch fluctuations, although all informants, both fishermen and members of the Fisheries Department, stress that these are considerable. This is in accord with the results of biological research on the dynamics of exploited fish populations in other areas (Beverton and Holt 1956, 1957; Bottemanne 1959) but fisheries research in Sri Lanka has not yet reached a position to substantiate these claims. Gahavälla fishermen claim that the 1970-71 catch was better than the preceding year, but argue that it was still slightly below the average annual catch of around Rs.200,000.

The average haul during 1970-71 resulted in a cash sale of Rs.225 which is about a third of a ton of fish. Even during the poor fishing of cycle one the average haul was Rs.120. Fishermen estimate prospective catches in cash, rather than numbers of fish, and do not set the net if the prospective return is less than Rs.25. They point out that a catch of this size would be distributed among the shore crew rather than sold, and thus net owners who did not work would receive nothing (see below). Moreover, when fishing is poor, men can earn more by handlining or rock fishing, than *madella* fishing.

During 1970-71, less than 8 per cent of the catches were under Rs.25, and most of these small catches were the first of the morning. The fishermen say that the first catch on the *varaya* side is normally the best of the day and unless fishing has been poor for a long period, the net due in this position is always used. This initial catch sets the pattern for the rest of the day: if it is a good one, around Rs.250, and especially if it is mainly *hāl mässa*, following nets will be used immediately their turns fall due; if it is smaller, around Rs.50, later nets will be used only if a shoal is spotted entering the harbour.

Seven hundred hauls were completed during the season, an average of little more than two per day. The average number of turns per net per cycle was less than three, although some nets were used as many as nine times in a single cycle. The reasons for this disparity are discussed below, at this point it is sufficient to note that the fact that the average net was used only seven times during the year and the most heavily utilized net was hauled on only 18 occasions, demonstrates an excessive number of nets.

One of the arguments used by advocates of the abolition of *madella* fishing, is that it gives a very poor return per man-hour (Canagaratnam and Medcof 1956). Even if this argument were true it has limited weight in a society with a heavy labour surplus, but in any case the Gahavälla data do not support it. On the basis of the labour inputs in Table 6.5 the cash return per man-hour was Rs.3.70. Using the formula of Rs.33 per hundredweight plus 10 per cent for home consumption, this converts to a return of 12 pounds per man-hour, which compares more than favourably with other coastal fishing techniques in Sri Lanka (cf. Administration Report, Director of Fisheries, 1940-50).

Table 6.4. also indicates considerable fluctuations in the results of individual nets. In both cycles two and three, some nets were not used at all, while the top ten nets received more than Rs.5,000. Over the three cycles the top net received Rs.7,762, while the least successful net received only Rs.38. This marked maldistribution of the catch is shown more clearly in Table 6.5.

TABLE 6.5. DISTRIBUTION OF MADELLA CATCH AMONG PARTICIPATING NETS

Number of Nets	Total Catch	Percentage of Catch	Cumulative Percentage
	Rs.		
Top 10	48,900	31	31
11-20	25,100	16	47
21-30	20,400	13	60
31-40	16,700	11	71
41-50	13,700	9	80
51-60	9,900	6	86
61-70	7,700	5	91
71-80	6,200	4	95
81-90	4,700	3	98
Bottom 9	3,000	2	100

Less than a third of the nets receive two-thirds of the catch - while the least successful third of the nets receive only nine per cent of the annual proceeds. Although fishing enterprises are notoriously risky, this is an extreme case. For example Firth (1966:383) found that although the yield from liftnet fishing in Malaya fluctuates markedly throughout the year, the catch of the most successful net was only five times larger than the least successful. By contrast the most successful *madella* had a catch 200 times greater than the bottom net.

While there are differences in the skill of individual net crews, these have very little influence on the annual operating results. Whether a particular net has a successful year is almost solely a function of its position in the net sequence.[10] In 1970-71 the ten most successful nets occupied positions 18 - 27 in the net sequence and 16 of the top 20 nets occupied positions 11 - 28.

Annual Returns

One of the reasons for the excessive number of nets is shown in Table 6.6, the annual operating results of the average individual net.

Even with the grossly excessive number of nets the average net still gives a profit (excluding labour costs) of Rs.803. If the net is worked by the owner, this is a return of 21 per cent on the investment and even if the owner pays wage labour it still gives a return of 7 per cent. As other avenues of investment for rural capitalists are being closed by government legislation, it will be appreciated that despite the large numbers of nets, the beachseines are a very attractive investment.

In view of the fluctuations in the return to individual nets, a comparison between the returns of each net and its operating expenses is the most satisfactory basis for an evaluation of annual operating results. If the nets are worked by their owners, nearly forty nets do not cover their operating costs, and a further thirty nets have profits of less than Rs.1,000. In contrast, the ten most successful nets have profits greater than Rs.4,000. If the net is worked by wage labour, only half made a profit, but the ten most successful have average profits of Rs.2,500, which is more than double the average annual income.

TABLE 6.6. ANNUAL RETURNS, AVERAGE INDIVIDUAL NET

		Owner Worker[a]	Wage Labor
Cost		3,875	3,875
Cash Sales			
Less:	Wages[b]		508
	Running Costs	670	670
	Interest[c] (3%)	116	116
	Total Expenses	786	1,294
Return on Finance			
	Total	Rs. 803	Rs. 295
	Percentage	21%	8%

[a] The distinction between owner and wage labor operated nets is discussed below.

[b] One-third of the cash sales less running costs. This sum includes only the 'hired man' share, stacking and redyeing are included in the running costs.

[c] The larger owners include interest on invested finance when calculating operating results, small owners do not. Three per cent may appear to be a low figure for the opportunity costs, but given the indirect economic benefits large owners derive from ownership it is realistic.

Risk and Uncertainty

Fishing is everywhere regarded as an industry embodying substantial risk and uncertainty (Beverton & Holt 1957; Turvey & Wiseman 1957). Gahavälla beachseining bears out this point to a marked - almost grotesque - degree. Not only do annual yields fluctuate, but 40 per cent of the catch is taken during an unpredictable flush period of about a month. The number of nets is five times the optimum with the result that the average net is used only seven times a year. The community pays a heavy cost for the excessive nets: if there were eighteen nets Gahavälla would take the same catch and lift its annual profits from Rs.80,000 to Rs.143,000. Moreover the catch is unequally distributed. Although differences in skill and effort are insignificant, nearly half the nets fail to cover their operating costs, while the few which are successful make substantial profits.

Although Knight (1921:19) distinguished measurable or quantifiable uncertainty which he called 'risk', from non-measurable or non-quantifiable uncertainty for which he reserved the term 'uncertainty', the distinction plays little part in contemporary micro-economic theory. Studies of peasant societies in particular, have treated the terms as if they were synonymous, or have replaced them with a third term such as 'subjective probability' (Wharton 1969). There are two reasons for this. Firstly, many studies deal with responses to government sponsored innovations and given the level of information available to the peasants, their responses, as Cancian (1972) notes, are most accurately characterised as 'taking a chance' rather than 'taking a risk'. Secondly, the distinction is often a function of time: as the time scale increases uncertainty shades imperceptibly into risk.

Nevertheless, a distinction between risk situations where the actor might calculate the approximate odds of a particular outcome, and uncertainty situations where he cannot, has considerable analytical value. Successful strategies can only be developed in a risk situation and a fundamental adaptational problem of peasant societies, particularly those with maritime economies, is to develop institutions which convert the uncertainties inherent in the ecology into economic risks.[11] For example, given the information available to Gahavälla fishermen it is impossible for them to calculate even approximate odds on such events as a big catch for an individual net, or the month when the flush will occur. But, as will be demonstrated in Chapter 11, it is possible to calculate the odds against a net making a profit and to use this as the basis of an investment strategy which will ensure an annual profit despite environmental uncertainties.

Moreover, the distinction between the uncertain consequences of the environment and the risks created by particular institutional frameworks, directs attention to the real source of Gahavälla's problems. The economic characteristics of modern Gahavälla beachseining have their origins in the ecology of Gahavälla fishing, but they are not ecologically determined: the current situation in Gahavälla cannot reasonably be represented as an inevitable outcome of the relationship between environment and forces of production. Nor is it a product of the technical aspects of the forces of production, beachseining is no more conducive to capitalist relations of production than other methods of fishing. Understanding modern Gahavälla beachseining requires an appreciation of the process by which equitable rules of procedure, developed in the context of simple commodity production in a rural economy with a low population and low level of economic activity, produced great inequalities in the distribution of the product once the relations of production were transformed.

CHAPTER 7

THE ORGANISATION OF BEACHSEINING

Accompanying the introduction of the *nuldella* was a new system of ownership. Whereas the earlier *madell* were made from local materials and, like the *oru* used in coastal and deepsea fishing, were individually owned, the new beachseines were beyond the reach of even the wealthiest fishermen. Consequently, a system of share ownership developed. Initially the share system worked on an *ad hoc* basis: individuals gave varying amounts towards the purchase of the net and disputes over revenue and the responsibility for repairs were common (Wright 1868). It appears that in fishing communities near the major market of Colombo, the incipient share system quickly collapsed and the nets were taken over by individual capitalists,[1] but in the more isolated regions, including Gahavälla, the concept of share ownership and control became firmly entrenched. Well before 1900, Gahavälla beachseines were being operated within a complex share system with a series of norms governing the rights and obligations of the owners, the relative shares of labour and capital, and rights of access to the fishery. Nowadays the interpretations of these norms is changing and the share system itself appears to have a limited future, but in the meantime rules of procedure developed about a century earlier provide the moral parameters of Gahavälla beachseining.

Reviewing Leach's very influential book *Pul Eliya*, Wijeyewardene (1966) made the critical point that while dry zone ecology must play an important part in any explanation of *Pul Eliya* social structure, the impact of the ecology was mediated by ethical and moral norms. Sri Lankan social structure must be analysed, not in terms of a simple opposition between the constraints of economics and the constraints of morality and law (cf. Leach 1961), but in terms of a complex interaction between them. A series of increasingly sophisticated studies of Sri Lankan land tenure (Codrington 1938; Pieris 1956; Leach 1961; Obeyesekere 1967) have indicated that most Sri Lankan communities share similar moral concepts concerning the ownership and control of economic resources.

Obeyesekere's (1967) ideal model of Sri Lankan land tenure contains three elements: the concept of the estate as a common property domain in which the co-owners are also kinsmen, the use of genealogies to allocate floating shares in the estate, and a system of rotation to equalize environmental effects. Such a model seems intuitively well suited to reservoir irrigated rice farming, but similar models are also used to organise other types of agriculture, including rain watered or river irrigated rice (Obeyesekere 1967), shifting cultivation of dry grains (Leach 1961), and village gardens or tree crops. As we will see, the model is equally applicable to the very different ecological niche of coastal fishing.

The Share System

Each net is divided into eight shares called *kottas* or, less frequently, *pangu*.[2] An essential feature of *kottas* is that like stock market shares they refer to the enterprise as a whole, not to particular portions of the net. When new nets are constructed or old nets are repaired it is usual for shareholders to contribute ready made sections of netting, but once the net is in operation individuals have no particular rights to the sections they have contributed.

The fishermen claim that the reason for the eightfold division is that eight is the minimum sized crew and that the division stems from an earlier period when shareholders alone worked the net. Observation suggests that the first part of the claim at least is correct, although under present conditions of abundant labour most nets are now worked by a permanent crew of nine. Three of the nets introduced in 1964 (see Chapter 10) have nine shares, and the shareholders lists from the now defunct beachseine sites at the nearby villages of Nilwella and Kudawellekele indicate that a nine-share net was common. Gahavälla informants suggested that the reason was that these were more exposed beaches and the crews therefore needed the extra man.

An individual may hold more than one share in a net and a share is often held by more than one person. For example, two siblings who inherit two shares from their parents will often register each share jointly; each thus retaining a one-sixteenth share in two nets rather than a one-eighth share in one net. The motive is both to share the risk of not participating in the flush period and a moral notion that inherited property should be jointly shared by all siblings, not divided among them. In 1971, 5 per cent of the shares were jointly owned, mostly by pairs of siblings.

Women are eligible to register shares and indeed owned 17 per cent of them in 1971. They are not, however, permitted to participate in the operation of the net nor in the division of its proceeds, and therefore have to surrender *de facto* control to a male nominee. In some areas in Sri Lanka many of the small fish traders are women, but Gahavälla women play no overt part in fishing and seldom visit the beach (Stirrat 1973).

Shares may be freely bought, sold, and used as security for various forms of mortgage. In former years they were often the most valuable item inherited, and, less frequently, were included in dowry payments. Although shares are freely transferable, in the sense that the other shareholders in the net do not have a legal veto over a prospective sale, the other shareholders do have a strong practical veto. Shareholders must work closely together and few men would buy a share in a net where the other shareholders strongly objected to the sale.[3]

I was told that formerly a group of elderly shareholders who were still working the net would often buy a surrendered share and give it to a reputed hard worker, allowing him to defer repayment until after a good catch. It was claimed that this was a common way for a poor man to acquire his initial share. But my informants were unable to think of any cases in the past thirty years, although they cited several earlier cases. If this was a common practice, then the ease of recruiting additional labour on a wage basis is probably the reason for its demise.

Since 1933 an appointed official, the *Patabändi Arrachi* has been responsible for compiling an annual list of shareholders. On a date announced by the beating of tom-toms, he inspects each *madella*, decides whether it is to be registered, and records changes in ownership.[4] The Rs.2 fee for the changes in ownership is paid to the *Patabändi Arrachi*. Registration is a tense occasion and a contingent of police is present to prevent fights. Regulations require each *madella* to have both an *orua* and a *maduwa*, and while most have a *maduwa* only forty-three nets have their own *orua*. Immediately prior to registration, competing factions petition the District Revenue Officer pointing out deficiencies in their opponents' nets, but the present *Patabändi Arrachi* is an old man who wants to avoid trouble, and registers all nets presented to him. In 1971 there were 108 nets listed in the shareholders lists compiled by the *Patabändi Arrachi*, but only ninety-nine nets actually exist. The other nets have been burnt in faction fights during the past three years and the shareholders have yet to replace them. When one of these 'phantom' nets is due to be used its turn is taken by the next in the sequence.

It would appear that registration was formerly also a ritual occasion, and a performance of the coconut smashing ritual, *pora pol*,[5] was financed by a levy on each net. But since the death of Nicholas Ediriweera (see Chapter 10) *pora pol* has not been held, and well before his death it had entertainment rather than ritual connotations. In the past the shareholders in each net (*kottas kārayō*) were possibly also close kinsmen, but it is now unusual for close kin to own shares in the same net and in most cases the *kottas kārayō* has no functions outside the economic context. The exceptions are the forty-two nets controlled by one of the three political factions which dominate village life.

Access to the Water

With a total of ninety-nine nets, only eighteen of which can be used in a day, the rules governing access to the water are obviously of great significance.[6] The following are the principles by which net owners decide when their turn is due. All nets are named and each owner is aware of the names of the nets immediately preceding and following his in the sequence. The fishing area is divided into two fishing stations: the *varaya patte* (harbour side) and the *galaha patte* (rock side).[7] The net cycle begins on the harbour side. A net can be used on the harbour side at any time during the day after the net immediately preceding it in the cycle has been used. After a net has had the dawn turn on the harbour side, it is entitled to the dawn turn on the rock side on the succeeding day. Subsequently, it may be used on the rock side at any time of the day once the net immediately following it in the sequence has been used. In addition the net with the dawn turn in either fishing station must be used before midday or forego its rights. I have defined a net cycle as the period between the use of net number one in the dawn turn on the harbour side.

The sequence of net use over a period of five days, in each of which there were four nets used on both fishing stations, is shown in Table 7.1. It will be appreciated that the situation is considerably more complex in practice, because the number of nets used varies from day to day, and on some days more nets are used at one fishing station than at the other.

TABLE 7.1. SEQUENCE OF NET USE

	Fishing Station							
	Harbour				Rock			
Day	Morn.——			Night	Morn.—			Night
One	9	10	11	12	8	7	6	5
Two	10	11	12	13	9	8	7	6
Three	11	12	13	14	10	9	8	7
Four	12	13	14	15	11	10	9	8
Five	13	14	15	16	12	11	10	9

The moral principle underlying this system, as stated to me by informants, is one of equal opportunity.[8] As opposed to a more simple system, for example the single use of each net in strict rotation, it meets four conditions.

(1) The two fishing stations are not equally desirable; most of the big catches come from the harbour side, although the average catch on the rock side during a period of poor fishing is usually larger.

(2) All turns of the day are not of equal value; the biggest catch of the day is usually the first turn on the harbour side,[9] and fish caught in the morning bring higher prices.

(3) The number of hauls during the day is not constant; during periods of poor fishing no nets at all may be used, in good periods, as many as eighteen. Nor is the speed of the haul constant; nets with big catches are hauled more quickly, in part because more people participate, in part to give the fish less chance to escape. Thus a system allocating access at a set time of the day would be inefficient.

(4) A disproportionate amount of the total labour input is concerned with preparing the net for the haul and restacking it afterwards; a system in which each net was only used once would be an inefficient use of labour.

Disputes about the sequence are rare and I did not witness any. According to informants, disputes only occur if a large shoal is spotted at dusk, or on a moonlit night. As no nets are usually in use at this time, any crew which is prepared to launch their *orua* can do so and occasionally more than one net may be launched. Disputes over delays in hauling the net are more common. During the flush period a craft launched late in the day often pauses at sea, especially if the crew have spotted a shoal just outside the harbour, and other crews fear missing their turn.

Although this system gives equal opportunities to all nets it does not result in equal returns, especially over the short term. During the flush season, which lasts only a month, the nets whose turns are due not only get bigger catches, they are also hauled on more occasions. For much of the year, only three nets are used each day and thus a net is unlikely to be used on more than two occasions in each net cycle. But in the flush season, between ten and eighteen daily hauls are made on up to eighteen successive days, and individual nets may receive up to nine turns in each net cycle. In 1970-71 only twenty-five of the ninety-nine nets received turns during the flush period. It is clear therefore that the annual returns of any net are governed, almost solely, by its position in the net cycle. If its turn is due during the flush period it will make heavy profits; if it is not, it will be lucky to recover its production costs.

The disparity between the moral notion of equal opportunity and the great differences in individual returns is due solely to the large number of nets. As long as the total number of nets was less than twenty, all nets received relatively equal returns and the system was an efficient and equitable means of regulating access to the water. But as the number of nets increased, the distribution of the catch became more and more unequal.

Although this system does not give equal returns over a single year, returns should even out over a longer period. Because there is no fishing on the quarter-moon holiday (*poya*), a net cycle takes about 105 days to complete. This means that a particular net's turn is not tied to any point in the year, and over a four year period each net will be used in each month. As the fishermen are unable to predict the flush period with any great accuracy, each net has an equal chance of good catches each year.

The Net Crew

Most nets have a permanent crew of nine men (one for each shareholder plus an extra man paid by the crew as a whole) who under the supervision of the *marrakalai* are responsible for all operations of the net. The term *marrakalai* has two connotations. First, it refers to the role of fishing expert (Firth 1966) who remains in the netlaying craft when the beachseine is hauled, directs the shore crew with hand signals and decides when the cod-end should be opened. It also refers to the man who organises the net crew, supervises the sale of the catch, and collects money from the buyers.

In the 42 nets controlled by one of the three factions, the two roles are separated. The fishing expert is normally the oldest man in the crew, for this is the least physically demanding task and the fishermen place little emphasis on differences in skill. The marketing and organisation role is the preserve of the faction leader or his nominee, who alone makes such decisions as when the net will be launched, whether extra men will be taken on, the price at which the catch is sold, and what repairs are needed. Other shareholders, whether members of the faction or not, have little control over the net's operation, and this is one of the reasons why men do not like to buy shares in a faction controlled net. While the two roles are usually performed by one man in the nonfaction nets, all significant decisions are reached by consensus among the shareholders.

Apart from these two roles there is no permanent division of labour within the net crew; a man may row on one occasion and remain ashore or serve as netlayer on the next. The only exception is that a crew that anticipates chasing a shoal will place its youngest and fittest men at the four oars.

In addition to the crews, there is a group of twelve other men who have permanent associations with particular nets. These are poor men with reputations as hard workers who have some disability which prevents them going to sea: two are deaf and dumb, one has a club foot and the others suffer from sea-sickness. These men have a semi-permanent relationship with about four nets each and participate only in the hauling operations. They are not given a specified share of the catch, but receive a small cash payment when the proceeds are distributed and, if the net does not employ a 'ninth' man, carry out the wage labour tasks of stacking and redyeing.

The crews are responsible for setting and hauling the net, irrespective of the prospects of a good catch. If they are unable to participate they must provide a substitute and on most occasions they comprise the whole net crew, with perhaps the aid of a few bystanders to launch the *orua* and a boy to coil the net. When fishing is very good, however, most of Gahavälla's male population gathers on the beach. As soon as it is apparent that the net has a good catch - (which can be ascertained when the *marrakalai* ties the *orua* to the centre of the net), many of these men join in the hauling and later, when the fish are prepared for sale, loudly demand fish for their efforts.

The regular net crews have a very ambivalent attitude towards these 'helpers'. While accepting that heavy catches require extra men after the *maduwa* is dropped, they point out that many more men than are required join in and most make only a nominal contribution.[10] In 1970-71 the rights of 'helpers' to a share in the catch was a constant source of disputes and, during the flush period, some nets sold the catch as a unit to avoid distributing fish to men other than regular crew members.

The Kuli Kārayō

When discussing the selection and organisation of the permanent netcrew, the fishermen draw a distinction between men who own shares (*kottas kārayō*) and men who work on a wage basis for the owners (*kuli kārayō*). Although ownership of a share carries the obligation to work the net when required, owners can deputise other men to work on their behalf. In 1971, 64 per cent of owners worked all their own shares, but many of these men were only small owners, and half the total shares were worked by *kuli kārayō*. The owners who employ hired labour are a disparate group with disparate motives: women who must employ men to work on their behalf; men living outside the village; men who derive most of their income from non-fishing activities; and village faction leaders who use the shares to provide employment for their clients.

For analytical purposes it is useful to divide the *kuli kārayō* into two categories each based on different relations of production. First there are men who work for close relatives; mainly sons working shares owned by a parent, and men working their brother's, sister's or brother-in-law's shares. The sons working their parent's share are mostly married men no longer living in their father's house. The sons operate the shares and take all the proceeds, giving gifts of money in return, but because of the strongly held belief that sons should not own their father's property while he is still alive the shares remain in the father's name. After his death they are registered by the mother, and only after her death transferred to the son's name. The practice of men working shares owned by their siblings or brothers-in-law is another stage in the developmental cycle of inheritance. As with other property, heirs are often unwilling to make a formal division of the shares they have inherited. In part this is due to the difficulty of making a division acceptable to all, but there is a belief that children have an obligation to maintain their parent's property as a whole, sharing equally in its benefits. The usual practice is for the son who was working the shares before the parent's death, to continue doing so, dividing the proceeds with the other siblings. But this arrangement seldom outlasts the first big catch, when the man working the shares is unwilling to distribute all the money on the grounds that some should be reserved for repairs. The outcome is normally the sale of the shares to the operator, who because he is in *de facto* control, pays only a nominal price.

Female shareholders, especially relatively young widows, have special problems in controlling their shares, because of the exclusion of women from any active part in fisheries. This problem can best be elucidated by looking at a particular example.

> Nicholas Ediriweera owned sixteen shares when he was killed by Sunil Mudalali in the course of a dispute over fish prices, (see Chapter 10) and ownership of his shares passed to his widow W.G. Laisyhamy. Two of Laisyhamy's brothers are *madella* fishermen and eight of the shares were given to them to work. Although she feels that her brothers do not remit the full amount due to her, Laisyhamy is reasonably happy with the arrange-

ments. The remaining shares, which are in nets in which several of the shareholders are clients of Sunil Mudalali, Laisyhamy gave to her sister's husband's two brothers to work. Although she would prefer to have given them to her brothers, she felt that if they attempted to work on a net controlled by Sunil they would be continually harassed. Her brothers-in-law, on the other hand are very tough men associated with David Mahattea's faction, who while they are able to maintain control of the shares, give her only a nominal payment. Laisyhamy has been trying to sell the shares for several years but her problems are well known and she cannot get a reasonable price.

In these situations there is not a clear distinction between shareowners and wage labourers. Many of the men both own shares and work others on a wage basis, and often 'hired men' are the potential heirs of the share owner. Approximately 30 per cent of the shares worked by the *kuli kārayō* are governed by such relationships. But there are situations in which the *kottas kārayō*/*kuli kārayō* distinction involves a class relationship.

Of the eleven largest shareholders in the village, who together contol 19 per cent of the total shares, only one works all his own shares. Seven of the others receive the bulk of their income from *madella* shares, but employ men to work at least some shares on their behalf, while the remaining three gain the bulk of their income from other activities and work all their shares with wage labour. For the ten men who do not work all their own shares, ownership of the shares has two advantages; it is an investment which gives a safe and reasonably good return, and it gives them a mechanism for recruiting and maintaining a political following. For the three men who receive only a small part of their income from the ownership of *madell* shares, the primary motive for the acquisition and retention of these shares is the maintenance of their political following. Although some of the hired workers are relatives of the owners, the basis of their recruitment is political allegiance, not the kinship tie. The ways in which the 'hired man' position is used to recruit and maintain a political following, can be illustrated by looking at the shareholdings of the cores of the Danny Wijenaike and David Mahattea factions.

Unlike the other two factions, members of the Wijenaike faction gain most of their income from beachseining. Podisingho Wijenaike and his relatives (see Fig.7.1) own ninety-two shares. Five of the sons work all their own shares, but Danny, the faction leader, works only six of his thirteen shares. Two of the remainder are worked by his brothers, two by his ZHB and the remainder by members of his faction core who live nearby but are not close relatives. Danny himself works two shares owned by his wife. Podisingho, although nearly seventy, works six of the seventeen shares he owns; six are worked by his three sons and the remaining five by two members of Danny's faction.

Danny's father-in-law, A.G. Mendis, who is closely associated with Danny's faction owns eleven shares. Five of these are worked by Mendis' son and four by a member of Danny's faction core. One of Mendis' sons is a fish trader who is unable to work his own shares; these are worked by Danny's brother and a member of Danny's faction.

This example indicates the conflict between economic and political goals faced by some faction leaders. Danny told me that although his family group (*pavul kattiya*) could work all the shares they owned, it was better to give some out on 'hire' and thus increase the size and unity of his following (*pirisa*). At the same time he has moral obligations to his brothers and nearly half the shares given on hire by Danny and Podisingho are worked by Danny's brothers. Mendis, a man without political aspirations, would prefer to have all the family-owned shares worked by family members, but as he himself is too ill to work very often and one of his sons is a fish trader, there is only one son to work the shares. As the shares are clustered in adjoining nets the son cannot work them all and thus they are given to members of Danny's faction. Mendis' position should be contrasted with Danny's brother-in-law, T.M. Peter, who by a series of judicious investments has succeeded in spreading his shares sufficiently for him and his siblings to work them all.

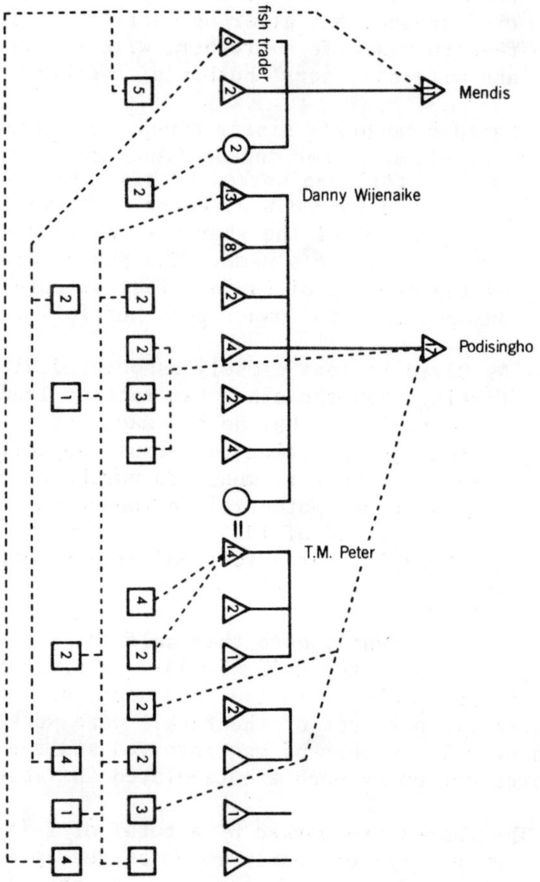

FIG. 7–1: DISTRIBUTION OF HIRED MEN POSITIONS AMONG MEMBERS OF THE WIJENAIKE FACTION CORE

The figures within the kinship symbols are the number of shares owned. The figures within the squares represent shares worked on a hire basis, with the dotted lines indicating the owners.

> Most of David Mahattea's income is derived from the operation of buses and vans. When, in the course of an abortive attempt to enter the fish trade (see Chapter 10), he initiated the introduction of twenty-five new nets, he preferred to lend associates the money to buy shares rather than buy them himself but he retained a total of twelve shares. Initially these shares were not allocated permanently to particular men, but after he married, David assigned them to his wife's brother, wife's sister's husband, and wife's sisters' husbands' brothers (two).
>
> David's mother's sister owned six shares, which were controlled by her deceased husband's brother (W.A. Peter) and worked by his sons. After a dispute David forced W.A. Peter to leave Gahavälla and took control of the shares which remain in his mother's sister's name. The shares are now worked by two members of David's faction core, but David ensures that the owner gets her full share.
>
> As David is less closely associated with *madella* fishing than the other two faction leaders, it is not surprising that he has made less use of the 'hired man' position to recruit supporters. But by lending supporters money to purchase shares he does have a strong potential influence on beachseining, and at the end of 1971 was negotiating to buy Laisyhamy's shares for some of his supporters to work.

In 1971 slightly more than half the shares were regularly worked by the *kuli kārayō*. If close relatives (brothers, brothers-in-law, and sons) are excluded, 136 shares (18 per cent of the total) were worked by wage labour. The number of men involved and the number of shares worked by each are tabulated in Table 7.2.

The shares are worked by a total of fifty-two men with an average of nearly three shares apiece. The men with three, four and five shares are the close associates of the faction leaders. They do not own shares and nearly all their income is from their work as wage labourers. Most of the men with only one or two shares on hire also own shares on their own behalf, but in most years their earnings from wage labour are more than one-third of their total income.

TABLE 7.2. SHARES WORKED BY THE *KULI KĀRAYŌ*

	Number of Shares Worked					
	1	2	3	4	5	Total
Number of Men	12	16	10	8	6	52
Total Shares	12	32	30	32	30	136

An important point is that seven men operating a total of twenty-three shares, had owned these shares in 1964. It is becoming increasingly common for men faced with heavy expenses to sell their shares with the proviso that they be allowed to continue working them on a wage basis. Often the transaction takes place over two years, with a mortgage in the first year. The agreements have no legal status, however, and these men are just as dependent upon the share owners as other wage workers.[11]

Division of the Catch

When the fish are auctioned on the beach the 'secretary' - this term is used only in a joking manner by the fishermen, but it provides a convenient label - records the price per box, the number of boxes taken and the buyer. Occasionally a bystander buys smaller quantities of fish belonging to the net crew as a whole and these sales are also recorded. About three months later when the money has been collected from the buyers, the shareholders meet to divide the proceeds.

The principles governing the distribution of the catch are straightforward. From the total cash receipts, 'expenses', wage payments, and a small sum for the secretary, are deducted. The remainder is divided into eight parts; one for each shareholder. If the net employs a 'ninth man', the division is into seventeen equal parts, with the eight shareholders receiving two parts and the 'ninth man', one part. Apart from the wage payments for dyeing and restacking, there are no special payments or extra shares for specific roles in the net crew. But despite these apparently straightforward principles, accepted by all fishermen, the division seldom takes less than four hours and often leads to fights.

The difficulty is to obtain agreement on what the catch was worth, for problems in recovering the money from the buyers postpone the division until three months after the net was used. The initial procedure is for the secretary to read out the details of the sales to each of the main fish buyers, for each of the catches, and while arguments are common, consensus on this point is usually reached. In addition, the secretary must account for money that he has received for sales to private individuals on behalf of the net crew and it is this latter sum that provokes many of the disputes. After the buyers have bid for the fish and the price has been accepted by the sellers, bystanders often take small amounts of fish from the general catch, paying one of the net crew or promising to pay later. In the excitement, it is often not clear whether the crew member concerned is selling part of the general catch, in which case the money should go to the crew as a whole, or selling part of the fish allocated to him for household consumption, in which case the money received belongs to him. Moreover, if the fish is sold on behalf of the net crew and the buyer later reneges on his promise to pay, the other shareholders may demand that the crew member selling the fish make up the deficit. With large catches, it is impossible for the secretary to keep count of all such transactions and he may be accused of retaining the money for himself.

While agreement is usually reached on the sum due from the fish traders, the total amount is seldom received. The secretary may be unable to obtain all the money due from small fish traders, who have spent the proceeds. Large traders may 'cut' the price (see Chapter 8) alleging that they made a loss on the deal or (especially if the catch was a large one) claim that they can afford to pay only part and will pay the rest later.

Moreover, a common practice is for the large traders to recover small advances to individuals by deductions from money owed to the net in which the individual is a shareholder, rather than directly from the individual concerned. It is impossible to give a firm statement on the average amount missing for these reasons, but in the eleven distribution meetings I witnessed, the amounts ranged from Rs.7 to Rs.618; 3 to 19 per cent of the total proceeds.[12]

Once agreement has been reached on how much money is to be divided, the next step is the deduction of the 'expenses' - small sums owed to the *kade* near the beach. If a *madella* is used in the early morning, the net crew often has a small meal of tea, rice noodles or bread, and bananas at a tea *kade* followed by a cigarette or cigar. This costs about Rs.4.50 for the entire crew and is charged to the net as a whole. With a big catch the crew may also share a bottle of arrack (Rs.10 to Rs.12). Problems arise because some crew members do not drink arrack. Payment for cotton or pieces of net purchased outside the village, and the wages for dyeing and restacking the net, are also deducted at this stage. The secretary does not deduct a set sum for himself, but takes what is over after a rough eight-fold division is made. Thus if the amount to be divided is Rs.1,016, it will be divided into eight shares of Rs.125 with the extra Rs.16 going to the secretary.

If the catches were good, there are few disputes, other than those concerning the total amount of the expenses. But if the catches were bad, the poorer crew men often argue that payment of the expenses should wait until the next cycle. This is especially true of wage payments, for crew members are naturally unwilling to see a man receive Rs.7.50 for three hours' work stacking the net, when their own return for 25 to 30 hours' labour is less than Rs.10.

The division of proceeds between the shareholder and the *kuli kārayō* seldom takes place at the major meeting, indeed it is unusual for both men to be present. There was considerable disagreement among my informants, not only concerning the principle which should govern this second distribution, but also concerning the current practices. The divergence in informants' statements reflects both differences in the current distribution practices among various nets, and differences in the status and composition of the *kuli kārayō*.

A generally accepted norm is that two-thirds of the proceeds should go to the shareholders and a third to the wage worker. But some informants argued that the *kuli kārayō* should receive the whole proceeds if they were less than a certain amount (usually Rs.250), and others that a 50-50 share was applicable in such cases.

My impression is that where the *kuli kārayō* are close relatives, the distribution seldom follows the 'norm'. If the hired man is a young son of the owner, his father takes all the proceeds, clothing and feeding the son in return, and as the son grows older the positions are reversed. When the division is between siblings or brothers-in-law, the person who is nominally the hired man in fact controls the share, meeting the running costs and paying the owner a small amount once a year. Even in a good season, the payment is unlikely to exceed a quarter of the proceeds less the repair costs.

Where the owner and 'hired man' are also patron and client, the arrangements are equally diverse. The two-thirds/one-third division is accepted as a norm, but practices differ according to the economic standing, source of income and political ambitions of the patron, and the client's economic position and the strength of his ties to the patron. In some cases the client takes complete control of the net, retains all proceeds and gives formal gifts to the owner on festivals; in others, the hired man has no responsibilities for the maintenance of the net and receives only one-third of the proceeds irrespective of the amount.

An arrangement whereby the client receives all proceeds and meets the maintenance costs if the catch is less than Rs.250, but takes only one-third and relinquishes the obligation of meeting the maintenance costs with larger catches, has been introduced by the faction leaders, David Mahattea and Sunil Mudalali. From their point of view, it has the considerable advantage that while they do not have to supervise their nets and appear to be taking a benevolent attitude to their followers, they remain the major beneficiary of any large catches.

Because of differences in the way in which the proceeds are distributed, men may work on several nets under quite different arrangements. D.V. Suganapala is an atypical, but instructive example. He is a hired man on six nets: (1) Owned by his brothers. Suganapala receives one-third and has no maintenance obligations. (2 & 3) Owned by David Mahattea's mother, but supervised by David Mahattea. Suganapala gets one-third before maintenance expenses are met. If a third is less than Rs.25, David makes up the difference and meets the maintenance costs. (4 & 5) Owned by David Mahattea. Suganapala takes all the proceeds, meets the maintenance costs, and gives David a formal gift of about Rs.50 every New Year's Day. (6) Owned by his mother. Suganapala takes all proceeds and meets the maintenance costs, but with his two brothers provides food and clothing for his mother's household.

Fragmentation and Inequality

The organisation of Gahavälla beachseining exhibits a striking paradox: operating procedures derived from an explicitly equalitarian ideology result in gross inequalities in the distribution of the catch. The key to this situation is the excessive number of nets.

Beachseining in Gahavälla is regulated by a tenurial model which is found in many other Sri Lankan and South Asian communities and which evolved in the context of subsistence agriculture. In the pre-capitalist Gahavälla economy these regulations were an efficient and equitable means of controlling participation in the fishery, but the common property elements were a vital weakness in the transitional capitalist economy. In an agricultural economy both fragmentation of the resource and additional investment and labour which does not increase the overall income, are constrained by the physical apportioning of the resource. Physical subdivision of farm plots below a certain level is impossible (and the economic limits on subdivision are reached well before this point), while increased labour or finance in the face of falling marginal products hits hardest at those responsible. Fisheries, however, lack these 'geographical' constraints: fishing time can be subdivided almost indefinitely, and even if the marginal product is zero, households which increase their labour inputs will reap a greater harvest at the expense of other community members. When it is used to regulate participation in a fishery rather than a form of agriculture, the Sri Lankan tenurial model permits individual households to maximize their incomes at the community's expense.

Gahavälla fishermen clearly understand the most important of these processes: soon after my arrival I was told that the community's problems were due to the excessive number of nets and this was reiterated on numerous occasions. But they also understand that the ninety-nine nets arrayed along Gahavälla's beach are only a material metaphor of far more important changes in social relationships. And these changes they are powerless to reverse. Whitehead (1948:17) wrote that the essence of tragedy 'is not unhappiness. It lies in the solemnity of the remorseless working of things'. We can begin to understand Gahavälla's tragedy by looking at the answers to two questions: What are the historical circumstances that lead to such a large number of nets? Why are the numbers not reduced?

CHAPTER 8

MONOPSONIES AND MARKETING

While any capitalist from a village shopkeeper to the owner of a large textile mill may be addressed as *mudalali*, for most of the people along the coast the term connotes the *malu mudalali*: the wholesale fish trader. These men differ in their wealth, in their range of economic interests and in the extent to which they use offices, book-keepers and the other parapher-nalia of the modern business, but some features are common to all. Perhaps the most significant is that they are all 'entrepreneurs'. Most are from the wealthier fishing families and family finance was important in es-tablishing their businesses. Nevertheless, their present wealth is a product of their own activities, not inherit-ance. They see their businesses as intensely personal enterprises which will cease with their deaths and have encouraged their children to take up other occupations, not to join them. Despite their strong desires for the social mobility of their children, they have made few attempts at personal social mobility through the adoption of the status indicators favoured by the landlords of the rural elite (Obeyesekere 1967:224). All the *mudalali* wear Sinhalese clothes, characteristically complemented by ornate gold jewellery, and use colloquial and egali-tarian speech. Their kinship and social relationships are with other *mudalali* and with members of the villages in which they reside, and apart from political alliances, they have little contact with the westernised elite of the rural towns. Many *mudalali* are respected members of the villages in which they live, but all are formidable men; their successes are as much due to their ability to enforce loan repayments, to discourage competition from other traders and to withstand abuse and occasional attacks from fishermen, as to their bargaining, book-keeping and general business skill.

An important aspect of the fish marketing structure is the extent of trust between *mudalali*; a sharp contrast to the relationship between *mudalali* and fisherman. In both the Colombo and Tangalla regional markets, the *mudalali* relies on local agents to remit a fair share of the proceeds. He has few opportunities to discover if reported prices are correct and for that matter cannot recover money due in the event of a dispute, for no receipts are given. But disputes appear to be very rare. One of the reasons is that the amount which could be obtained by misrepresenting the price is comparatively small compared to the 10 per cent commission on large and regular supplies of fish. The other, and I believe the more important reason, is that the *mudalali* involved in such arrangements are usually close friends. Certainly some *mudalali* are far richer than others and the richer men may serve many of the functions of a patron, but these relationships lack the asymmetry and associated patterns of deference which characterise patron-client relationships in other spheres of Sri Lankan life. Business between *mudalali* is conducted in an egalitarian atmosphere and the relationship is underwritten by mutual gifts, by attendance at ceremonies at each others' houses and, occasionally, by marriages between their children.

The Structure of the Market

Mudalali buying fish at Gahavälla Beach may choose between four markets: (a) the central markets in Colombo; (b) retail markets in the small towns along the Matara-Hambantota road; (c) retail markets in the small towns to the west of Matara; (d) local villages served by petty traders using bicycles. These four alternatives do not exhaust the possibilities - at times fish is sold in the interior towns or along the roads to the East Coast - but the amounts are insignificant. Each of the four markets differs in its entry conditions, marketing costs, returns and profits.

Fish sold in the Colombo market bring large profits, usually around 100%, but only the large varieties such as tuna and kingfish which are suitable for preservation in ice, are consigned, while catches of less than 200 pounds do not justify the transport costs. In 1970-71 slightly less than 8 per cent of the total fish landed in Gahavälla was suitable for sale in Colombo and most of this was sent there. The fish is initially carried by van to Matara, where an agent assembles the small consignments, ices and boxes the fish, and forwards it to a Colombo *mudalali* by rail or lorry transport. After the fish arrives at Matara, all marketing costs are met by the Colombo *mudalali*, who deducts a flat fee of Rs.8 to Rs.10 per box for this service. The fish are auctioned in the Colombo market and the proceeds, less a 10 per cent to 15 per cent commission, held by the *mudalali* for collection. While the Colombo market is not very important to Gahavälla middlemen in terms of the amount of fish they sell there, marketing in Colombo does serve other important functions. All of the traders in the Tangalla region market their fish through a single Matara *mudalali* operating in the Colombo market and during a year this man received a fee on more than 2,000 tons of fish. In return he gives numerous small loans at low interest and by using his extensive political connections, provides opportunities to purchase new vehicles, gear and spare parts, and to obtain vehicle route licences.

The retail markets in the towns west of Matara are mainly supplied by local mechanised boats and for most of the year the Gahavälla fish traders do not attempt to compete. Prices are similar to those in the Tangalla markets, marketing costs are higher, and by the time Gahavälla fish is carried to these areas it is beginning to decompose. But the mechanised craft do not fish regularly during the south-west monsoon, and if the flush in Gahavälla occurs before the end of the monsoon, Gahavälla middlemen can avoid a glut in the Tangalla region by selling fish in this area. The usual practice is to transport the fish (uniced) by van, pausing at the municipal market in each town. Some bargaining is permitted, but if the local retailers are unwilling to meet the seller's minimum price he quickly moves on. These sales are invariably for cash. In 1970-71 very little Gahavälla fish was sold in this area and most selling trips were excuses for joy rides in the fish vans.

Slightly more than half the fish bought by Gahavälla *mudalali* is sold in the retail markets in the small towns of the Tangalla region. These markets are also supplied with fish from locally based mechanised boats, but there is little competition between the two: although fish from the mechanised craft is more popular, it is 50 per cent to 75 per cent more expensive and the minimum sale portion is twice as large. Local councils have rules that all incoming fish must be auctioned and 5 per cent of the auction price must be paid as a market tax. If the sums paid in tax represented a true auction price, then fish would be very cheap - about Rs.10 per hundredweight - but the council rules are ignored. The *mudalali* delivers the fish to an agent in the market using his van for large loads and bicycles for smaller ones. The agent, who usually acts for more than one *mudalali*, either turns the fish over to bicycle traders for sale in the villages, or gives it to stall holders for retail in the market. Some *mudalali*, usually small operators, sell the fish to the agent, but normally the fish is sold on the *mudalali's* behalf and the agent takes a 10 per cent commission for his services. The *mudalali's* profit after the deduction of the agent's commission seldom falls below 30 per cent or exceeds 60 per cent. There is normally a two-day delay in payment, the agent collecting the money from retailers the day after the sale and turning it over to the *mudalali* next day.[1]

The remaining third of the *mudalali's* purchases are retailed in the villages within three or four miles of Gahavälla by the bicycle *kārayō*. The composition of the bicycle *kārayō* changes with the seasons. During periods of good fishing, almost every otherwise unemployed man who owns or who can hire a bicycle participates, and often more than forty are gathered on the beach. Only eight men derive the major part of their income from bicycle trading, however, and for eleven months of the year only those men are to be seen. The bicycle traders are all very poor. For eleven months only small amounts of fish are available, prices are high and profits are low, while the entry of marginal workers during the flush month further restricts their income. Most of the men who are permanently employed as bicycle traders suffer from some disability - usually sea-sickness - which prevents them from fishing, but two are younger men who see trading as a more desirable and potentially more profitable occupation than fishing. This is rather a forlorn hope, for the earnings of the most successful bicycle trader are well below the earnings of a successful fisherman.

The general poverty of the bicycle traders - few would have Rs.25 in ready cash - severely restricts their opportunities to purchase fish. They can buy only the smallest catches because even in concert they can only raise small cash payments and they are poor credit risks. Their incomes from fish purchased directly from the fishermen are very low. On an average day one might purchase Rs.8 worth of fish and after cycling for six or more miles, sell it in 25 cent portions for a total profit of Rs.2. This is not sufficient for even a subsistence income and most bicycle traders additionally act as retail agents for one of the *mudalali*.[2]

There are several possible financial arrangements between a bicycle trader and *mudalali*. The most popular, as far as the bicycle traders are concerned, is for the *mudalali* to buy the fish on the trader's behalf in return for a flat fee. The bicycle trader obtains relatively large amounts of fish (up to 100 pounds) which he retails at larger than usual profits, and after paying the *mudalali's* fee, can make up to Rs.15 for a day's work. From the *mudalali's* point of view this arrangement gives an easy return, for as he is purchasing the fish on credit, he in effect receives a 5 per cent levy on the sale. But the *mudalali* makes larger profits under other systems and he only enters this arrangement when the bicycle trader is a close associate, and then only when comparatively large amounts of fish are available, at a high price, late in the day.

The most common arrangement is for the bicycle trader to retail fish on the *mudalali's* behalf. If the fish is to be retailed locally, the *mudalali* fixes a total resale price about 25 per cent higher than the wholesale price and the bicycle trader keeps any profits above it. In the case of a loss the *mudalali* may still demand his full price. If the fish is to be carried to the markets in the nearby towns, the bicycle trader is given a small fee for carrying the fish. Most bicycle traders prefer this, for by making several trips in a day they can earn almost as much without risk of a loss.

The obligations of the bicycle traders to the *mudalali* are not limited to these functions. They are expected to help count and sort the fish on the beach, to carry fish to storage areas and to help load the van. The bicycle traders are also expected to support the *mudalali* in bargaining for fish and to aid him in any disputes or fights that occur on the beach. All advantages lie with the *mudalali*, for in addition to providing an efficient and profitable means of disposing of fish in the local markets, the presence of a group of committed followers provides important support in his often fiery relationships with the fishermen. His obligations in return are limited to providing some semblance of regular employment, occasional small gifts of fish, liquor and cigarettes, and very occasionally, small loans or gifts of money. The bicycle traders, however, have little choice other than becoming clients of a *mudalali*. They can make higher profits on fish they purchase directly from the fishermen, but only the *mudalali* can ensure the regular supply of fish that is necessary for a tolerable income.

The *mudalali's* market choices are guided by clear considerations. Colombo is the most favoured market but only a small proportion of the catches is suitable for sale there. The bulk of the catch is sold in the Tangalla regional markets, but when a glut leads to lower prices, fish may be diverted to the towns west of Matara. Small catches of fish landed late in the day, are retailed locally by the bicycle traders.

Gahavälla *mudalali* do not preserve fish. Nowadays, fish drying is limited to migrant fishing camps, where men occasionally dry fish to take home. None of the fish transported by local *mudalali* is iced. Fish for sale in Colombo is not iced until after it is received in Matara and fish that has to be stored overnight for retail is normally first sold to retail traders, who ice the fish on their own behalf. There are several reasons why Gahavälla *mudalali* do not ice fish. As the nearest ice factory is twenty miles away, ice would have to be purchased before the size of the catch was known and this would result in considerable waste. The beachseine catch is landed alive and intact and thus gives the dealers more time for transportation than the mechanised boats' catch, which is often considerably damaged in the nets and has been dead for up to eight hours when it is landed. Nevertheless, the non-use of ice does place some constraints on the marketing process: it prevents the *mudalali* from taking full advantage of potentially profitable markets in the interior and it adds weight to the role of the bicycle traders in disposing of excess fish relatively quickly.

The lack of preservation is one reason why the marketing costs of the *mudalali* are very low. In most cases costs are limited to petrol and wear and tear on the van, while when selling through the bicycle traders the costs are limited to occasional gifts and loans. But although the marketing costs for established traders with their own vehicles are very low, they are a considerable barrier against new-comers. When they are available, the hire charge for vans carrying fish between Gahavälla and Tangalla is Rs.25 and to Matara, Rs.40. A second-hand van in reasonable condition cannot be bought for less than Rs.18,000 and the repayments alone will amount to more than Rs.500 per month.

Gahavälla fishermen argue that they are exploited by the *mudalali* and in my view their claim is correct. While the *mudalali's* average profits are not excessive from the standpoint of capitalist enterprises, they conceal occasional bonanzas which may increase his annual income by a tenth (see below pp.178) and provide him with a far higher standard of living than any fisherman. The major Gahavälla *mudalali* acknowledges an income of about Rs.6,000 after the deduction of all expenses, including household and legal expenses. An alternative view is provided by calculating his income on the basis of his purchases. Assuming an average profit of 25 per cent, his income in the year 1970-71 was more than Rs.20,000; twelve times greater than the Gahavälla average.

Buying Fish at Gahavälla

Fish from the beachseines is never weighed prior to retail sale. The bulk of the catch is retained in the net during the bidding and in most sales the selling unit is the box. The 'boxes' are disused soap boxes which, when filled level with the brim, hold eighty to

100 pounds depending on the species. After the price has been agreed upon, additional fish are added to top up the box. The extent to which additional fish are added depends upon negotiations between buyer and seller and full boxes of the same species may differ by up to 10 per cent. Generally speaking, full boxes weigh between ninety and 110 pounds.[3] Cane baskets, used for small catches, contain about thirty-five pounds. Large fish are sold individually.

The filling of the first box is the signal for the start of the auction. Unlike the procedure described by Firth (1966) for the Malays, the sellers do not normally make counter offers, but indicate their preferences by their reaction to the bids. A low bid is greeted by a series of ribald comments; a bid approaching the desired price by studied indifference, or by suggestions that the price should be lifted a little. Most sales follow a predictable pattern. The fish traders make two or three initial bids, each about 15 to 25 per cent below the prices received in earlier sales. The sellers react with abuse. The next bid approaches the price paid in the previous sale, and if it does not meet with a hostile reaction, the *mudalali* makes a slightly higher offer and begins moving the catch. If the sellers still object, the *mudalali* may offer another one or two rupees, but is unlikely to go higher. In most auctions there are only five or six bids and the sale only takes a couple of minutes. As traders usually arrange to split the catch rather than bid against each other, the sellers must accept the final bid if it is at all reasonable.

Once the price for the first unit is agreed, the *mudalali* is entitled to buy the entire catch at that price. Occasionally, when the catch is very large, the successful bidder may take only part of the catch and the remainder is then available to other traders at the same price. If there are no takers, the remainder is re-auctioned. Re-auctions are strongly opposed by the fishermen, because the second auction invariably brings a lower price and men who have bought earlier will attempt to pay at the lower price. This gives an important tactical advantage to the local *mudalali*. If they have been forced to bid high by competition from outsiders, they can delay in loading the fish and, when the competitors have left, demand that the remainder be re-auctioned, thus buying the bulk of the catch at a lower price.

After the *mudalali* has emptied the first box it is returned to the net to be reloaded. Usually two men from the net crew are deputised for this task, filling the box with large armfuls of fish. These men are under constant pressure from the bystanders to distribute fish without payment; other members of the net crew, men who have joined in to help pull the net, and relatives or acquaintances of net crew members, all demand a share. At times there is a yelling, struggling mass of more than fifty people all demanding fish, while small boys creep in and out of everyone's legs, stealing any fish they can lay their hands on.

If the catch has been a good one, the usual practice is to halt the sale when no further full boxes remain in the cod-end. If no large fish have been set aside for the net crew, each crew member takes about two and a half pounds and the rest of the catch is distributed in smaller lots to people who have helped in the net handling, or who shout the loudest. Most of the fish given to the net crew and bystanders is not immediately taken home but is redistributed on the beach. Some is gifted to friends and relatives by members of the net crew, but the bulk is sold, both to people who require fresh fish for their own meals and to the bicycle traders. There is considerable competition among buyers, and prices are sometimes more than twice as high as in the main sale. As up to three months may elapse before the proceeds from the main sale are received, the Rs.1.50 to Rs.2 each crew member receives from the sale of his share of wet fish, is an important source of income.

In recent years the beachseine fishermen have become increasingly resentful of the custom of distributing fish without payment to casual helpers, relatives of the net owners, and other bystanders. The resentment is particularly marked among wage workers for their individual share of a sale of Rs.100 is less than Rs.12, while as much as Rs.30 or Rs.40 worth of fish from the catch may have been distributed without payment. One means of restricting the amount distributed is to prevent men other than the new crew working on the net, another is to continue the sale until the net is empty. This has the disadvantage, however, that a box containing seventy-five pounds is likely to be described as three-quarters full by the fishermen and one-half full by the *mudalali* with a consequent dispute over payment. Another possibility, used about a dozen times in 1970-71, is to sell the catch as a whole without dividing it into boxes, but in such cases the price tends to be lower, because of uncertainty about how much fish the net contains. On all but one occasion when the net was sold as a whole, the unit price was considerably lower than usual.[4] Disputes over the distribution and selling of fish are common; seldom did a week pass without a heated argument around the net.

Fishermen's Selling Strategies

The fishermen have a clear and explicit notion of a just or reasonable price, *mila denna honda* (a price good to give at), which in the case of *hāl mässa* (anchovies) the main beachseine catch, is around Rs.40 per box.[5] When questioned, fishermen say that the *hāl mässa* should bring about Rs.40 per box and attribute the lower average price to the rapacity of the *mudalali*. Included in the fishermen's notion of a just price is the idea of a reasonable return for labour and capital and the knowledge that in buying fish at this price, the *mudalali* will seldom make a loss. If the *mudalali* wish to buy at a lower price, they should justify their stand in terms of the lateness of the day, the lack of transport, or similar reasons.

The fishermen lack the exact knowledge of local market conditions which the *mudalali* gain from daily market visits, but this is not very important for bargaining. The catch from the beachseines does not compete on the local market with fish caught by other methods and although the retail price of *hāl mässa* ranges from 40 cents to Rs.1.40 per pound over the year, the price alters only slightly from day to day. For most of the year, the retail price hovers about the Rs.1 mark, dripping to 40 cents if there has been a big catch at one of the important beachseine centres and rising to around Rs.1.40 during the three month period of poor fishing. As long as the last week's price is known, daily retail prices can be predicted fairly accurately.

When selling individual catches, fishermen fix their ideas of an acceptable price by referring to the previous day's sales. When fishing is poor, they seek a price slightly above the prices paid on the preceding day; if fishing is very good, their efforts are bent towards matching the previous day's price. The crews of nets used later in the day seek a price approximating the early catches but, as is discussed below, many variables other than market conditions have to be taken into account and price fluctuations over a day are considerable. Although auctions are seldom an arena for competition among buyers, they serve an important function in communicating the notions of acceptable prices held by the fishermen and *mudalali* and in decreasing the margin of difference between the two.

The fishermen's main sanction against the *mudalali* is the possibility of selling the catch themselves. If the catch is large, a van may be hired to take the catch to a local market, or a *mudalali* from a neighbouring village may be asked to sell the catch on a commission basis. I witnessed only four examples of the fishing group marketing the catch themselves but I was told that it was common several years ago during a prolonged dispute between the fishermen and the *mudalali*. Small catches, especially during periods of poor fishing, can be divided among the net crew members with each selling his own share, either on the beach or in the neighbouring villages. Perhaps a fifth of the off-season catches are disposed of in this manner.

The fishermen receive a return which approximates their notions of a just price for both the largest and smallest catches. Their difficulties arise with the catches between 100 and 400 pounds, which are too small to justify the expense of a van and too large to sell themselves.[6] As most catches fall within this range, the fishermen are dissatisfied with the prices they receive and highly critical of their exploitation by the *mudalali*.

Mudalali's Buying Strategy

Although the retail price of the beachseine catch remains relatively constant, there are considerable fluctuations in the prices paid at Gahavälla beach. While it is common for the price to exceed Rs.100 per box, small catches landed late in the day may bring less than Rs.20 per box at auction. These price fluctuations can be discussed in three contexts: seasonal variations, variations during the day, and differences due to the composition of the shareholders' group.

Some price fluctuations are the result of seasonal factors and the prices received for the first catch of the day show a regular pattern.[7] Between November and May the price per box hovers around the Rs.40 mark, with catches of more than 250 pounds going as high as Rs.65 and very small catches selling at Rs.30. When fishing falls off at the beginning of June, the price for the small catches lifts to around Rs.40 and for big catches often exceeds Rs.100. Prices fall sharply during the month of very good fishing around October. If the first catches of the day are very large, say 1,000 pounds, the price may be as high as Rs.65, but smaller catches, as well as catches later in the day, are unlikely to fetch Rs.30.

It is not uncommon for the best unit price of the day to be three times higher than the poorest. To some extent the prices paid for any catch are a matter of chance events but some general norms can be established:

(a) The initial catch of the day usually brings the highest price for the wholesale buyer has the widest choice of retail markets;

(b) Prices fall after noon and especially near dusk, for the fish may have to be iced overnight. In such cases marketing costs increase, the standard of the fish falls and it has to be sold in competition with fresh fish the following morning;

(c) Catches approaching a van-load bring higher prices;

(d) Large catches of prized species sell at higher prices because they can be transported to Colombo;

(e) During the flush period, traders from other areas who have not been able to buy fish locally visit Gahavälla late in the day and hold prices at higher levels than would otherwise be the case.

The effects of these factors on daily prices are most apparent during the flush period. In the off-season they are not important, for most catches are retailed in the immediate area and even late in the day there is an unsatisfied demand.

While the price fluctuations discussed above can be accounted for by supply and demand, other variations are clearly the result of political considerations. As was pointed out in Chapter Five Gahavälla political life is dominated by three factions or *kattiya*. Men give their allegiance to a *kattiya* on various grounds - kinship, past or future favours and friendship - but one of the most important ways of recruiting a following of committed supporters, is to employ them as hired workers for beach-seine shares owned by a faction leadership. One of the *kattiya* is led by the main Gahavälla fish trader, Sunil Mudalali, and this faction owns at least one share in forty-nine nets and a majority shareholding in twenty-four nets.

In approximately two-thirds of the nets, where the shareholding is controlled by one of the factions, the faction leader or his nominee arranges the sale of the fish. He alone decides whether the bids are to be accepted, how much fish is to be added to top up the box, and the extent to which fish is distributed among net crew and bystanders. The selling procedure is the same with these hierarchically organised nets as with the others, but the crew members take their cues from the leader. In the nets controlled by the local *mudalali's kattiya*, the *mudalali* is effectively both seller and purchaser. The remaining nets, owned by men who are not associated with any of the factions, lack internal cohesion and a clearly recognised leader. During the auction the crews of these nets often squabble amongst themselves, some shouting that the buyer should take the fish, others demanding that the price be increased.

There are several situations in which the composition of the net crew affects the price. First, during the auction the *mudalali* may offer a slightly lower price (seldom more than Rs.5 per box less) and rely on one of his faction members among the net crew to persuade the others to accept it. If the client tells his patron to take the fish, other crew members are inhibited from physically intervening by the fear that they will have to face the *mudalali* and his henchmen unsupported. Secondly, after the price is agreed upon, the box is topped up. Often this involves the addition of only three or four handfuls of fish, but at other times the fish are covered with a light sprinkling of sand and more fish added, until the box cannot be moved without spilling large amounts. If one of the *mudalali's* faction is filling the box, he may get 10 per cent more fish than otherwise.

The most important consequence of the composition of the net crew is in relation to the practice of price-cutting *rävula kapana* (cutting the beard). When the *mudalali* pays for the fish which he purchased some months earlier, he may try to justify a lower price by arguing that he has made a loss on the deal. Fish traders seldom attempt to cut the price to nets where members of their own faction have shares, for they will have purchased the fish at a lower price in any case. Nor do they attempt to cut the price to nets owned by other powerful factions, because they are frightened of retribution. But net crews lacking internal cohesion and where the shareholders are not allied to one of the major factions - perhaps a third of the total - consistently receive less than 90 per cent of the price agreed upon.

In discussing a similar practice of price-cutting among the Malay fishermen, Firth (1966:208) states that:

> ...the practice has the effect of evening out the profit-and-loss fluctuations for individuals. The losses of the middlemen tend to be distributed over the general body of producers as well. But on the other hand the knowledge of the middlemen that they can cut if they lose allows them to bid higher than they otherwise would, so that if they get a profit the producer in effect has also benefitted.

The capital of the average Malay middleman in 1939 was so low that a loss on the deal would have wiped him out.

Firth's argument is clearly applicable to some of the coastal villages west of Matara where the catch is auctioned and where there is considerable competition among numerous small retail sellers. In these areas the practice of 'cutting' is accepted by *mudalali* and fishermen alike. It is also possible that the origin of the system in Southern Sri Lanka was a situation of small traders with little capital similar to that of Malaya. But in today's Gahavälla 'cutting' does not serve an 'insurance' function. The *mudalali* seldom make a loss and if they do their capital is more than sufficient to bear it. Further, the cutting is directed at only some of the nets. In my view, the purpose of 'cutting' is to increase the profits of the fish traders in situations where the fishermen are without power to retaliate.

In the absence of accurate data on the actual prices per pound, and on the ratio of the bids to the money actually received by the net crews, it is difficult to present a quantitative account of the consequences of 'cutting' and other *mudalali's* strategies for individual nets; but some general remarks are appropriate.[8] First, nets associated with factions other than the *mudalali's* faction, receive the highest bids, and the smallest amount of fish to the boxes, and seldom suffer from cutting. Thus these nets receive the highest returns for their fish. Secondly, nets of the *mudalali's* faction receive the lowest bids, add most fish to the boxes, and seldom meet price cuts. Their unit prices are up to 10 per cent below the first group. Thirdly, nets which are not associated with any faction receive relatively high bids, add relatively little to the boxes, and are hardest hit by price-cutting. Their returns are probably slightly higher than the nets of the *mudalali's* faction.

In many fishing communities, for example Malaya (Firth 1966) and West Africa (Hill 1970), fish traders operate on credit and pay only after they themselves have received their money. In most of these cases the period between the sale and the payment is only a few days, but in Gahavälla the proceeds are often not received for more than three months: the *mudalali* pays for the previous catch only after the net has completed its turn in the following cycle. Delaying of payments in this manner gives a double advantage to the *mudalali*. He can buy large amounts of fish with only small amounts of capital and gain a powerful, if implicit, hold over the net crew, for if they refuse to sell him fish on the next occasion the net is used, the *mudalali* may further delay the payment.

There appear to be three reasons why the long delays in payment are tolerated by the fishermen. First, the average beachseine fisherman owns shares in five nets and if they are equally distributed throughout the net sequence, he will receive some income at four-week intervals. Secondly, individual fishermen may obtain some of the money due before the net group as a whole is paid, although a condition of such 'advances' is a closer relationship with the *mudalali* than the fisherman might otherwise desire. Thirdly, the delayed payment reduces the area of uncertainty in the planning of expenditure. If the fisherman was paid immediately after the sale he would not know how long the money must last, for he cannot accurately predict the size of future catches; whereas under the delayed payment system, he acquires accurate knowledge of his income up to three months in advance of its receipt and can plan his expenditure accordingly. One might argue that the delayed payment system is an adaptation to conditions of uncertainty, but the fishermen do not see things this way. As far as the fishermen are concerned, any positive aspects are much outweighed by the advantages given to the *mudalali*.

Building a Monopsony

Although *Karāva* are renowned for their entrepreneurial abilities and local men had been selling dried fish in the interior villages since 1900, the *malu mudalali* is a post-war phenomenon in Gahavälla and the adjoining villages. It was only after 1940 that the prices and volume of fish gave the opportunity of a high income for fish traders. The ready access to motor transport in these years led to intense competition and during periods of good catches as many as thirty *mudalali*, each with his own van, gathered on Gahavälla beach. There was spirited competitive bidding for catches and nearly all payments were cash. Only three Gahavälla men participated in these sales: most of the *mudalali* were from other areas and visited Gahavälla only when catches were heavy. For the remainder of the year, the catch was handled by the three Gahavälla traders, buying on credit and taking fish on a regular basis from nets in which they or their relatives owned shares. From the fishermen's point of view this was a good arrangement. During the low season they, in effect, received a fixed price and when the catches were large men from other areas entered the market, raising prices and paying cash.

The competition among fish traders and the practice of cash payments for major purchases continued for approximately twenty years, but since 1960 the small fish trade in each of the villages east of Matara has been dominated by alliances of two or three *mudalali* who do not compete against each other and who buy on credit.

This monopsony situation can be explained to some extent in purely economic terms. First, since 1960 there has been an increasing and unsatisfied demand for fish in Sri Lanka. Fish is the main source of animal protein in the Sri Lankan diet and the increase in fish production, following mechanisation, did not keep pace with demand. Retail prices rose considerably in the small towns near the fishing villages, with the result that high profits and regular incomes could be made even from the small daily sales outside the flush periods. Secondly, after the Sri Lankan Government restricted motor vehicle imports in 1960, the prices and hire charges of motor vehicles rose considerably, restricting the entry of marginal workers into fish wholesaling. Whereas previously men with Rs.500 to Rs.1,000 could buy considerable amounts of fish and use hired transport to carry it to the markets, after 1960 it became increasingly difficult to obtain transport at short notice and when it was available, the hire charges were far greater than the transport costs of *mudalali* using their own vehicles. Thirdly, once the mechanised craft were established, wealthy *mudalali* could obtain larger and more regular profits by establishing 'tied boat' arrangements with the owners of the mechanised craft (see Chapter 3). Consequently, the wealthy *mudalali* (especially those from deep-sea villages) who had provided most of the competition during the previous two decades, turned to the mechanised craft to the exclusion of the small-fish trade.

The increase in the value of fish after 1960 was thus accompanied by a drop in the numbers of established *mudalali* interested in the small fish trade and a strengthening of barriers against newcomers. But it would be false to argue that the monopsonies are merely a reflection of economic circumstances: fish trading is still a very profitable business and barriers against newcomers are not insurmountable. An examination of the recent history of the Gahavälla fish trade indicates the ways in which the economic domination of the *mudalali* is maintained by social and political relationships.

Becoming a Mudalali

The marketing of the beachseine catch in Gahavälla is controlled by J.A. Sunil (Sunil Mudalali) and two of his brothers, J.A. Lantis and J.A. Punniyadasa. In 1970-71, the brothers bought 83 per cent of the fish sold in the main sales from the beachseines as well as most of the large catches from inshore fishing. The brothers do not normally discuss prices prior to sale. With small catches only one brother bids, but with large catches they pretend to bid against each other. They take their cues from Sunil Mudalali however, and after the price has been agreed upon, each brother takes a portion of the catch. Apart from the bidding and then only with large catches, the brothers do not co-operate in marketing. Each is responsible for making his own payments to the fishermen and to some extent they sell their fish in different markets. Sunil is the wealthiest partner and handles about two-thirds of the fish.

According to his own account, Sunil's entry to fish trading was something of an accident. After leaving school, he went to work for a Matara fish *mudalali* operating in the Colombo markets. There he was involved in a brawl and had to return to Gahavälla to avoid prosecution. One evening in 1959, a net owned by his family had a very big and unexpected catch of striped tuna; more than 2,000 fish weighing about two pounds each. When the fish were auctioned, none of the local fish traders were interested in buying and, on impulse, Sunil bought the entire catch on credit for a mere 25 cents apiece. Borrowing a van, he sold the fish in the Colombo market for Rs.2.35 each, a clear profit of more than Rs.4,000. Elated by his success, he continued to buy fish, consigning much of it to his ex-employer in Colombo and by 1961, with the aid of a loan from this man, was able to buy a small van.

At this time, Sunil estimates he was buying about 50 per cent of the fish landed in Gahavälla. Because of his close relationship with the Colombo *mudalali*, he was able to offer high prices for the large varieties of fish, and he also had a lien on the catch of the twenty-seven nets in which his family owned shares. One of the three *mudalali* who had been prominent in the 1940-60 period had retired, and the other two were both elderly men, lacking Sunil's business ability and contacts.

Between 1962 and 1965, however, Sunil and his six brothers became involved in a series of increasingly violent disputes. The origin of these disputes had little to do with the fish trade, but eventually a prominent beachseine fisherman (Nicholas Ediriweera, see Chapter 10) was killed in a dispute over fish prices. Acquitted on the murder charge, Sunil was later gaoled for six months after a police jeep was fire-bombed in his father's compound. This sentence and several other cases of arson, assault and attempted murder, cost the family considerable sums of money. Although his brothers took over Sunil's business, they were afraid to bid aggressively and the wealthy trader David Mahattea began buying much of the Gahavälla catch. Sunil had borrowed large sums of money from the *mudalali* in Colombo, but his family still had to sell or mortgage most of their nets to meet the legal expenses.

When Sunil returned from gaol, however, he quickly reestablished control. David Mahattea stopped buying fish after his mother-in-law was killed and two other *mudalali*, W.A. Peter and W.A. Dawith, who were slowly building up a business, had left the village after a dispute with David. As far as I can ascertain, Sunil was not directly involved in either of these disputes, but they added fuel to his reputation as a violent man with whom it was dangerous to compete.[9]

There are several reasons why Sunil and his brothers have been able to maintain control since 1966. Wealthy *mudalali* from other villages provide little competition. These men are too involved with the catch from the mechanised craft to worry about the comparatively small catches from Gahavälla. Smaller *mudalali*, men with a single van, occasionally visit Gahavälla but are usually unsuccessful. The fishermen demand cash because they feel it would be difficult to collect on credit sales from people living outside Gahavälla, while Sunil bids up the price to unprofitable levels. Nor does Sunil have much competition from others in Gahavälla. Many of the fishermen would be happy to see him eliminated and there have been three attempts to kill him, but attempts to compete against him have met with little success. Part of the reason lies in Sunil's business ability. He has a well organised marketing system with extensive contacts in all important retail outlets, he has a larger amount of capital than any of his business rivals, and he owns a freehold van. People bidding against him must pay lower prices to make equivalent profits and few have sufficient capital to withstand the occasional loss. Moreover, Sunil and his brothers have a strong and well-earned reputation for violence and because of their relationship with the bicycle *kārayō* always have a big following nearby. In contrast, the fishermen are fragmented. Sunil's faction has shares in a third of the nets and ownership of the remainder is dispersed among members of the other two factions and the independent fishermen.

Other *mudalali* do occasionally compete, however, and in 1970-71 succeeded in buying 17 per cent of the beach-seine catch. Many of these purchases were late in the day when Sunil and his brothers were not interested in buying, but one man, W.A. Peter, competed directly against them and achieved some initial success. An examination of the competition between W.A. Peter and Sunil Mudalali is a clear demonstration of the way in which a combination of bargaining skills, patron-client relationships and threats of violence are used to discourage competition.

W.A. Peter was not clearly associated with any of the dominant faction leaders, but his wife was the biggest money-lender in the village and through her he had access to two or three thousand rupees in ready capital. Although he lacked transport of his own, one of his wife's brothers is a *mudalali* in a nearby village and Peter was able to use his vans to transport fish to Colombo. He was closely related to two bus drivers, so he could use the buses to transport boxes of fish to the town markets, and he also built up a close relationship with two of the more irregularly employed bicycle traders.

When Peter and his brother left Gahavälla after the dispute with David Mahattea, they established a small fish trading business at Tissamaharama. In 1969, at his wife's urging, he returned to Gahavälla and was encouraged to enter the fish trade by the faction leader, Danny Wijenaike, who promised he would sell the fish from his faction's nets on a credit basis. During the first six months of 1970, Peter bought only small amounts of fish, late in the day. But as time passed he began to compete more directly, concentrating on catches of 100 to 200 pounds which could be transported by bus. Initially paying cash for all his purchases, by the end of 1970 he was making large purchases, especially from the Wijenaike nets, on credit.

Sunil's initial reaction was limited to bidding up the price when Peter was trying to buy, but as Peter became more successful and especially after he began buying on credit, Sunil attempted to buy all the fish landed. There was little difference in bargaining skills between the two men; Sunil was unable to prevent Peter buying and on several occasions he himself was forced to buy at unprofitable prices. Several members of Sunil's faction then organised a petition to prevent the bus drivers from illegally carrying fish and, using his political contacts, Sunil forced the local manager to stop the practice. Peter was also subjected to a considerable amount of abuse and threats of violence from Sunil's supporters, but appeared unconcerned and continued to buy increasingly large amounts of fish.

Competition between the two men came to a head late in December. The catch was a large one: 2,300 *ginnätti* (leather jackets), a very popular fish which brings around Rs.1.20 at the Tangalla market and sells in Colombo at more than Rs.2. The shareholders in the net were not closely associated with any particular faction, although another of Sunil's brothers, Martinsingho, owned and worked a share. When the bidding began, Sunil and his brother Punniyadasa entered bids of 40 and 50 cents per fish. The net owners greeted these bids with laughter and abuse; an old man, the *marrakalai*, told Sunil that if he could not do better than that he was wasting his time and should go and 'fuck dogs'. Sunil then bid 53 cents followed by 55 cents, and, as the crew members discussed whether they should accept the bid, offered 60 cents and began counting the fish prior to removal. However, the *marrakalai* told him to stop; they were not selling yet.

Among the forty or so people watching the sale was W.A. Peter, sitting with a few of his relatives on a nearby *orua*. The *marrakalai* asked him if he was interested in buying and Peter offered 65 cents. Sunil who was becoming increasingly angry, said he would give 70 cents and several of the net crew began to argue that this should be accepted. The *marrakalai*, however, turned towards Sunil and shouted that this 'dog fucker' had bought Rs.1,300 worth of fish from them earlier in the year and they had received only Rs.1,200; if they sold to him at 70 cents, how much would they get? The two men began abusing each other, but Sunil's brother Martinsingho, intervened, suggesting that they give the fish to Sunil for 65 cents on the condition that he pay cash. The net crew seemed agreeable and Sunil recommenced counting the fish. Peter then climbed up on the canoe and shouted in a rage that he had also bid 65 cents and as he would also pay cash, the fish should go to him. Sunil and Peter hurled abuse at each other but when it turned out that neither carried sufficient money to pay cash, the net crew decided to divide the catch between them at 75 cents. Martinsingho argued that as Peter was only a small trader (*punchi mudalali*), he should pay cash, but was unsuccessful in converting the remainder of the crew to this view.

The two men then began counting the fish. When the count was half-way completed, Sunil, whose supporters had been gathering and now equalled Peter's in numbers, accused Peter of taking all the large fish. A scuffle broke out and Peter tried to knife his opponent but was restrained by his supporters. Sunil completed loading his share of the fish into his van and then drove it straight through the middle of Peter's fish, destroying about twenty of them and forcing Peter and his helpers to leap aside.

A few minutes later, while Peter was still awaiting transport, Martinsingho announced that he had not agreed to the price and therefore wanted his share of the fish. The other crew members argued with him but he remained adamant and was supported by his followers who by this time numbered about twenty. The *marrakalai* asked Peter to give Martinsingho a share of the catch. Under protest, Peter counted out one-eighth of the catch, and included the twenty fish damaged by the van. Martinsingho refused to accept them. It was not his fault, he said, that the fish had been destroyed. A further heated argument ensued and it seemed that a general brawl might develop but eventually, on the urging of the *marrakalai*, Peter replaced the damaged fish with whole ones.

After most of Peter's supporters, believing that the dispute had been settled, had drifted away, Martinsingho suddenly asserted that he had not been given enough fish. His share was one-eighth of the total catch and as Sunil had left, he wanted one-quarter of Peter's purchase. Peter refused, but when Martinsingho and one of the bicycle *kārayō* tried to attack him, he ran away saying that he would not buy any of the catch. The net crew was called together, another auction was held and Sunil and Martinsingho's brother, Punniyadasa, bought all the fish, including Martinsingho's share, at 60 cents.

A week later Peter was severely assaulted as he returned home from a gambling party and did not attempt to buy fish again. The net crew eventually received 60 cents apiece for their fish, with Sunil justifying his 15 cent cut by claiming a loss on the deal. Neither Sunil nor his brothers would pay for the fish destroyed by the van; those, they said, were Peter's responsibility.

Monopsonies and Violence

The recent history of Gahavälla fish trading can be presented as the biography of one man and Sunil's personality and character undoubtedly did much to shape the precise pattern of events. It would be wrong, however, to regard Gahavälla as atypical for this reason. Similar monopsonies have been established in the other southern coast fishing villages and the events in Gahavälla are but one version of a much broader social process.

An analysis of the formation of these monopsonies might reasonably begin with the macro-economic structure. In the mid-fifties the increased demand for fish in conjunction with improvements in communications and preservation, widened the market and increased the profits in the small fish trade. At the same time, the established *mudalali* were turning towards the larger profits in marketing the catch from the mechanised boats and this opened the way for the emergence of a new group of fish traders. A decade later, restrictions on motor vehicle imports and subsequent shortages of transport, were substantial barriers against new entrants. This analysis, however, merely brushes the surface: deeper understanding requires a switch in focus from economic to social factors.

Several aspects of the social organisation of fish marketing contribute to the dominant position of the local *mudalali* in each village. Both net crews and fishermen as a class, are riven by faction cleavages which prevent them from bargaining effectively against the *mudalali* or marketing the catch themselves. The *mudalali*, by contrast, always has a large body of committed clients to serve as a claque in the bargaining process and as henchmen in arguments or fights. The custom of buying on credit inhibits sales to *mudalali* from outside the village, for the fishermen feel that they would have difficulty in recovering the money. The most effective constraint upon the extension of an established monopsony to a fresh village is the personalised structure of the *mudalali* enterprise: the structure of their businesses and the organisation of the market makes it imperative that they buy the fish in person.

The most significant point, however, is the importance of violence, or more accurately, the threat of violence, in maintaining the position of the *mudalali* against competitors and fishermen alike. The economic transactions are conducted within a framework of accepted norms, but underlying these is the constant threat of violence if either party oversteps the narrow limits of accepted competition. The *mudalali* is the more powerful, but the threats are not unidirectional; just as the fishermen are constrained, so too are the *mudalali*. Nor is the violence limited to threats, the two major challenges to the Gahavälla monopsony ended in homicide.

CHAPTER 9

THE 'TRADITIONAL' VILLAGE

When anthropologists have not avoided history we have usually dichotomised it. Ethnographers in Sri Lanka, as elsewhere, have sought the 'traditional' village; a field site remote from the metropolis and free from the obvious signs of economic change - transistors, motor bikes and coca cola - which might support our claims to have reconstructed the 'real' social structure. Such illusions are usually harmless conceits, but they cripple attempts to explain social and economic change. There is little point in describing the impact of modern technology on a traditional society, when the traditional society has been transformed by a century of colonialism.

The Sri Lankan villages studied by modern anthropologists undoubtedly differ in numerous, if as yet unspecified, ways from their pre-colonial predecessors. In Madagama, a village as remote as any, Obeyesekere demonstrates that land tenure, agricultural practices and social stratification were radically altered by 19th century colonial legislation. Similarly in Gahavälla: the social changes which resulted from the emergence of capitalist relations of production in the 1940s, were but the most recent phase in a process of social change which began in the mid-nineteenth century. In one sense Gahavälla in 1940 was not even the same community as a century earlier; very few descendants of the 1850 inhabitants remained.

This and the following chapter attempt to reconstruct Gahavälla's economic history. The dividing point between the two chapters is 1940, the year in which capitalist relations of production entered Gahavälla fishing. Before 1940 the economic logic governing the fisheries was production for use, and Gahavälla had a semi-subsistence economy. A household's primary aim was to secure its subsistence needs, and agriculture and cottage industries played an important role alongside fishing. Fish was certainly sold, but much was preserved or retailed by family members and the cash was only part of the household's income. After 1940, market production transformed the economic organisation of fishing and the household economies of the fishermen. Cash sales became the major income source of fishing households; capitalist entrepreneurs controlled fish marketing, and began to dispossess the fishermen from the means of production by increasing the number of nets and buying shares; and a rural proletariat emerged. The year 1940 is a convenient dividing point in the consideration of these changes, but it is not arbitrary. The development of capitalism was, of course, grounded in earlier events, but the combination of the war, better communications, and an ice factory, crystallised it remarkably quickly.

As this and the following chapter deal with historical materials it is perhaps worth emphasising that they are intended as contributions to social anthropology. Although my personal opinion is that there should be no intellectual division of labour in the study of societies such as Sri Lanka - an historian concerned with Sri Lankan rural history runs severe risks of misinterpretation if he does not draw upon the numerous studies of contemporary Asian peasantries to formulate his questions; while anthropologists dealing with contemporary societies cannot afford to ignore the historical processes which produced them - nevertheless, the division does exist. Larkin (1971:784) notes that 'history seeks the particular in events and human society and culture, while other social disciplines are most frequently concerned with generalizations about the human response'. The last phrase is slightly misleading when applied to social anthropology, for the continuing *rationale* of the discipline has been to describe other cultures in terms familiar to readers within the Western intellectual tradition, without destroying the particularity of the culture in the process, but the question does draw attention to an important difference between history and anthropology. Despite the use of historical data this is not an exercise in history: the intention is to sketch a broad social pattern not to describe the precise sequence of events.

Nineteenth Century Settlement[1]

At the beginning of the nineteenth century, Gahavälla was an isolated fishing settlement of less than fifty inhabitants surrounded by heavy jungle; by 1900 it was a prosperous village, with an economy based on tree crop agriculture and beachseining, and a population approaching 500.

In 1824, at the time of the first British census (Bergman 1827), the census area of Nakulagamuwa, incorporating Gahavälla and the three adjoining villages, had a total population of 231 and apart from Tangalla (920), was the biggest population centre in Hambantota district.[2] All of the people in Nakulagamuwa were of the *Karāva* caste, but *Karāva* amounted to less than 15 per cent of the Hambantota district's population, which was overwhelmingly *Goigama*. By 1871 (Williams 1873) the population of Gahavälla and the adjoining village of Moraketiara had grown to 392. Most of Gahavälla was covered in bush and scrub, and the track along the side of the lagoon connecting Gahavälla with Kudawellekele had not been built. The Gahavälla population was concentrated in two areas. At the mouth of the Sinimodera River, in the hamlet known as Kottetawa, was a small settlement of perhaps 100 persons, drawing a living from line-fishing and the cultivation of small gardens in the bush. The census does not report any fish trading (although it does for the neighbouring villages) suggesting that the fish was mainly consumed in the village. Judging from the records of land sales between 1870 and 1890 and evidence in a land case encompassing this area which was decided in 1898 (No.462, Tangalla Court), people living in Kottetawa around 1870 were members of three *pelapata:*[3] Mutu Malage, Ullius Hewage, and Mawelle Hewage. One indication of the fate of these early settlers is that the two latter *pelapata* today comprise only three households. Mutu Malage is still a large *pelapata* but most of its members are descended from later Kudawellekele immigrants and do not regard themselves as close kinsmen of Gahavälla Mutu Malage.

Closer to the main provincial highway and including part of the modern village of Moraketiara, was a larger settlement of about 300 people. The evidence in the partition case indicates that by 1850 much of this area had been planted in tree crops, mainly coconut and breadfruit; the paddy fields which later exceeded 17 acres, were in the process of being formed out of a swampy estuary; and the remainder of the land was used for *chena*[4] cultivation. Members of the two *pelapata* which dominated Gahavälla and the nearby villages at the end of the century (Ediriweera, and Ediriwickramasuriya) began buying land in 1867 and had considerable landholdings by 1878. The ancestor of Sunil Mudalali also began buying land about this time.

TABLE 9.1. GAHAVÄLLA'S POPULATION

	Male	Female	Total
1871	208	184	392[a]
1891	248	192	440[a]
1901	248	220	468
1911	304	283	587
1921	302	294	596
1931			752
1970			1,031

[a] Including Moraketiara. In 1970 Moraketiara's population was 832.

Sources: 1871 (Williams 1873); 1891 (Lee 1892); 1901 (Arunachalam 1902); 1911 (Denham 1912); 1921 (Turner 1923); 1931 (Turner 1931); 1970 (District Revenue Office Records).

In the twenty years after 1871 the Gahavälla population increased by 13 per cent to a total of 440. This period also saw the establishment of a small settlement on land near the southern headland, in what is today the centre of Gahavälla. Lemon de Silva, who is regarded as the founder of this part of Gahavälla and whose sons are credited with the introduction of the beachseines, first appears in the land records in 1869, when he claimed title to 27 acres of Crown land which he had purchased in 1853. He appears to have been a minor official from

Weligama, a *Karāva* village on the South-West coast, who purchased the land as an investment during his official career. The land was willed to three of his sons and, according to local stories, Lemon de Silva did not himself live in Gahavälla. It would appear that his three sons, who later took the *pelapata* names of Mawelle Arrachige, Abraham Gallipatige and Paranamanage, arrived in Gahavälla about 1870, because their marriage certificates dated 1873, 1876 and 1882, all give Gahavälla as their place of residence, and the actual marriages took place some years earlier.

Even at this time the inhabitants of the area were on less than friendly terms with the central government. In 1873, following a series of assaults and a murder, the Government Agent imposed a punitive squad of police on the villages of Nakulagamuwa. The maintenance costs were supposed to be met by a levy of Rs.2.50 on each household, but the police had considerable difficulty in obtaining the money (Administration Report, Government Agent, Hambantota, 1874).

The 1901 census (Arunachalam 1902) was considerably more detailed than its predecessors. The population of Gahavälla was 468 and 231 persons lived in Moraketiara. Thus the population of the two villages increased by 50 per cent in the period of only ten years and was to rise by more than 40 per cent in the next decade.[5] The adult (over 15) male population was 113, and the occupations listed are: agriculture 53, traders 24, fishermen 57, others 15. The occupations total 149 suggesting that nearly half the men had more than one. It is clear that by 1901 fishing was important in the village economy, but Gahavälla was by no means a single-product village. As many of the fishermen were also agriculturalists, cultivation of dry grain must have provided a large proportion of the village cereal consumption. The traders were engaged in salting fish and selling it in the interior villages, but there was also substantial trade in cattle and coconut products.

Although the data is less than comprehensive, it is clear that the thirty years before 1900 saw considerable economic and social changes in Gahavälla and these were accompanied by substantial population increases. There are two documented events which probably account for most of these changes: the introduction of the beachseines and the establishment of an arrack and toddy tavern.

The First Beachseines

Gahavälla fishermen hold that the sole rights to beachseining off Gahavälla beach belong to descendants of the three brothers who introduced the nets around 1880. While they do not argue for a single founding ancestor (and many are unaware that the three were brothers), informants are adamant that the founders of the Paranamanage, Abraham Gallipatige and Mawelle Arrachige *pelapata* brought the nets to Gahavälla and that fishing rights descend from these three men. The land records indicate that these men were the sons of Lemon de Silva and there is a further, less widespread, tradition that the first beachseine was brought to Gahavälla as the dowry of one of his sons. In the modern system, the first beachseine in the sequence is *Nilvälla orua* (*orua* from Nilvälla). Dinoris Paranamanage, whose marriage was registered in 1882 when his bride was thirty-two years old[6] did take a bride from Nilvälla, suggesting that the tradition may be accurate and the beachseine was introduced to Gahavälla shortly before 1880. This is in accord with what is known from other sources about the history of the beachseines in Sri Lanka (see Chapter 6).

The *madell* must have greatly increased the efficiency of fishing in Gahavälla. In Gandara, a village ten miles towards Colombo, the beachseines resulted in a 500 per cent rise in fish production over four years (Government Agent, Matara, Administration Report, 1886), and Gahavälla's more favourable environment suggests even greater increases. As beachseining was a seasonal activity and the fish were caught alive, it would seem particularly suited to the relatively high status Buddhist agriculturalists living in Gahavälla. Difficulties in marketing the catch would have blunted the impact of the beachseine on the village economy, but as early as 1900 two results are evident: at least seven large masonry houses were built between 1891 and 1901, all but one of them by beachseine fishermen, and there is clear evidence of a change in marriage patterns after 1890.

A study of Gahavälla birth and marriage certificates[7] between 1869 and 1885 shows that inter-village marriages almost invariably led to virilocal residence. In contrast, 70 per cent of the seventy-six inter-village marriages recorded between 1895 and 1905 led to uxorilocal residence and in all but one the husband came to Gahavälla. The names of the persons involved in the marriages show that with the exception of two of Garuhamy's daughters (see below), the females were daughters of beachseine fishermen. After 1910, however, uxorilocal post-marital residence is once again very rare. The timing of these dramatic changes support the supposition that high profits and an increased demand for labour generated by the beachseines was the main reason for the upsurge in uxorilocal residence. The population at the time the beachseines were introduced was probably too small to use them efficiently and marriage may have seemed an appropriate way to recruit labour.

Garuhamy's Tavern

The beachseines increased the resource base of Gahavälla's economy and stimulated population growth: Garuhamy's arrack tavern changed the pattern of land use and stimulated social stratification. A.G. Garuhamy had been employed by an arrack renter near Matara, but in 1891 or 1892 he purchased the arrack licence for a tavern in Tangalla and shifted it to Gahavälla, building his tavern where the main provincial highway joins Moraketiara.

As the 'Report of the Commission of Enquiry into Arrack Renting' of 1887 demonstrates, arrack selling was an extremely profitable business. In 1885 there were 198 arrack taverns in the Southern Province alone, one for each thousand adults, paying rent of Rs.228,500. Arrack could be bought from the distillers for Rs.1, tax amounted to Rs.2 and the sale price was as high as Rs.7, giving Rs.2 to Rs.5 per gallon profit on the 600-odd gallons sold in a year. In 1898 profits were further improved when the number of taverns was cut by two-thirds. Garuhamy also held a distiller's licence and this was even more profitable. The commission estimated the total costs of production of a gallon of arrack (including the rent of the coconut trees and the collection of the toddy, but excluding capital costs), at less than six cents per gallon as against a wholesale price of Rs.1.

Soon after his arrival, Garuhamy began purchasing large areas of land and planted it with coconut, presumably to provide toddy for his stills.[8] His purchases in Gahavälla between 1898 and 1914 totalled thirty-seven acres, and checks in Sinimodera and Moraketiara show further purchases amounting to nearly fifty acres. This was in addition to very large purchases in less settled areas, for according to one of his descendants his total land-holdings exceeded 350 acres. There are other indications that his business was highly profitable: in 1901 he completed a massive house, surrounding the two acres of grounds with an eight foot masonry wall, and constructing two ornate wrought iron gates.

In his masterly account of land tenure in Madagama, a village in the interior of Southern Province, Obeyesekere (1967) documents the effects of the grain taxes and various Crown Land Ordinances on the pattern of property-holding within Low Country villages. The high taxes on grain forced villages to sell paddy land, while the Crown Land Ordinances prevented village expansion into unoccupied land. Consequently, land was accumulated by the families who controlled the local level posts in the colonial government: in Madagama such men accumulated more than half the village paddy lands in less than two decades. Obeyesekere emphasises the relationship between land ownership and the control of local colonial posts. The local headmen were appointed from among the larger landowners and their appointment facilitated the acquisition of further land. As the headmen were *de facto* assessors for the grain tax and the critical witnesses in any attempt to establish a land claim on the grounds of continuous occupation, they could ensure a steady flow of land onto the market. In some cases the dominant landlord families established marriage alliances with similarly dominant families in other villages. The outcome was the *peläntiya:* a status group of landlords, divorced from the immediate production process, and practising a neo-feudal life-style.

Obeyesekere suggests that a similar process took place in other areas of the Southern Province and his thesis does broadly describe events in Gahavälla, although the emphasis is different: grain taxes, to take an obvious point, were unimportant. In 1914, A.G. Garuhamy, the arrack renter, and Dionysius Ediriweera, the Village Headman, owned 36 per cent of Gahavälla's land. In the next five years their children acquired a further eleven acres, giving 44 per cent by 1920.

Dionysius Ediriweera belonged to the Ediriweera-Ediriwickramasuriya *peläntiya,* most of whom lived in Moraketiara and Sinimodera. The founder of the Ediriweera *pelapata* was a clerk in the District Revenue Office in Tangalla, who purchased large areas in Moraketiara and Sinimodera between 1865 and 1870 and planted them in coconut and paddy. Later there were three marriages between his children and the children of a man called Ediriwickramasuriya who owned sufficient land to be appointed Village Headman in 1871. Dionysius was the child of one of these marriages and after the Nakulagamuwa Village Headmanship was split into two parts, became Village Headman of Gahavälla in 1902, although he did not take up residence until 1908. Between 1908 and 1914 he purchased two and three-quarter acres, most of it in very small lots, and after the Village Settlement (see below), purchased a further eight acres. This was three-quarters of the land sold to claimants under the Waste Land Ordinance, and while there is no reason to suppose that Dionysius had any special claim to the land, the average price was less than Rs.8 per acre.

Ediriweera's major allies were the other members of the *peläntiya* living in Moraketiara and Sinimodera, but there is also evidence of an attempt at marriage alliances with A.G. Garuhamy, the wealthiest man in Gahavälla. In 1906, Garuhamy's daughter married one of Dionysius's sons and in 1907, another daughter married into the Ediriwickramasuriya *pelapata.* Earlier, one of Garuhamy's sons had been appointed *Market Constable* in Sinimodera. The attempted alliances were evidently unsuccessful, for no further marriages are reported and no other children of Garuhamy acquired government posts.

The land purchased by Dionysius was on the Gahävalla-Moraketiara boundary, but there is some indication of similar events in the more central areas of Gahavälla. Lemon de Silva had purchased considerable land here while he was in government employment in Weligama. When Garuhamy began buying land around 1895, the sellers were not de Silva's descendants, but men from small towns, particularly Matara, who had purchased the land direct from the Crown. I have no data on the occupations of these men, but the lots all exceeded an acre, and the land was covered in scrub at the time Garuhamy purchased it. This suggests that the land had been bought for speculation, rather than use.

Garuhamy's initial purchases, which exceeded seventeen acres, displaced few peasants, although they must have restricted the area available for *chena*. The purchases after 1900, particularly those following Land Settlement under the Waste Land Ordinance, which had begun in 1904, were of a different order. Most were small shares in areas of undivided land,[9] the sellers were poor men living in Kottetawa and the prices were very low. The outcome was that twenty acres of subsistence *chena* cultivations owned by numerous poor peasants became one man's coconut plantation. *Chena*, which with fishing was the basis of the poor peasant economy, was in effect eliminated in Gahavälla. I am not sure what happened to the erstwhile *chena* cultivators after their land was sold. On the basis of oral history it appears that a few left Gahavälla, but most built houses on the strip of land bordering the foreshore and earned a living from inshore fishing and labouring on the beachseines. Around 1920 most of the remaining families in this area became deep-sea fishermen, using gear rented from landlords living in Moraketiara and spending six months of the year as migratory fishermen on the East Coast south of Trincomalee. Some have since taken up permanent residence on the East Coast, especially in Puttalam. It is difficult to provide an accurate account because few present-day Gahavälla citizens will admit descent from the *chena* cultivators, and as poor men the *chena* cultivators left few traces in the land or other records.

Why did these small peasants dispose of their land? The grain tax was not an important factor: it had been abolished in 1892, before the sales in question occurred, and although in theory applicable to dry grain as well as paddy, was seldom enforced. The land sales by poor peasant owners between 1900 and 1914 were a product of the implementation of the Crown Land Ordinances in a community where the population was growing rapidly.

The various Crown Land Encroachment Ordinances, promulgated between 1840 and 1907, provided that all uncultivated land should be deemed Crown Land. Officers appointed by the governor visited each village, carried out a survey (the Final Village Plan) and compiled a Register of Settlements in which all land within the village boundaries was classified under three headings: (a) Declared Crown Land, (b) Admitted private, (c) Sold to villagers. Claimants to land had to substantiate their claims by deeds, tax receipts or evidence of continuous occupation, and if the claim was accepted, the boundaries of the land were delineated approximately and title granted. If the claim was rejected the claimant could buy the land. Any remaining land was assigned to the Crown.[10]

The land settlement programme was initiated in 1904 in Gahavälla and the Final Village Plan and Register of Settlements were published in August 1914. This radically changed the context of Gahavälla land sales. It had previously been difficult for men like Garuhamy to purchase land from *chena* cultivators: boundaries were not fixed; areas were measured in terms of sowing rates rather than acres; claims were based on continuous occupation rather than deeds; and as a result of bilateral inheritance, there were numerous owners of even the smallest areas. After the Village Settlement: approximate boundaries and acreages were established; the Settlement Plan was proof of title; and while fragmentation of land through bilateral inheritance remained a problem, a partition case would establish exact entitlements. Men like Garuhamy could now speculate in the land 'sharemarket' and amass large holdings.

It remains to be explained why, as the land settlement applied to the whole of Gahavälla, land sales were mainly limited to Kottetawa. The answer probably lies in Kottetawa population increases between 1891 and 1911.

In 1901, there were eighty-nine families in Gahavälla, about thirty of whom were engaged in *chena* cultivation on the twenty-three acres of Kottetawa. This is an average of more than half an acre per family and supplemented by inshore fishing, was probably sufficient for a subsistence living.[11] Between 1901 and 1911 the Gahavälla population increased by 25 per cent. In addition to the uxorilocal marriages of the beachseiners an important reason for the increase was immigration from the even more densely populated village of Kudawellekele to Kottetawa. Thus by 1911 *chena* cultivation in conjunction with fishing could not provide a subsistence income for the people of Kottetawa. Many of Garuhamy's purchases were foreclosed mortgages and it appears that *chena* cultivators ran up bills in his tavern and had to sell their land to meet them.

Gahavälla in 1914

The publication of the Final Village Plan marked the end of one phase in Gahavälla's history and a description of the village at this time provides a useful bench-mark for the discussion of the following half-century. By 1914 the village had been surveyed into named areas of land, most of them marked by fence lines. The total area was fixed at 132.25 acres and by 1914, 78 per cent of the land was privately owned, the rest belonging to the Crown.[12]

The Register of Settlements divides the land into three categories: gardens (which included house sites) planted in tree crops; *chenas* planted in dry grain such as Indian corn, *kurakkan*; low jungle and scrub not used for cultivation. Overall, 50 per cent of the total village area was gardens and a further thirty-seven acres was utilised for *chena* cultivation. The Crown Lands were areas along the jungle-covered southern headland, and the lagoon side of the Gahavälla-Moraketiara road suitable only for house sites.

Within Gahavälla there were marked differences in the pattern of land use. The house sites of the grandsons of Lemon de Silva and his grand-daughters who had married uxorilocally, were on the seaward side of the Moraketiara-

TABLE 9.2. LAND USE AND LAND TENURE IN 1914

Land Use	Acres	Percentage
Gardens	65.50	50
Chena	49.75	37
Jungle	17.00	13
Total:	132.25	100
Tenure		
Private Ownership	89.75	67
Crown	28.50	22
Sold to Crown by Claimants	14.00	11
Total:	132.25	100

Kudawellekele road. These men were engaged in beach-seining and trading and their house compounds were reasonably large (more than quarter of an acre) and planted with tree crops. Most houses were of wattle and daub construction, but by 1911 there were at least six substantial tile-roofed masonry houses.

The lands called Areotottawatta (which is still planted in coconut and breadfruit) and much of Kottetawa was a plantation owned by A.G. Garuhamy, his brothers and their children. In 1914 some of this land, especially the sections closest to the beach, was used for *chena* or occupied by houses, but it was rapidly being planted in coconut. The northern portion of the land was unoccupied except for Garuhamy's own house, but the southern block was being divided into small gardens by those of Garuhamy's brothers' children who had married into the beachseine families. Apart from the two areas owned by the Village Headman, Ediriweera, the rest of the village was not subdivided by fences. There were several small 'squatter' settlements, the largest of them on a narrow strip along the foreshore in Kottetawa: small groups of wattle and daub houses owned by *madell* labourers and in-shore fishermen.

Several of the wealthier villagers owned land in Sinimodera and Moraketiara and increasingly their children left to settle there. Most of this land was under tree crops. Garuhamy, for example, owned a coconut plantation 100 yards wide extending almost the full length of the Sinimodera frontage of Gahavälla Beach, as well as several smaller parcels elsewhere.

Gahavälla was a highly stratified village in 1914. The economic elite were the landowners deriving most of their income from the sale of tree crops. Garuhamy was certainly the wealthiest: his arrack tavern plus his landholdings in the three villages alone would have placed him among the wealthiest men in the Tangalla region. The other large landowners were the close relatives of the Village Headman, and, perhaps, one or two of the richer beachseiners. In all this group amounted to no more than six households - less than 10 per cent of the population, - and owned almost two-thirds of Gahavälla's land.

The political elite was the Moraketiara based Ediriweera-Ediriwickramasuriya *peläntiya* plus their allies from Sinimodera. Between 1890 and 1910, internal segmentation accompanied by name changes divided the *peläntiya* into five constituent *pelapata*, but they still controlled local level politics and between 1880 and 1937 the office of Village Headman in all three villages was held by a *peläntiya* member. Informants claim that the *peläntiya* adopted all the trappings of the traditional Sinhalese feudal system: respectful terms of address were used by other villagers towards them, they were worshipped on New Year's Day and in return distributed gifts of clothes and agricultural produce on festival occasions.

About fifty middle peasant households owned the beachseines, which judging by reports from other nearby fishing villages, were probably the major contributors to the village economy. Informants often described the beachseiners of this period as *eka pavul kattiya* (a family group): a kin group comprising the descendants of the three founders and their affines who married endogamously and settled their disputes on a kinship basis. The genealogies I collected tend to support these claims. Within the beachseiners the beginnings of economic differentiation were already apparent: some men had begun trading coconut products, cattle, and fish (salt or dried), and had begun building expensive masonry houses.

At the bottom of the heap, and probably comprising more than half the population, were the original Gahavälla inhabitants living in Kottetawa with the later immigrants from Kudawellekele. Occupying small mud houses along the foreshore, these households obtained a precarious living from lagoon and inshore fishing, supplemented by small amounts of garden produce and occasional work as beach-seine labourers and coconut harvesters.

By 1914 Gahavälla was well along the path in the transition from a subsistence economy based on dry grain cultivation and a little fishing, to a market economy based on tree crop agriculture and the sale of dried fish. *Chena* cultivation had almost been eliminated: much of the land was privately owned and used for tree crops and house sites while the unoccupied land was not suitable for cultivation. The original inhabitants had been displaced from their land and along with later, similar migrants, eked out a marginal existence on the fringes of the village economy. The *peläntiya* class had reached their zenith: their large landholdings were sufficiently profitable to support an affluent lifestyle. The beach-seiners were a prosperous community who were not fully exploiting the fishery and could supplement their incomes by cultivation and trading.

The Decline of the Landlords 1914-1940

The landlords dominated Gahavälla's economy for only a short period. By 1931 the population was 752, a density of more than 3,500 per square mile[13] (Turner 1931). The expansion of coconut and other tree crops into *chena* lands ceased around 1920 and during the following two decades the coconut plantations began to be subdivided into dwelling sites. The total acreage under tree crops (excluding house sites) was less than twenty-three acres in 1930, much of it in areas such as the headland which were unsuitable for houses. In 1940 five households still derived most of their income from agriculture, but their landholdings were not in Gahavälla. The land use transition from *chena* to tree crops, and then to house-sites, was stimulated by population growth and accelerated by five partition cases between 1919 and 1933 which fragmented A.G. Garuhamy's thirty-seven acres into more than 100 separate holdings.

The changes in land use had obvious effects on the economy. In 1931 fishing was the major locus of production, although the manufacturing of coir rope and other coconut products had become increasingly prominent during the previous decade. The land planted in tree crops had so diminished that most of the raw materials for manufacturing coconut products had to be imported and while subsistence agriculture was still an important source of papaw and plantains, as it is today, cultivation of grains had ceased. By 1940 almost all of Gahavälla's cereal requirements were imported, much of it from overseas.[14]

grain import

Fishing produced most wealth, but trading undoubtedly provided most of the village's cash income. Using Gahavälla as a base, several beachseining families established substantial trading enterprises. Two families began to finance migratory fishermen at the deep-sea fishing sites within the Yala game reserve, sun-drying the catch and marketing it along with salted and dried fish from Gahavälla, in the interior villages of the Southern Province. Another household, Andrea Hennedige Matteshamy's, took control of coconut-coir manufacturing, buying coconut husks from the villages near Matara and converting them into coir in Gahavälla. Around 1930 the margin of the lagoon was occupied entirely by soaking pits for the husks owned by Matteshamy. Other traders established small retail shops in the areas in Hambantota being brought under paddy cultivation, particularly near Walasmulla and Tissamaharama. Although these men spent most of their time elsewhere, their wives and children stayed in Gahavälla, their houses were built there, and their earnings strengthened the village economy.

The economic changes were accompanied by demographic changes. Immigration had almost ceased by 1911 and from this point Gahavälla has probably had a nett population loss from migration. Emigration during the 1914-1940 period took several forms. The heaviest emigration was among landholding families dependent upon tree crops where land fragmentation and lower prices had lowered their standard of living. Some took up new paddy land in the settlement schemes in the south-east dry zone; others planted coconut in the as yet unsettled belt four to five miles behind the coast. A mission school had been opened in Sinimodera in 1908 and some of the pupils of this school and a convent in Tangalla, entered the government service as minor clerks and school teachers. Initially, these men retained their land in Gahavälla and attempted to combine government service and coconut cultivation, but the more successful were eventually transferred elsewhere on promotion. Today the landlords who dominated the economy at the turn of the century are represented by only ten households: the descendants of Garuhamy's children who married beachseiners.

There was less migration among the fishing and trading families. The beachseines could absorb considerable labour and most children from this group joined their parents or became traders. Although the position of the Kottetawa fishermen had become increasingly bleak with the end of *chena* cultivation and the increasing pressure on employment within the fishing industry, there was initially little emigration. Their main opportunity for employment was as tenants or labourers on the new paddy lands, a prospect which they apparently found unattractive. When they turned to deep-sea fishing around 1920, however, many began settling in the migratory fishing areas along the East Coast, especially in the villages south of Trincomalee.

Gahavälla social stratification in 1940 differed considerably from twenty-five years earlier. Many of the landlords' descendants had left, and the biggest landholder owned less than six acres. The remaining families attempted to assert their high status, but except for the few who supplemented their landholdings with salaries, lacked the necessary economic base. The beachseine fishermen had split into two groups. The majority were making a subsistence living from fishing, although population growth was reducing average household incomes. The small number who had given up beachseining in favour of trading formed a new economic elite and as they extended their alliances through marriage, were becoming a political elite also.

The social mobility of the successful beachseiners was aided by an increased emphasis on village identity among the three villages of Nakulagamuwa. Prior to 1921, all three had a single headman and men living in one village commonly owned land in another. But by 1940, each village had its own headman and land was mainly owned by the inhabitants. In 1937, the trader and coir manufacturer, A.H. Matteshamy, became Village Headman in Gahavälla, the first headman in any of the three villages from outside the Ediriweera *pelapata* and their allies. The traders were following the same avenue of upward mobility as the earlier landlords, acquiring land and educating their children for white collar employment, but because little land was available, their progress was considerably slower.

Beachseining, 1914-1940

Beachseining had become the main form of production by 1914 and by all measures, except the income received in cash, was the basis of the village economy. As far as I can ascertain from oral histories and genealogies, all of the men engaged in beachseining before 1940 held rights of access, either by descent or marriage. Some fishermen were the descendants of the men who had married uxorilocally before 1910, but most were the descendants of the three founders.

There is consensus that shares were rarely sold at this time and that the price of the few shares that were sold was always lower than the cost of construction. Share inheritance was also relatively unimportant, for the maintenance costs of a share over five years was equivalent to the cost of a new net. In any case sons gradually took over the operation of the nets as their fathers grew older, and the legal transfer following the death of both parents was a purely formal acknowledgement of existing arrangements. As a dowry, the importance of the share transfer between father-in-law and son-in-law lay not in the economic value of the share, but in its confirmation of the son-in-law's rights to fish at Gahavälla Beach.

Although there was no limit on the number of nets, and anyone holding access rights was entitled to construct a net and use it at Gahavälla Beach several economic considerations inhibited construction of new nets. Before 1939 beachseining remained a semi-subsistence activity. As much as 40 per cent of the catch was consumed in the village and although perhaps half the catch was dried (much of it for later sale in the interior villages) the prices for dried fish were very low. There was little surplus finance available in the village and no incentive to invest in gear other than the minimum required to provide employment. Further, it must have been clear that once the number of nets exceeded those that could be used in a day, additional nets would not increase the total catch and profits would decrease even further. As the fishermen were essentially a single kinship group, it is reasonable to suppose that informal agreements were partially effective in restricting the number of nets. Nevertheless, the nets did gradually increase from around twenty in 1920, to thirty-six in 1938 (see Table 9.3).

Apparently the main impetus for the increases in nets was demographic pressure. The Gahavälla population grew by 70 per cent between 1901 and 1931 and a greatly disproportionate increase occurred among beachseining families. Before 1910, the beachseiners, handicapped by a severe labour shortage, had encouraged their sons-in-law to live in Gahavälla, and by 1931 many of these mens' children were themselves marrying. Because exploitation of the fishery resource was tied to the eight share system, sons from large families had to construct additional nets if they wished to continue beachseining. A hypothetical example will make this clear. If there are twenty nets, a man with one share will receive 1/160th of the annual catch. But if after his death his two sons take joint ownership of his share, they each receive only 1/320th of the catch, whereas if one joins in the construction of a new net they each receive 1/168th. Thus, although the construction of new nets was clearly uneconomic from the viewpoint of the community as a whole, there were good reasons why individual fishermen, especially those from large families, should construct new nets. The optimum number of nets was reached before 1920 and the consequent increase involved additional investment of which the marginal product was zero.

TABLE 9.3. INCREASES IN NUMBER OF NETS[a]

Year	No. of Nets	Source of Information
1970-71	108	Registration List.
	99	Personal Observation.
1967	108	Informants.
1964	83	Registration List.
1957	77	Informants.
1946	77	*Patabändi Arrachi's* Notebook.
1945	71	*Patabändi Arrachi's* Notebook.
1938	36	*Patabändi Arrachi's* Notebook.
1933	32	*Patabändi Arrachi's* Notebook.
1920	20 (?)	Informants.

[a] The figures after 1946 are accurate. The earlier figures are mainly derived from notes kept by the then *Patabändi Arrachi* (1933-57), but cross-checks with informants' accounts suggest that any errors are small.

The tendency towards an increase in the number of nets as a result of population growth was partially offset by other factors. The most important is that many sons could not afford to finance new shares and were forced into other less desirable fisheries such as deep-sea fishing or handlining. Further, as the number of nets increased, the probability of any particular net participating in the flush period decreased, and men unable to meet the maintenance costs of their share following a poor year dropped out in favour of newcomers. As the returns from other fisheries were very low, it was very difficult for men in either category to amass sufficient finance to return to beachseining.

Taken together, these factors support the inference that although finance that would otherwise have been used for the construction of additional nets was redirected into the acquisition of relinquished shares, the rate of population growth was too high to permit the system to reach an equilibrium. As increasing the nets did not produce larger catches, a point would eventually be reached where ownership of a single share was insufficient to sustain life and large numbers of men were forced to find other occupations. The function of the rights of access concept was not to limit the number of nets, but to ensure that outsiders did not construct nets for use on Gahavälla beach and thus accelerate the fragmentation process.

In 1933 the government introduced legislation to register beachseines throughout Sri Lanka and only men with a licence were permitted to fish off a particular beach. Although the government accepted that in some areas fishing rights were not individually owned but belonged to the community as a whole, it was uncertain as to how joint ownership could be translated into legislation (Anon 1922). In most sites beachseines were by this time owned by one or two men. In these cases the government simply issued licences to the owners and crystallised the *status quo*. In the few sites on the west coast where each net had several owners, fishing cooperatives were established which quickly became either bankrupt or mere facades for the activities of a capitalist elite. But in areas along the southern coast (including Gahavälla) where share ownership was widely distributed throughout the community, the fishermen refused to form cooperatives. As a compromise the government limited the number of nets at any site to those in use in 1933 and codified the criteria for allocating access to the water.[15]

This legislation effectively destroyed the notion of rights to access. Whereas previously all people in the community had the right to build nets and participate in the fishery, now men could participate only by buying a share in an existing net. The legislation also permitted sales of shares to men without hereditary rights to the fishery and many of the share sales following 1940 were to such people. The legislation would have had the positive effect of limiting the number of nets but this proviso was not enforced and nets had increased to thirty-six by 1938.

The 1938-39 season was the last in which the beachseines operated within a semi-subsistence economy. In 1935, according to the *Patabändi Arrachi's* notebooks, one man in Gahavälla owned three shares and six men had two shares each. If it is true that the remaining participants owned only a single share each, then as many as 208 households[16] derived part (in most cases the major part) of their income from beachseining.

The living standards of the beachseiners must have dropped steadily during this period. The number of men and nets engaged doubled, as did the production costs, while the volume of the catch probably remained constant.[17] Nor did the value of the catch increase substantially: dried fish prices rose by only 25 per cent between 1920 and 1938 (Government Agent Reports, Hambantota 1920 and 1938) and wet fish prices remained static. The increasing population in the nearby agricultural villages was a good market for wet fish, and this decreased the percentage that had to be dried and increased the overall price, but the fishermen could not take full benefit. Their marketing range was limited by the speed of the *pingo* carriers and the rate of decomposition, as well as by seasonality: during the flush period the catch was far larger than the local market could absorb.

Accompanying the decline in average income from *madella* fishing was a decline in other sources of income. In 1914 the average *madella* fisherman owned a quarter acre and its coconuts, plantains and betel provided both cash and items for household consumption. By 1938, the same area was occupied by at least double the number of households. There were employment opportunities in the trading ventures and, for women, in coir manufacturing, but it is unlikely that these gains balanced the losses.

By 1938 the share system governing *madella* production was apparently on the point of collapse. Although the value of the catch had not significantly increased in the past two decades, the production costs and the number of households dependent upon the catch had more than doubled. The Gahavälla residents were aware that there were too many nets, but neither the common kinship of the *madella* shareholders, the economic constraints on the construction of new nets, nor restrictive legislation, was effective in containing the growth. Fragmentation of ownership had forced some members of the beachseining households into other occupations, but the majority had managed to retain their shares. Sales of shares were becoming more frequent, but as there were few incentives for the accumulation of shares, the sale price was lower than the cost of construction.

A Semi-Subsistence Economy

Man cannot live by fish alone, but this in itself does not justify the common equation of fishing villages with market economies. While the percentage of the catch which reached extra-village markets gradually increased, fisheries production in Gahavälla before 1940 retained a subsistence rather than a market orientation. At the end of the nineteenth century Gahavälla traders were retailing substantial quantities of dried and salted fish in the interior villages, but this was a surplus in the strict sense of the term: fish remaining after Gahavälla's subsistence needs had been met. As the population increased and Gahavälla became more dependent upon the adjacent agricultural villages for its basic foodstuffs of grain and tubers - hence the term semi-subsistence - more of the catch was sold as fresh fish. This, however, did not lead to market-orientated fishing: transport and preservation techniques limited the size of the markets and the prices providing few incentives for the entry of large-scale fish traders or for the accumulation of beachseine shares. It is, perhaps, worth stressing that the absence of capitalism, 'modernization' or 'development' in this period was not due to an absence of achievement orientations or the barriers created by traditional social structures. Gahavälla *mudalali* had established substantial enterprises in other fields in the 1920s; they ignored beachseining because it did not provide opportunities for capital accumulation.

CHAPTER 10

CAPITALISTS AND CAPITALISM

World War II brought new economic opportunities to the people of Gahavälla. Several families established small businesses near the army camps; men who could speak a little English acquired jobs as drivers and clerks in the rapidly expanding government establishments; and the increased demand for coconut products, especially the woven coconut thatch used for temporary constructions, brought wealth to others. The most important economic changes, however, were developments in fish marketing which tied Gahavälla to the national economy at a time when the village was increasingly dependent upon fishing, and small scale agriculture and cottage industries had almost disappeared. By the end of the war production for exchange had replaced production for use, and extra-village agencies were beginning to take control of local production.

In 1938 the production and distribution of Gahavälla fish was essentially the concern of individual households. The beachseines were owned by the men who worked them; catches were divided among the net crew and consumed, dried or retailed by the crew members' households; and only the surplus produced during the flush season could be purchased by fish traders. Five years later Gahavälla fishing practices were determined by the logic of the market: most of the catch was sold as fresh fish to a new group of fish traders; additional nets were being added each year; and wealthy non-fishermen were buying beachseine shares as investments. The process by which peasant owner-operators lost their shares and capitalists accumulated them was firmly established.

Fishing for the Market 1940-1964

The parameters of the Gahavälla beachseine economy changed radically in 1940 when better communications, the availability of ice and increased demand, rapidly lifted the value of the catch. Fish prices more than doubled throughout Sri Lanka during 1940-41, but an equally significant factor in Gahavälla's case was improved access to the national market. In 1939 the road linking Gahavälla to the main Southern Province highway was widened to take motor traffic and in the same year an ice factory was established in Matara. Lack of motor transport prevented Gahavälla fishermen taking immediate advantage of these marketing opportunities, but this was remedied in 1940 with the beginning of the government sponsored Fish Sales Union. Although the activities of the Fish Sales Union in areas near Colombo have been severely criticised (MacDonald 1954), there is no doubting its beneficial effect on more isolated villages such as Gahavälla. The Union provided transport, which could also be hired by private middlemen, and its guaranteed price scheme set an effective floor to the fish market.

Whereas prior to 1940, as much as 30 per cent of the total catch from Gahavälla was being sold to fish driers at a price of less than Rs.3 per hundredweight, and as much again was preserved within the households, by 1944 all of the catch excepting that required for immediate consumption, was sold in fresh form at prices that seldom fell below Rs.15 per hundredweight. Thus the beachseine fishermen saw prices increase more than four-fold in less than four years and instead of having to wait until the dried fish was sold to receive their yearly cash income, were paid immediately. The deep-sea and inshore fishermen also benefited, for they were able to take advantage of the particularly high prices for larger varieties of fish.

A less desirable consequence was an immediate increase in the number of nets; between 1940 and 1945 nets nearly doubled to seventy-one and in 1945 a further six were added (see Table 9.3). There were three main reasons for this spectacular increase. First, the increased prices made *madella* shares a very profitable investment. If a man could scratch a subsistence living from a single share in 1938, by 1940 the same share would have given a very large return. Although the marginal product of additional finance remained at zero, the amount of profit had substantially increased, and thus the return on the investment was very high. The beachseines were converted from a technology used by peasant fishermen for a subsistence living, to a channel for very profitable investments by capitalists. Second, there was much more money available in the fishing community. While the benefits of the increased fish prices were not equally distributed, there were now several people with large amounts of money and few avenues for investment. Third, as the number of nets began to increase, individual shareholders were forced to join in the construction of new nets, for otherwise their equity in the total catch would diminish. At the same time the profits from the shares they already held were sufficiently large to leave a surplus for investment. Thus once the process of net construction began, it took on increasing momentum as each individual attempted to maintain, or if possible increase, his equity in the catch.

The structure of the share system was consequently radically altered. The owner-operator with only a single share was replaced by entrepreneurs with up to twelve shares, many of them worked by wage labour. In 1945, there were six men with ten or more shares, and a further eight men with five or more shares. In other words the ten biggest shareholders owned 14 per cent of the total shares in 1945 as opposed to 6 per cent in 1938. But the true holding of the entrepreneurs was closer to 30 per cent for many registered shares in relatives' names.

As the capitalists began to take control of beachseining, smaller owners found it increasingly difficult to retain their shares. With more nets, the time any individual net spent in the water was shorter and its chance of participating in the high catch period was reduced. This increased risk did not affect the larger owners who could spread their shareholdings throughout the sequence, but for the holder of a single share it meant that when the total number of nets exceeded seventy, he could expect to participate in the flush period in only one year in three. In one of the other two years he would receive only a bare subsistence living and in the third, his returns would not cover the production costs. If he did not have access to further finance, and most did not, it was inevitable that he would lose his share. Consequently net sales became more frequent and as many of these sales were to men who were not descendants of the original owners, the final nails were hammered into the coffin of the 'rights of access' and the kinship basis of the shareholder's group destroyed.

By 1945 the *madella* fishing economy had taken on most of its present features. The shares were a profitable investment, even where the owner had to pay labour to work the net; the number of nets was considerably larger than could be worked in any one day; the system of allocating turns in conjunction with the very short period of high catches, led to a very unequal distribution of the catch among individual nets; and the peasant operator was being forced out by the capitalist entrepreneur.

The changes in net ownership also led to changes in the relationship between share owners and hired men. Prior to 1940 most shares were worked by their owners or by the potential heir of the owner, and while some of the entrepreneurs who introduced new nets between 1940 and 1946 were not themselves fishermen, they normally gave their shares to close relatives among the fishermen to operate. Thus the market economy did not result in immediate changes in labour relationships; most hired men were relatives of the shareowners and many were, or would become, shareowners in their own right. The development of the shareowner-shareworker relationship into a markedly asymmetrical relationship was a gradual response to three factors. First, the one-third share of the hired man amounted to a considerable sum when the net was successful. Second, small owners displaced by the entrepreneurs were forced to seek alternative employment and employment prospects in other fisheries and other industries were increasingly bleak. Third, village level political leaders began to use the beachseines to recruit and maintain a political following.

Between 1946 and 1964 there were several attempts to limit the number of nets. In 1946, the fishermen sent a petition to the Government Agent in Hambantota asking that the regulations promulgated in 1933 to restrict the number of nets, be enforced. The petition argued that there were already too many nets in Gahavälla, that men had to wait too long for their turn, and that the catches were too small to cover their expenses. Earlier petitions in 1940, 1942 and 1945 had been ignored, but the Government Agent accepted this one and agreed that the nets that could be used in Gahavälla in future would be limited to the seventy-seven nets registered in the 1946 season.

On the surface it appears that the impetus for the 1946 petition, as with the earlier ones, came from the smaller owners who had seen their equity being constantly diminished over the past decade. This was certainly the view of the Government Agent, who stressed the point in granting the petition. Reference to the discussion of the petition in the *Patabändi Arrachi's* notebooks (which would have been given to the Government Agent for his perusal) indicates that six nets had been introduced in 1946 which was a very poor season and all owners had realised that it was no longer profitable to build new nets. Examination of the signatures to the petition, however, reveals that the 1946 signatories, although mainly small fishermen, included the three largest shareholders in the village, and one, P.M. Rossiappu (see pp.216 below), has a rather different view of events. He claims that the large shareholders realised that they did not need to add nets to increase their control of the catch, because large numbers of shares were being sold by small owners unable to meet the maintenance costs. These shares could often be bought for less than the cost of constructing a new net, and even when the price was higher, buying these shares was in their long term interests. Thus, according to Rossiappu, the large shareholders made an informal agreement to support the petition. I was unable to corroborate Rossiappu's account but it is certainly plausible. Although it was not enforced completely the 1946 decision did restrain increases in nets: whereas forty had been added in the previous six years, only seven additional nets were constructed in the ensuing eighteen years.

Between 1946 and 1955, there were also several attempts to reduce the nets, either by increasing the number of shares in each net or by introducing a cooperative system along the lines of the Tangalla Fisheries Co-operative.

None of these attempts were successful, mainly because the small shareholders felt that both alternatives would eventually result in the loss of their rights. In the case of the cooperatives this was a realistic view because the Tangalla cooperative, as with most others, eventually became a front for large net owners (MacDonald 1954). The proposal to reduce the number of nets to twenty, but increase the number of shares in each net to twenty-four, also failed. It failed partly because small shareholders felt their shares would be embezzled, partly because agreement could not be reached on procedures for amalgamation, but mainly because by this time the right to work a net had a high value in itself for small net owners, and a crew of twenty-four was regarded as too large to be efficient.

In most of the *padu* in Sri Lanka where beachseining is carried out today, the fishing is controlled by one or two licensees, who own the nets, take all the proceeds of the catch, and pay the crew on a wage basis. If the system used in Gahavälla was once common to all beachseine *padu* in southern Sri Lanka, why is the system found only in Gahavälla today?

The main reason is that before 1940, Gahavälla, unlike the other beachseining centres, did not give opportunities for high profits. In the more profitable *padu* which were linked to the main communications networks, rapid expansion in the number of nets (a post-1939 development in Gahavälla) had occurred much earlier. Because of the lack of any limit on the number of nets the share system had collapsed and the elite had gained control well before 1930. Thus, the licensing system introduced in 1933 merely confirmed the elite's control. But in Gahavälla there was no economic incentive for share accumulation before 1940, for the few men with ready finance could more profitably invest in trading enterprises. By the time the accumulation of shares became profitable, several competing factions were attempting to acquire shares and it was impossible for a small elite to gain control, over the short term at least. In other sites, the number of nets has been held to an optimum level, but only by limiting ownership to a small elite. In Gahavälla the system of widespread individual shareholdings has been partially preserved, but only by increasing the number of nets far beyond the optimum level.[1]

The New Capitalists

In 1946 when the scramble to build additional nets appeared to have finished, six men owned ten or more shares. These six men owned around 15 per cent of the 616 shares at that time, while their close relatives owned a further 10 per cent. One man quickly lost his shares gambling and has no surviving relatives in Gahavälla, but it was possible to compile reasonably complete life histories of the other five: three were the fathers of the modern faction leaders and truncated biographies of the other two are presented below.

The careers of these five men have many points in common, but three facets of their careers set them apart from most fishermen and probably facilitated their accumulation of shares. Perhaps the most important is that while all but one had owned *madella* shares before 1940, fishing was not their main source of income: three were traders and manufacturers of coconut products, one was a dried fish trader, and the other's family had both relatively large landholdings and wealthy affines. Moreover, at least three of their wives had substantial earnings from money-lending and land. These men were already relatively wealthy when the beachseines became highly profitable and their initial share purchases were not financed from fishing income.

In a social sense, also, these men were on the margins of beachseining: none were closely associated with the kingroup that had previously dominated the *madell*. Two were descended from men who had come to Gahavälla following uxorilocal marriages around the turn of the century, and another was a descendant of the landowning *peläntiya*. The remaining two, M.A. Don Charlis and P.M. Rossiappu were sons of the founders, but in recent years had had prolonged and bitter conflicts with other members of their *pelapata*. It is reasonable to suppose that their marginal status, in conjunction with their independent source of income, made them unsusceptible to any informal agreements limiting the number of nets.

The final point is that, with one exception, the men had sons or other close male relatives who could work their shares. Investing in the beachseines therefore did not require them to give their full attention to fishing at the expense of other profitable activities. Other factors were important in particular cases: Rossiappu, like Sunil Mudalali two decades later, wanted to control the nets to ensure a regular supply of fish to sell. But in terms of understanding the social process, the critical point is that the inflation in net numbers was initiated, not by beachseiners, but by an emerging group of capitalists. A brief account of the careers of two of these men indicates both the motives for share accumulation and the methods by which it was accomplished.

Rossiappu

P.M. Rossiappu was born about 1896 and spent ten years at the mission school in Sinimodera where he acquired a reasonable command of English. Rossiappu's father was one of the men who introduced *madell* to Gahavälla and Rossiappu, along with his three elder brothers, was given a beachseine share by his father.

Rossiappu did not enjoy working the *madell* and after he married the daughter of another *madella* fisherman in 1920, used his wife's dowry and some money borrowed from her family, to begin a fish trading business. He purchased fish during the flush season, it was dried or salted by his wife and her sisters, and once a year he travelled by ox-cart to the villages near Ratnapura to sell it. His capital was very small and he could not afford to establish the patron-client links characteristic of the two or three larger fish traders, but consanguines and affines had sufficient shares to ensure a regular supply of fish and, because they were his relatives, he could delay payment until after the dried fish was sold.

At this time his wife was probably the major contributor to their household's income. She ran a tea *kade*, purchased and resold coir made by women in the village, leased jewellery from her dowry for weddings and other ceremonies, and was a small-scale money-lender and *sittuwa* (revolving credit organisation) organiser. Around 1936 Rossiappu's father died and in the property dispute which followed, Rossiappu became estranged from his brothers and parallel cousins.[2] Cut off from his major source of fish in nets owned by his brothers and other consanguineal kin, he purchased ox-carts and other equipment and began bringing coconut husks into the village, having them spun into coir and selling the coir in Matara. He also continued a small fish-trading business based on fish from his affines' nets.

When World War II created a new and highly remunerative market for coconut products, Rossiappu was quick to capitalise on the opportunities, increasing his sales and obtaining an old motor truck. After the ice factory was established in Matara, Rossiappu began backloading small amounts of ice and selling fish to the market *mudalali* in Matara. After the track linking Gahavälla to the main road was improved, other fish traders from Matara and Tangalla began to buy fish in Gahavälla and the prices rose quickly. In 1940 Rossiappu owned only one *madella* share and unable to buy fish caught in his relatives' nets, was quick to appreciate that additional nets would give a double return: not only could he wholesale a larger proportion of the catch, but he would also make large profits on the shares themselves. In 1941 he financed three new nets (24 shares), distributing some shares to his mother's brother and his wife's brothers (to be paid out of the catch), giving three shares to each of his eldest sons, and retaining six for himself to be worked by his younger sons. The finance for these shares came from both his wife's and his own savings and from his early profits as a fish trader - none of it was borrowed. As the shares were in sequential nets he initially had some problems in obtaining sufficient labour from among his kinsmen to work them efficiently, but within a year he had managed to exchange two of them for nets in poorer condition which were better placed in the sequence.

In the four succeeding years Rossiappu financed sixteen shares in three additional nets, in each case in conjunction with his wife's brothers, and by 1945, after a series of sales, purchases and trades, had spread his shareholdings throughout the net sequence. Of the 568 shares extant in 1945, Rossiappu had thirty-four registered in his own, his wife's and sons' names, and including shares owned by his mother's relatives and his affines, controlled fish sales from eighteen nets, by far the greatest number of any fish trader in the village. In 1946 he was forced to sell eighteen shares, mainly to his wife's brothers, to purchase a van, but by 1950 he had twenty-two shares, controlled the sale of fish from about twenty nets, and owned a new van. In addition he claims to have markedly increased his status by taking a leading role in the 1946 petition limiting the number of nets.

From this point his fortunes began to decline. According to his wife the major reason was his heavy drinking and gambling, but while this was probably a contributing factor, a more important reason lay in their attempts to convert their economic success into social status. They purchased an acre of land and began building a large house of brick and mortar. In 1951 marriages were arranged between their two eldest daughters and the sons of wealthy *mudalali* from neighbouring villages. By the standards of the time the dowries were enormous: the eldest daughter received the van and Rs.2,000 in cash as well as the usual complement of jewellery and household equipment, and the second daughter's husband, who settled in Gahavälla, was given six *madella* shares.

A common investment of the Sinhala-speaking capitalists who emerged during the war period was an English education for their children. Most of Rossiappu's children were too old for this, but the youngest son was sent to a prestigious college in Galle. As a result of his English education, he obtained a government post and in 1953, when working as a clerk in a police station was charged with bribery. The charge was dismissed after an appeal to the Supreme Court, but the case cost Rossiappu more than Rs.5,000. This wiped out his savings and he had to sell nine shares to pay lawyers' fees and other expenses.

Concurrently his business enterprises were becoming less profitable. Rossiappu had long since abandoned coconut trading and his wife had also lost some of her earlier energy. Their household's main sources of income were seven shares, registered in Rossiappu's name but operated by his sons, and the fish-trading business operated in partnership with his son-in-law. Rossiappu's contribution to the business was negligible, but competition among fish traders was very keen and the nets which Rossiappu and his relatives controlled provided the bulk of the fish for the partnership. The relationship between Rossiappu and his son-in-law became increasingly strained, because although the son-in-law was doing most of the work and the van had been transferred to him as dowry, Rossiappu demanded half the proceeds. After a very bad fishing season in 1957 or 1958, the son-in-law took the van and began a fish-trading and vegetable business near Tissamaharama.

About the same time relationships between Rossiappu and his sons reached breaking point. Together the family owned seventeen shares and although only seven were registered in his own name, Rossiappu behaved as if he owned all the shares and his sons were merely wage labourers. Although his married sons, two of whom had independent households, did all the work associated with the shares, Rossiappu customarily participated in the distribution meetings and gave an arbitrary portion of the income to his sons. Around 1958, they took full control of the shares registered in their names, and when Rossiappu lost two of his shares at a gambling party, forced him to transfer the remaining shares also.

In 1970 Rossiappu was in many ways a tragic figure. He owned no shares at all, his wife had sold or pawned all her jewellery, and he lived on gifts from his sons and daughters. His large house had never been completed, and he lived in its crumbling ruin, roofed only with thatch. Even the land on which it stood had been sold and he might be thrown out at any time by the owners. In the meantime, his wife and his two youngest daughters who had never married, lost no opportunity to remind him of the suffering he had caused them through his drinking and gambling.

Nicholas Ediriweera

Nicholas Ediriweera, born around 1915, was the youngest son of a family which boasted that they had never been fishermen. His grandfather was one of the earliest settlers in Moraketiara, and his father, who was Village Headman for Gahavälla, Moraketiara and Sinimodera between

1903 and 1918, owned extensive areas of land in all three villages. Nicholas' three elder brothers all entered government service and until 1950, or thereabouts, their descendants owned considerable areas of land in Sinimodera and Moraketiara.

In 1934 Nicholas married W.G. Laisyhamy, the daughter of a wealthy *madella* fisherman and trader, and the cousin of W.G. Sammiappu.[3] The Ediriweeras were strongly opposed to this marriage: Nicholas was only twenty, the W.G. *pelapata* had a reputation as criminals, and the high status of the Ediriweeras would ensure a large dowry if a marriage was eventually arranged. Nicholas went ahead with the marriage despite his family's objections, and his father, who died soon after, publicly stated that he no longer recognised Nicholas as his son and he would have no rights to inherit.

Nicholas was given two *madella* shares as a dowry and when fish prices increased in 1940, pawned his wife's jewellery to finance two further shares in a net being constructed by his father-in-law. Between 1940 and 1944 he obtained six additional shares: two from the profits of a very good catch by one of his nets in 1943; two with a loan from his father-in-law; and two with money borrowed from Rossiappu in return for a promise to sell him the fish. When his father-in-law died in 1952, Nicholas gained control of two more shares which his wife inherited, giving him twelve in all. Unlike Rossiappu, Nicholas was not a leader in the share speculation between 1940 and 1946: in acquiring shares he was merely following a lead set by his affines.

Soon after his father died without making a will, Nicholas forced a partition case over his father's landholdings in Gahavälla. In the 1956 judgement, Nicholas was assigned the rights to one-twentysecond of the land, less than a quarter acre, and the produce from seventeen coconut trees. When he attempted to collect the produce, however, he was abused and assaulted by his brother who occupied the compound. In retaliation, Nicholas, his wife's cousin Sammiappu, and other affines, invaded the house one evening, smashing most of the contents and badly injuring the brother and his wife. Charges of assault, attempted murder and unlawful assembly were laid and

Sammiappu, who had a previous conviction, was jailed for 18 months.

Nicholas was forced to mortgage six shares to J.A. Podisingho (Sunil Mudalali's father who was the largest shareholder of the time), to raise money for Sammiappu's trial. The mortgage was under an early system whereby Nicholas retained the shares and all the proceeds but had to repay both interest and capital within a year (see below pp.228). After nothing had been paid for three years, Podisingho demanded that the shares be transferred. Nicholas refused, but late in 1959 repaid the capital plus one year's interest.

By 1960 Nicholas lead a powerful faction based on a core of his wife's brothers, and was regarded as the leader of the beachseiners in their attempts to prevent Sunil Mudalali establishing a monopsony in beachseine marketing. A big man by any standards, over six feet tall and weighing about 200 pounds, and a very skilled bargainer, Nicholas was able to force up the prices in auctions on the beach and had sufficient henchmen to prevent the fish traders later cutting the price. When the previous incumbent died, Nicholas took over control of the *pora pol* ceremony, and with the 'profits' from the ceremony and a big gambling win, purchased a further four shares, giving sixteen in all.

Already on poor terms with the Jayaweera's because of the mortgage, Nicholas's activities on the beach brought him into open conflict with Sunil's faction. He was charged in several cases of assault and arson, as well as an attempt to kill J.A. Podisingho, but was acquitted and, because he lived very frugally, was able to meet all the expenses without disposing of his shares. Although estranged from his own family, he had powerful allies among his wife's kinsmen.

The denouement was late one evening in 1961. A net in which Nicholas and two of his faction owned a share each, had spotted a shoal of mackerel tuna entering the bay and despite the heavy sea launched their *orua* and made an unexpected, exceptionally large, catch. It was already late and as the heavy surf made it difficult to haul the net, it was dark when the cod-end was finally hauled into the shallows. Word spread rapidly through the village and a big crowd gathered, including Nicholas who, although he seldom worked his shares, usually acted as spokesman for the net crew in the auction. Sunil Mudalali pointed out that while it was too late for the net crew to sell the catch in Tangalla, he had transport and ice and would pay a good price for the fish which he would sell in Colombo. Nicholas, who was very drunk, refused, saying he would rather see the fish rot on the beach. The five shareholders who were not members of Nicholas's faction protested that this was the best catch they had had for many months and they needed the money. Nicholas refused to let Sunil take the fish, and when it became clear that no other potential buyers were present, staggered into the water and attempted to untie the lacing rope which would allow the fish to escape. As he bent over, someone, probably Sunil, stabbed him several times in the back and when he fell, several of the net crew pounded him with oars. The crowd then fled and Nicholas and the fish were left rolling in the surf. Sunil was acquitted on a murder charge, apparently on the grounds that Nicholas had drowned.[4] The shares which Nicholas had owned were inherited by his wife, Laisyhamy, but as was pointed out in Chapter 7, she is finding it difficult to control them.

Twenty-Five New Nets

The Government Agent's decision to accept the fishermen's petition of 1946 and prevent the construction of additional nets, certainly slowed the pace of net expansion but did not halt it completely. Between 1946 and 1964 seven new nets were added. This suggests that factors other than legal sanctions inhibited net construction after the rapid increase of 1940-46. The data on the sale of shares (see below) in conjunction with Rossiappu's testimony, supports the view that the entrenched capitalists had realised that their interests would be better served by accumulating existing shares rather than adding nets. By 1946 these men already owned about a third of the shares and further nets would water down their equity. At this stage they may well have felt that they would slowly, but inevitably, take control of beachseining in Gahavälla.

In the two years after 1964, however, there was another spate of net construction when twenty-five nets were added. The catalyst was the entry of a new entrepreneur into beachseining: David Mahattea. Early in 1962, David Mahattea, faced with increasing competition and decreasing profits in his vegetable wholesaling business, had sold his lorry and purchased two vans with the intention of entering the Gahavälla small-fish trade. Since the death of Nicholas Ediriweera the year before, Sunil Mudalali was firmly in control and David found it very difficult to buy fish in competition with him. Sunil's supporters owned shares in twenty-seven of the eighty-three nets and on the few occasions David succeeded in buying fish from these nets had had to pay high prices in cash. Although members of the M.A. *pelapata* owned shares in thirty nets, David was estranged from his kinsmen and received no advantages from their shareholdings.

Initially David attempted to buy shares, but competition both from Sunil's faction and other potential buyers forced up the price. In six months David bought only two shares at the very high price of Rs.500 each. At this time David was a close friend of another rising faction leader, Danny Wijenaike. The Wijenaikes had held large numbers of shares in the 1945-55 period, but seven sons drawing a living from the beachseines had gradually diminished their holdings. The year before Danny and his brother-in-law T.M. Peter had brought the first 'bible' nets to Gahavälla and now that 'bible' fishing was prohibited within the bay, they had nearly Rs.30,000 to invest in *madella* fishing.

In 1963 David approached the local MP, a Sri Lanka Freedom Party representative, and suggested that permission be given to construct additional nets. Posing as a representative of poor fishermen, he emphasised that many Gahavälla fishermen were without nets and had no opportunity to earn a living. The MP asked the District Revenue Officer to consider the proposal, but the DRO and the *Patabändi Arrachi*, who appear to have been acting dispassionately, reported that there were already far too many nets and suggested a cooperative as an alternative. Not surprisingly this suggestion was rejected by all the fishermen.

The Village Headman, a brother-in-law of Danny Wijenaike, pointed a way out of the impasse. He discovered that although the 1933 regulations limited the number of nets, they did not, as everyone had previously believed, prevent the construction of new nets. If too many nets were registered, there was provision for a ballot to decide which nets would be used, and nets eliminated in the ballot would receive first preference in the following year.

When the *Patabändi Arrachi* registered the nets at the end of 1964, members of David's faction presented four new nets and demanded that they be registered. The *Patabändi Arrachi* refused, claiming that the nets had been borrowed from fishermen at Devinuwara. A scuffle broke out and eventually the DRO and a party of police arrived to arbitrate. A spokesman for David's group said that the nets had been purchased from Devinuwara fishermen, that none of the shareholders in the new nets had more than three shares in existing nets and that thirteen had no other shares at all. It was unreasonable, he claimed, that a small group should be allowed to control fishing at Gahavälla and justice demanded that the new nets be registered. The DRO once again suggested a cooperative but when this proposal was rejected, directed the *Patabändi Arrachi* to register the new nets. David then returned the nets to their Devinuwara owners, from whom he had borrowed them, and four replacements were built. The ballot provision was ignored because agreement could not be reached on the appropriate number of nets: the thirty-two nets in use in 1933 when the regulations were promulgated, or the eighty-three nets of 1964.

In the 1965 national elections, the United National Party candidate won the local electorate with the aid of a large vote from Gahavälla. Danny Wijenaike who organised the UNP campaign in Gahavälla claims that in return for votes, the MP agreed that additional nets would be registered in 1965 and that the regulations would then be changed to bar any further nets. Although the friendship between Danny and David had broken under the stress of a hard-fought election campaign and they did not cooperate, associates of these two men controlled most of the shares in the twenty-one additional nets registered in 1965. Danny and his kinsmen financed shares on their own behalf, and David, whose primary aim was to obtain fish for sale, lent his supporters money to build nets. One reason for their success was that Sunil's faction who would have provided the major opposition, were otherwise occupied: four of the J.A. brothers spent most of 1965 on remand for a series of assaults.

The four nets first registered in 1964 were not used in that year. By that time they were completed, the flush season had finished and David and Danny agreed to postpone their use until further nets were registered in 1965. The new nets had been allocated numbers at the end of the net sequence and when the first turn of net 84 arrived in 1965 further problems emerged. As was mentioned above, David had preferred to finance net construction by others rather than register shares in his own name. Most of the shares in net 84 were owned by W.G. Sammiappu, his sons and sons-in-law. David had lent much of the money in the hope of gaining Sammiappu's permission to marry his daughter, but Sammiappu refused because of David's sexual relationship with another younger daughter. Despite Sammiappu's opposition David had recently married the eldest daughter and set up house with both sisters.

Sammiappu and some of his relatives owned net 1, in addition to net 84 and late one afternoon after net 83 had been used, they suddenly launched net 1, thus squeezing net 84 and the other twenty-four new nets out of the cycle. Sammiappu's action had wide support, both from Sunil's faction and from the unaligned small shareholders whose incomes would diminish by a third if the additional nets were used. As fishing was poor at the time the owners of the new nets did not protest very vigorously, but when the stratagem was repeated in the next cycle, Danny and David made it clear that they would resist future attempts.

When the first of the 1966 net cycles reached net 83, Sammiappu again launched net 1. This time Danny and his supporters launched net 85 in opposition and following a brawl at sea, the *orua* carrying net 1 overturned. Members of all three factions had gathered on the beach, and only the arrival of three jeep-loads of armed police, whom David had warned in advance, prevented a riot. The police remained in the village for the next three weeks ensuring that the new nets were used at the appropriate times.

Regulations freezing the number of nets at 108 were promulgated in 1966 and there have been no further disputes. David's fish trading prospered during 1966 and it appeared that he would establish a monopsony in Gahavälla, but after Sunil Mudalali returned from jail he fostered the increasing enmity between Danny and David. Eventually a number of Danny's nets were burned (probably by Sunil's faction) and believing that David was responsible, Danny instigated an attempt to destroy one of David's vans. The van was set on fire and in attempting to rescue her son who was driving it, David's mother-in-law (Sammiappu's wife) was killed. Frightened for his own life, and given the opportunity of a partnership with his sister's husband in ventures outside Gahavälla, David left Sunil in control.

The Share Market

One effect of the higher fish prices after 1940 was an expansion in the nets; another was the creation of a share market. Before 1940 there were few incentives for capitalists to accumulate beachseine shares: the nets were barely profitable when worked by wage labour and there were better avenues for investment. Men did occasionally sell shares, but the major consideration in arriving at the price was the condition of the net in which the share was held. After 1940, however, beachseining became a highly valued means of capital accumulation. Even when worked by wage labour, a beachseine share would give high profits and sale prices began to be calculated in terms of the size of the potential profit rather than the construction costs. At a later stage, an added motive for share accumulation was the belief that the share system was near to collapse and that when this occurred the largest shareholders would be able to take complete control, as had happened in neighbouring villages.

The data on share transactions presented in Table 10.1 are derived from a question in a property survey[5] and are subject to two major sources of error. As the property survey covered only 159 households, all of them in Gahavälla, it included a little less than two-thirds of the 1971 shareholders' households (although these households owned 71 per cent of the shares). The other point is that while most respondents gave accurate accounts of how many shares they held, some would not say how much they had paid and several claimed to have inherited shares which had been bought or obtained through a mortgage agreement.[6] Nevertheless, it is probable that Table 10.1 fairly represents the volume of sales and prices with the exception of the post-1964 period. For thirty-two shares the prices listed by the buyer could be cross-checked with the seller's accounts and showed close agreement.

TABLE 10.1. AVERAGE SELLING PRICE AND VOLUME OF SALES, 1921-70

Period	No. of Sales	Average Price	Range
Pre-1935	22	Rs. 56	Rs. 40-100
1935-1939	32	74	30-150
1940-1944	17	152	60-200
1945-1949	48	242	100-350
1950-1954	43	231	150-400
1955-1959	38	269	20-325
1960-1964	28	302	90-500
1965+	41	191	50-350

The table indicates that while all shares are approximately equal in value[7] the prices fluctuate considerably even within a five-year period. There are three main reasons for these fluctuations. First, when the property of a deceased shareholder is divided the son who had been working the share normally buys out his co-heirs. In such cases, especially if the joint owner is a married woman living outside the village, the payment is very low. Secondly, a man forced to sell his shares in an emergency has to accept a low price, especially if the sale takes place during a period of poor fishing. The third reason is that many of the 'sales' are more accurately described as foreclosed mortgages. When a share is mortgaged the mortgager receives less than half the market value of the share, interest is fixed at an annual interest rate of 40 to 60 per cent, and the share is registered in the name of the mortgagee. There is a verbal agreement that if the loan plus interest is repaid at the end of the year, the share will be transferred to the original owner. There are two possible arrangements for the working of the share during the period of the mortgage. Normally the mortgagee has full rights to the owner's portion of the catch, but the mortgager works the share and takes the hired man's portion. A second arrangement, which was common but is now rare, is for the mortgager to retain full rights during the period of mortgage, including all proceeds.

Modern mortgages give considerable advantages to the mortgagee. If the net has a poor season the mortgagee acquires a share at less than half its market value. If fishing is good he receives the sum lent, plus interest at 60 per cent, plus the owner's share (two-thirds) of the annual proceeds: an effective interest rate of 500 to 600 per cent. Consequently, few men who mortgage nets are able to redeem them. Even if the mortgagee is willing to extend the mortgage for a further year, after three or four years the interest exceeds the value of the share. I recorded details of fourteen mortgages within the past six years (undoubtedly only a small percentage of the total), and in each case the net changed hands at below the market price. Although cases of successful redemption of mortgages were reported for earlier periods, no informant was able to give an example within the past two decades.

It would appear that the change in mortgage procedures is a consequence of the penetration of capitalist relations of production into beachseining. In the past, the mortgagee was intent in recovering the loan, the share was of no value to him and was important only as a sanction. Nowadays, however, the mortgagee's hope is that the loan will not be repaid and he can acquire a share at low cost.

One further point which affects the data in Table 10.1 is the effect of inflation. The current price of a fully equipped *madella* and *orua* is Rs.3,875. Remembering that only two-thirds of the nets have *oru*, this gives an approximate construction cost of Rs.425 for each of the eight shares. Informants agree that there has been a marked increase in the price of coir, cotton and especially *oru*[8] over the past six years, and estimates of the value of a fully equipped net in 1965 ranged from Rs.2,000 to Rs.2,400: Rs.250 to Rs.275 per share.[9]

The costs of the nets at other points in the past are considerably more difficult to ascertain. Neither the 1950 fishing census (Director of Fisheries 1940-50), nor the 1941 Commission of Enquiry (Sammarakkody 1941) mentions the cost of fishing equipment. According to the 1922 Inquiry into the Fishing Industry (Anon 1922) a *madella* 'made of coir twine and yarn' cost Rs.500 and a new *oru* Rs.600 to Rs.700, placing the cost of a fully equipped *madella* with a second-hand craft at about Rs.800.

When these factors are taken into account, the volume of sales and the ratio between the sale price and construction costs over the past half century are consistent with the history of the share market outlined above. During the two decades when the market did not determine production practices, share sales were infrequent, were mainly between relatives, and were at prices considerably below the construction costs. The 1933 legislation which theoretically limited the number of nets, did not affect share prices. The average sale price in 1938 had changed little from twenty years earlier, and was about 50 per cent of construction costs.

The transition to a market economy in 1940 had an immediate effect on the share market. Although the volume of sales decreased, prices rose sharply, and by 1946 the average price was equivalent to the construction costs. Sales dropped because higher fish prices enabled even poor men to retain their shares. Prices rose because buyers were willing to pay a premium for shares in established nets.[10]

For the fifteen years after nets were limited in 1946 the volume of sales and prices continued to increase, until in 1962, just before new nets were added, two sales reached Rs.500, nearly twice the cost of construction. The two types of sales discussed above, are clearly apparent in the records of this period. Sales between relatives or (as was becoming increasingly important) sales by poor men unable to meet maintenance costs, were at very low prices, often less than half the construction cost. Simultaneously, wealthy men, traders and the remnants of the landowners, who had bought shares between 1940 and 1946, were selling them preparatory to leaving the village. These men received the high prices.

A further change is evident after additional nets were added between 1964 and 1966. Prices recorded since then have been lower than construction costs, in most cases at least 25 per cent lower. Share transactions since 1964 are analysed below, but two points should be mentioned: most sales are 'forced' and there is little competition among buyers.

An analysis of share volume and prices supports the account of the evolution of the share system, presented earlier. Until 1940, share prices were determined by the value of the fishing implement they represented, but once net limits were enforced, shares became of value in themselves over and above the costs of the cotton, coir and wood. Changes in market practices facilitated the entry of capitalist shareholders and this in turn, altered labour relationships in the industry and produced a class of wage workers. For a short period between 1940 and 1960, there was considerable competition to acquire shares and men who could wait for the best price made large capital gains. But after 1960, growing factional competition restricted the range of potential buyers and prices fell. Simultaneously small shareholders were forced to relinquish their shares and the volume of sales increased.

Economic Success and Social Mobility

The most important social development in the post-war period was the emergence of substantial numbers of Sinhala-speaking rural capitalists: the *mudalali*. Although businesses - trading dried fish, manufacturing coir rope, operating village stores - had been common in earlier periods, most were very small and gave similar incomes to fishing or agriculture. The successful, larger, *mudalali,* such as A.G. Garuhamy and A.H. Matteshamy in Gahavälla, quickly acquired land and attempted to merge themselves with local *pelantiya.* The business enterprises established after the war, however, covered a far greater range of products. The scale of the ventures and the wealth of the properties were much larger than before, and the number of households involved more than trebled.

The initial impetus for capitalist development in the coastal regions came from the trade in fresh fish. The families which had earlier combined petty trading with fishing were quick to appreciate the opportunities which the entrance of the local fishing communities to the national market created. As the demand (and the raw materials) for coconut products diminished, finance and skills were transferred to the marketing of fresh fish. Using kin connections to maintain a basic flow of fish in their home villages, *mudalali* competed fiercely for the catch in other villages. Later they sought to increase the supply of fish by financing 'bible' nets and importing mechanised boats from other areas. When the mechanised craft began to produce large catches of high value fish, the more successful *malu mudalali* abandoned the traditional craft and established 'tied-boat' arrangements with the mechanised craft.

A second generation of *mudalali* who became prominent after 1955, moved out of fish trading into other activities. Between 1955 and 1960, Gahavälla men with finance inherited or borrowed from close kin, established a cinema and bar at Beliatta, two paddy mills near Tissamaharama, vegetable and dry goods wholesaling along the Southern Province-East Coast roads, several gambling and liquor joints and three bus routes using converted vans. Other *Karāva* men (though none from Gahavälla), lacking the business contacts to compete with the Indians and Muslims who controlled retailing of general goods in the small towns, established 'hotels'[11] providing food for travellers. Men from coastal villages were not usually allocated land in colonisation schemes (Farmer 1957), but two Gahavälla men began small retail shops and later purchased land.

In recent years the activities of rural capitalists have been challenged by government policies promoting State Trading enterprises. State Trading Corporations have been established in the sectors of transport, paddy milling and marketing, the retailing of imported staple goods, and fish marketing. Although the corporations have been unsuccessful in eliminating the middlemen,[12] the *mudalali* feel that their businesses will eventually be taken over. Most businesses which are unaffected by the State Trading Corporations are illegal (alcohol and gambling), dependent upon government licences, or have been eliminated by local economic development (wholesaling vegetables on the East Coast).

For at least fifty years the people of the coastal villages have been eager to begin new ventures. Within a short time of opportunities arising through higher prices, better communications or new technology, Gahavälla men have taken up new occupations, adopted new technologies and established new forms of economic organisation. *Karāva*, and to a lesser extent *Durāva*, have a reputation as clever traders and in many of the interior villages a single household from these castes runs the village shop and buys paddy and other produce. The notion of the overly conservative peasant, refusing to take risks in the hope of future gains, is clearly inapplicable.

There are several reasons why men from the coast have sought new opportunities, even where these entailed difficult living conditions in distant areas. Population increases have had a critical effect at several points. Gahavälla's history might well be described as a cyclical process: population growth outstrips existing resources, this forces the development of new resources, and population growth continues. The rapid increase in *chena* cultivators between 1890 and 1915 was an important factor in enabling a few men to acquire much of the land and the consequent change from *chena* to tree crops. Twenty years later, natural increases among the families dependent upon tree crop agriculture forced the subdivision of land below economic levels and the emigration of many landlord families. Likewise, the beachseine families initially encouraged uxorilocal marriage as a source of additional labour, but by 1940 the number of households depending on beachseining had increased to such an extent, that the catch would soon have been insufficient for even a subsistence living. This was averted by the rapid increase in fish prices, but today the number of households dependent upon the beachseines is once again nearing saturation point.

For most of Gahavälla's history there have been few barriers against social mobility. The caste system, though lacking the social significance of Indian caste hierarchies, did impose some limits on economic opportunities: it is difficult to imagine a *Karāva* purchasing land in a village dominated by another caste, even if the expected profits were very large. But most new business ventures were essayed, either in occupations for which ascribed castes did not exist, such as trading, or in newly settled regions which lacked established local caste rankings. In a sense caste aided the economic development of the coastal villages, for it encouraged successful capitalists to marry and establish their homes on the coast, rather than at their place of business. Even today, the money remitted by *mudalali* to their wives and children, or spent during their own infrequent visits home, is an important addition to the village economy.

Nor was caste a significant barrier against the conversion of economic gains into social mobility. Most of the coastal businessmen's non-economic relationships were with other *Karāva*. The *Karāva* lack the ranked subsections which are found among the *Goigama* caste and in most villages the elite was itself of relatively modern origins.[13] As the political and social position of the elite was predicated upon its wealth, there was little to prevent its replacement by an economically more successful segment of the population.

While the social context of the *Karāva* villager during the colonial period appeared to aid, rather than hinder, social mobility through economic success, political and economic changes since Independence have made it difficult for *mudalali* to attain the social status and political power which they see as a prerogative of their wealth. Traditionally, social mobility in rural Sri Lanka was achieved by purchasing large areas of land, acquiring local colonial posts, adopting honorific surnames and a life-style based on feudal ideology, and establishing marriage alliances with similarly placed groups in neighbouring villages. In other words the creation of a *peläntiya*. A dominant class whose economic base is tree crop agriculture or tenant-farmed paddy, however, is especially vulnerable when land is restricted and the population is increasing. Once population growth forced excessive subdivision of landholdings, the landlords had only two ways of maintaining their position: they could buy land in newly settled regions and recreate a *peläntiya*, or they could take advantage of their English education to enter government service, medicine or law. Most landlords in the Tangalla region chose the latter alternative. Today the electoral-level organisations of both major political parties are controlled by descendants of the landlords, and although these men seldom directly intervene in village affairs, their influence through their professional skills and alliances with village-level leaders, is considerable.

The most successful of the pre-war *mudalali* attempted to follow the same avenue of social mobility as the landlords who preceded them. But because it was difficult to accumulate land, posts such as Village Headman were declining in importance and the population was rapidly increasing, *peläntiya* formation was impossible. A few *mudalali's* children did obtain low level government posts, but the success of the fathers was seldom consolidated by the sons.

The 1950s when the second generation of Sinhalese-speaking entrepreneurs was beginning to dominate the rural economy was a period of rapid social change and the general tenor of economic thought, especially in urban and government circles, was opposed to the activities of rural capitalists. It is probably true that the 'socialist' ideology espoused by both major political parties since 1956 is more Sinhalese-nationalist than socialist, nevertheless it has given birth to an ever-increasing volume of propaganda in which the *mudalali* is the prime villain. Nor have the attacks on the *mudalali's* economic position been limited to propaganda, most legislation concerned with the rural economy has been intended to eliminate rural capitalism.

Post-Independence changes in education providing for free education,[14] greater representation of rural children in higher educational levels, and for university lectures in Sinhalese and Tamil as well as English, seemed to provide opportunities for social mobility through employment in the civil service. The children of rural capitalists took advantage of these opportunities and comprised most of the rural youth who entered the universities after 1960. The growth of government employment during the 1960s did not keep pace with the increases in the numbers of educated youth, however, and few rural youth, educated in Sinhalese and holding an arts degree, acquired the jobs they desired. By 1970 the unemployment rate among males under twenty-five who had completed high school was estimated at 65 per cent (I.L.O. 1972). Children of *mudalali* formed the bulk of these unemployed and also of the participants in the 1971 'April Insurrection' which was the outcome (cf. Obeyesekere 1974).

CHAPTER 11

THE DEMISE OF THE PEASANTS

As the major theme in this account of Gahavälla beach-seining has been the emergence of capitalist relations of production, the analysis inevitably concentrates on the social origins of the rural capitalists and the strategies which they are using to acquire control of the means of production. This final chapter switches the emphasis from the capitalists to the peasants: it ascertains the extent to which peasant owner-operators have been displaced, examines the economic prospects of the survivors and describes the defensive strategies by which they are endeavouring to retain the shares they hold. The period under discussion is the seven years since 1964, when the last expansion of nets occurred.

Factions and the Share Market

The effects of faction competition on beachseining have been mentioned several times, but as faction control of nets is the major constraint on the market in beachseine shares, there is some value in a more systematic discussion of the economic consequences of faction ownership.

The economic advantage of faction-controlled nets can be broadly grouped under two headings: marketing and operations. The marketing advantages were discussed in Chapter 8. In brief, nets controlled by a faction (other than Sunil Mudalali's faction) receive higher bids from the fish traders, seldom suffer from price cutting and obtain the money due to them more rapidly. The major operational advantage of faction-controlled nets is the ability to switch gear from one net to another. Only forty-three of the ninety-nine nets actually in use in 1971 have their own net-laying craft. Whereas all but four of the non-faction nets have their own *orua*, about half the faction-controlled nets do not. Five of the nets added in 1965, for example, use a single *orua* and another *orua* is used by four nets. Using a single *orua* for more than one net gives a considerable saving in both construction and operational costs. *Maduwa* are also occasionally switched between nets, although every net presents a *maduwa* (no matter how decrepit) at registration. Knowing that gear can be switched between nets enables faction-controlled nets to take greater risks during hauling, for damage will not rob them of the remainder of their turns during the cycle. In 1971 Danny Wijenaike attempted to substitute another net for one damaged by arson, thus effectively using one net twice during a single cycle. But the small shareholders, appreciating that if Danny was successful, other factions would follow suit, and their equity would be further diminished, persuaded the District Revenue Officer to stop the practice.

In view of the economic advantages obtained by the faction controlled nets, it would seem sensible for the shareholders in each net to associate themselves with one faction or another. The reasons some do not, are in part related to the broader question of why some men avoid joining factions, and in part, a recognition that non-faction members owning shares in a faction-controlled net are in an economically vulnerable position.

It was noted earlier that a considerable number of men in Gahavälla find faction politics distasteful. Violence, which is an invariable concomitant to faction competition, is abhorrent to most of the population, including many faction members, and men must therefore have a very strong incentive to join a faction. Many men outside the factions have little to gain from faction membership: they have other sources of credit, are not involved in litigation, and have other channels of communication with the political and administrative organisations in the towns. Conversely, many of these men have little to offer the faction leaders and would always remain on the periphery. For most men the benefits of a follower - occasional gifts or small loans and intervention with extra-village authority - do not outweigh the disadvantages: the loss of control over their own affairs, the adoption of a subservient position in relationships with the faction leader, and the ever-present possibility of retaliatory violence from members of other factions.

Further some men who might otherwise join a faction are equally opposed to all three faction leaders because of past disputes. This is particularly true of the descendants of the three *pelapata* who originally controlled *madell* fishing, for although they own more than 200 shares, few are associated with a faction. These men see the factions as a destructive intrusion in Gahavälla affairs which was directly responsible for the excessive number of nets. While Nicholas Ediriweera was alive it seemed that some members of this group might form a fourth faction, and for a brief time W.A. Dawith and W.A. Peter united seven of the eight households in the W.A. *pelapata*. But today the only faction members drawn from the founding *pelapata* are four households of the twenty-one in the M.A. *pelapata* who are associated with David Mahattea.

A non-aligned shareholder in a faction-controlled net suffers several disadvantages. For a start it is difficult to avoid becoming associated with the faction in the eyes of the other villagers. Not only must a non-aligned shareholder work with faction members, but he must also spend a considerable time in their company: repairing the net, 'on call', drinking tea and gambling. There are, moreover, immediate economic disadvantages. In the first place the owner loses control of the way the net is used and the catch sold. In contrast to other nets where decisions are reached by consensus, decisions in the faction-controlled nets are made by the faction leader or his nominee. Not only does this damage the shareholder's self-esteem - a not inconsiderable point in a community of fiercely independent fishermen - it also leads to considerable monetary losses. In nets controlled by Sunil's faction the catch is sold at lower prices, while in other nets faction members who are not shareholders are often allowed to participate in the hauling and take considerable amount of fish for their 'services'. Burning nets is a common form of inter-faction aggression (thirteen have been burnt in the past five years) and in such cases non-faction members suffer with the rest.

While these are significant disadvantages, the main reason for avoiding shares in faction-controlled nets is the ever-present possibility of having to sell the shares at a low price. A man wishing to sell a share in a faction-controlled net has only one buyer, the faction leader, and because of this lack of competition the sale price of these shares is very low. The average share price over the past seven years was less than half the construction cost and the prices for the sales in faction-owned nets were much lower.

There are several methods by which non-faction members are forced to sell their shares. Faction members can make it very difficult for outsiders to operate their shares efficiently: denying information as to when the net will be used or repairs carried out; raising objections to any substitute the share owner attempts to employ; purchasing meals and arrack with the proceeds of the catch at a tea *kade* associated with the faction so that non-faction members won't participate. The cash flow can also be manipulated. Shareholders in an unsuccessful net often postpone repairs and expenses to the next cycle; a faction leader's insistence that expenses are deducted from the proceeds and that repairs be met immediately, forces small shareholders to seek high cost credit. In yet other cases the intimidation is more direct, the shareholder is abused, threatened and assaulted until he is frightened enough to sell the share for whatever it will fetch.

Two instructive examples of the ways in which men are forced out of the net group were the aftermath of arson. In the first case, three nets in which the majority of the shares were owned by Sunil Mudalali's faction were burned. The following year he announced that it was time for the nets to be replaced. Three non-faction members, each with a single share, protested that they could not afford the construction costs, whereupon Sunil Mudalali bought their shares for Rs.25 each. The second case was more blatant. David Mahattea and his supporters owned four shares in a net that was burned and when the other shareholders could not afford replacement costs, David and his followers simply took over the entire net. The ex-shareholders sent a petition of protest to the District Revenue Officer but David's political contacts ensured that it was ignored. At the end of the fieldwork Danny Wijenaike was making similar preparations for four of his nets which had been burned, but was unable to raise sufficient finance.

These situations presuppose that a particular faction controls most of the shares in a particular net. The goal of share purchasing, from the point of view of a faction, is to attain complete control of a net, but the number of shares required differs in each case. If the other shareholders are submissive men without a strong group of close kin, then as few as three shares may give effective control to a faction leader. The discussion of marketing in Chapter 8, for example, indicated that the presence of a single shareholder from his faction gave Sunil Mudalali a vital edge in his competition with both the net crew and the competing fish buyer. In less public contexts, or when the other shareholders are more assertive, even four or five shares need not assure the faction leader of control.

While it is not possible to say how many shares give control of a net, it is evident that owning more than four shares puts a faction in a strong position. The distribution of faction shareholdings is tabulated in Table 11.1. The data includes the shareholdings of faction followers as well as the faction core, but it should be regarded as indicating minimum holdings for individuals were regarded as faction followers only if all three of my informants on this topic agreed.

The attempts by faction to attain complete control of particular nets are immediately apparent. Overall, faction members own about half the shares and these are strongly clustered in particular nets. Twenty-two nets, all but three added in 1964-65, are entirely owned by a particular faction, and individual factions have majority shareholdings in a further twenty. Differences in the extent to which the faction leaders are economically dependent upon beachseining are obvious from the distribution of their holdings. The shares owned by David, who is interested mainly in maintaining his following and reaping the benefits of the occasional good catch, are distributed widely: in eleven nets his followers own only a single share. Danny, on the other hand, is

TABLE 11.1. DISTRIBUTION OF FACTION HOLDINGS AMONG NETS

No. of Shares		No. of Nets	
	David	Sunil	Danny
1	11	2	1
2	4	6	1
3	9	9	2
4	6	7	4
5	-	4	-
6	3	1	-
7	1	4	7
8	9	6	7
Total:	43	49	22

heavily involved in the day-to-day operation of the beachseines and most of his faction's holding is clustered in a few nets. If one of my informants had not insisted that Danny's brother-in-law, T.M. Peter, was not a member of Danny's faction, 80 per cent of the faction's shares would have been clustered in the fourteen nets which they own entirely.

Thirty-one nets, mainly owned by descendants of the founding families, have no faction owned shares. The remaining twenty-six nets, in which shares are owned by more than one faction, are the focus of intense competition with each faction attempting to gain a controlling majority. Non-aligned shareholders, fearful of the outcome of the competition, try to sell their shares and buy new shares in neutral nets, but few are successful: there were only eleven sales of this type between 1964 and 1971 and in each case the price was high.

Increasing Inequality

In 1964 there were eighty-three beachseines and by 1971 they had increased to 108. The distribution of shareholdings in these years is tabulated in Table 11.2.

TABLE 11.2. DISTRIBUTION OF SHARES 1964 AND 1971

Number of Shares	Number of Shareholders			
	1964 N=664		1971 N=864	
	No.	%	No.	%
1	30	16	26	16
2	35	19	15	9
3	41	23	31	19
4	29	16	15	9
5	13	7	8	5
6	12	7	12	8
7	9	5	12	8
8	4	2	7	4
9	3	2	10	6
10	3	2	11	7
11	1	-	2	1
12	1	-	2	1
13	1	-	4	3
14			2	1
15			-	-
16			-	-
17			1	-
18			1	-
	182		159	

One crucial point is immediately apparent, the shares are being accumulated by an elite. Although the number of shares grew by nearly a third during the period, the number of shareholders decreased by 13 per cent: from 182 in 1964 to 159 in 1971. In only seven years, at least twenty-three men were dispossessed of the means of production in a community which offers very little alternative employment. The drop in the number of shareholders lifted the size of the average holding. In 1971 the average shareholder held 4.9 shares (equivalent to 3.8 shares in the 1964 nets) as opposed to 3.6 shares in 1964.

While there is obviously increasing inequality, in the sense that the means of production are concentrated in fewer hands, at first glance there appears to be little difference in the distribution of shares among the surviving owners. The skewed distribution in favour of a small elite is readily apparent in both years, but it is not obvious that the skewing had increased during the period: in 1964 as in 1971, the bottom 25 per cent of shareholders held about 7 per cent of the shares.

The Lorenz curve of Figure 11.1 gives a rather different view of the changes. In 1935 the curve was almost straight because the vast majority of shareholders owned only a single share. The pronounced inequality in the 1964 curve reflects the situation discussed in Chapter 10: capitalists introducing additional nets and therefore diminishing the equity of the small shareholders. Increasing inequality between 1964 and 1971 is in part due to new nets, but is mainly a result of share sales. There is a tendency for the curves to merge at the ninth percentile, indicating that the proportion of shares owned by the top group has changed little. The medium shareholders, however, have bifurcated: while a few of the men who held between five and nine shares in 1964 have managed to increase their holdings, most have been forced to sell some or all of their shares.

Examination of the lists of shareholders and the changes in registration between 1964 and 1971 reveals a total of 217 transactions involving 181 shares.[1] The details of these transactions are summarized in Table 11.3.

Sixty-nine of the transactions directly involved inheritance arrangements. In most cases the shares were merely transferred from the previous owner to his heirs but there were thirty-four sales of inherited shares: twenty-six among the heirs and eight to outsiders.[2] In two cases shares were included in dowries.[3]

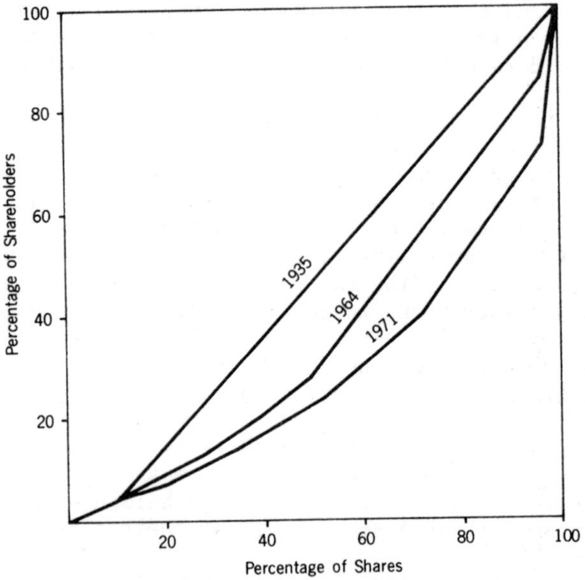

FIG. 11–1: DISTRIBUTION OF SHAREHOLDINGS
1935, 1964, 1971

TABLE 11.3. SHARE TRANSACTIONS, 1964-1971

	Number	Percentage
Total Transactions	217	
Less Inheritance	69	
	148	
Circumstances of Sales		
Extra-village Owner	14	9
Investment	35	24
Emergency Expenses	81	55
Unknown	18	12
Total:	148	100%

Circumstances in which shares were sold can be grouped into three broad categories. Ten per cent of the sales were by owners living outside Gahavälla.[4] As was noted in Chapter 7, the position of non-Gahavälla shareholders is becoming untenable as pressure on the resources increases: local men resent attempts by extra-village owners to work their shares (and this is difficult in any case because of uncertainty about when the net will be used), yet the employment of a Gahavälla resident makes it difficult to obtain the proceeds. Despite informants' claims that immediately after the war considerable numbers of shares were owned by non-Gahavälla residents, in 1971 outsiders held less than 4 per cent.

Thirty-five sales (24 per cent of the total) were for investment purposes: the owner sold the share with the intention of immediately buying a share in another net. This type of investment is discussed below, but twenty-four sales were to spread shareholdings more evenly, and eleven to relinquish shares in a faction controlled net.

Although I was unable to obtain details of eighteen sales, it is evident that the remaining 67 per cent were sold to meet emergency expenses. It would be misleading to break down these into sub-categories, such as medical expenses or a poor fishing season, for in most cases several factors were involved. It should be noted, however, that eight men sold twenty-two shares to meet legal expenses. Many of the sales were made in two stages, at least twenty-eight were foreclosed mortgages.

An analysis of the present occupations of the men who sold shares in this period supports the claim that the share sales do not represent the ebb and flow of economic fortune, but the inexorable process of capitalist accumulation. If shares sold for investment, by men living outside the village or who have since died, and by women, are excluded; twenty-four men who sold sixty-eight shares are known. Thirteen of these men are still engaged in *madella* fishing: seven who sold twenty shares now work as wage labourers, mainly on shares they once owned, and six work shares which they have retained. The remaining eleven men are now either without regular work or have become inshore fishermen. Two are old men who would probably be semi-retired in any case, but the other nine would still be beachseining if they had not lost the means to do so. In short, only six of the twenty-four men who sold shares to meet basic expenses between 1964 and 1971 still owned shares in 1971. This lends support to the hypothesis discussed below, that a man forced to sell one of his shares will rapidly lose them all.

What of the men who bought shares during this period? The most important point is that of the thirteen largest shareholders in 1964, only four[5] were among the twelve largest shareholders in 1971. The eight newcomers are all closely associated with one of the factions and apart from the faction leaders, include one member of Sunil's faction, two members of Danny Wijenaike's and two of David Mahattea's faction. Although the new members of the shareholders' elite gained substantial holdings with the additional nets of 1964-66, they have purchased 26 per cent of all shares sold in the last seven years. Other members of the three factions bought a further 31 per cent: eighteen sales to Sunil's faction, nine to Danny's and nineteen to David Mahattea's faction. Remembering that 24 per cent of sales were for investment purchases, it is evident that most shares which are sold are accumulated by the faction leaders and their close associates.

Three conclusions can be drawn from developments in the share market between 1964 and 1971: the middle peasants who have comprised the beachseiners for most of Gahavälla's history are selling their shares at an increasing pace to meet essential living costs; the distribution of shares among those who remain is becoming increasingly unequal; and the three leaders and their faction cores are rapidly taking control of the fishery.

Survival Strategies[6]

Studies of peasant agriculture reveal a remarkable resilience in the face of sustained population growth. Although farm sizes inevitably diminish, many poor peasants seem to be able to retain a small plot of land and in extreme cases, such as Java (Geertz 1963), the size of the average holding may even fall below that needed for a subsistence income. Population increases are apparently absorbed by increased labour inputs and higher yields, and while households with a high rate of growth are inevitably forced out, the transition to elite control of the means of production takes several generations.

Two critical economic factors which contribute to this resilience of peasant agriculture are: the positive relationship between increases in labour inputs and increases in yield, and the low maintenance cost of the major component of the means of production, the land itself. By contrast, the technology used in peasant fisheries imposes severe limits on the ability to lift yields through increased effort, and the means of production are both expensive to maintain and subject to severe risks of damage or loss. The history of Gahavälla fisheries suggests that these differences in the forces of production constrain the transformation of the relations of production. Instead of a gradual decline, it indicates that there is a critical size for a viable holding. Once this level is breached, the loss of the means of production is inevitable and an elite can displace peasant owners very quickly.

The process by which this occurs is well illustrated in the special case of Gahavälla beachseining. Consider a fisherman who owns five shares distributed equidistantly throughout the net sequence. The expected income from these five shares over a five year period is shown in Table 11.4.

TABLE 11.4. ESTIMATED EARNINGS FROM FIVE EQUALLY SPACED SHARES OVER FIVE-YEAR PERIOD[7]

Net Number	Year				
	One Rs.	Two Rs.	Three Rs.	Four Rs.	Five Rs.
1	463	52	87	148	232
21	232	463	52	87	148
41	148	232	463	52	87
61	87	148	232	463	52
81	52	87	148	232	463
Total	982	982	982	982	982
Production Costs	416	416	416	416	416
Income	566	566	566	566	566

Apportioning shareholdings throughout the net sequence neutralises fluctuations in the returns from individual nets. The owner can expect a similar income each year, irrespective of the point in the net sequence when the flush period occurs, for a poor return from one net is balanced by the high catches of another. As long as the income is sufficient to meet his household's needs, he has access to credit to cover short-term (less than one year) fluctuations in income, and no emergencies occur; he can retain his shares indefinitely.

Table 11.5 shows the estimated annual earnings of the same owner after he has sold one share (in net number 81). There are two main differences in the cash flow: not only does his average annual income fall by a fifth, it also fluctuates wildly from year to year. Even if the shareholder can adjust his expenditure to the lower income, he is faced with considerably more difficult problems of planning and saving. In *Year One* his income is greater than before and in *Year Two* it is similar, but in *Year Five* his income falls to 40 per cent of the five year average. The fifth year is crucial, for in view of the restrictions on credit outlined earlier, he will have to sell or mortgage one of his shares to meet his production and consumption expenses.[8] In fact the table conceals some of the management problems because it disguises the effects of uncertainty. The shareholder cannot put aside part of his income in a good year to meet the basic expenses of a poor year, for good and bad years do not follow in orderly succession.

TABLE 11.5. ESTIMATED EARNINGS FROM FOUR SHARES OVER FIVE-YEAR PERIOD

Net Number	Year				
	One Rs.	Two Rs.	Three Rs.	Four Rs.	Five Rs.
1	463	52	87	148	232
21	232	463	52	87	148
41	148	232	463	52	87
61	87	148	232	463	52
Total	930	895	834	750	519
Production Costs	332	332	332	332	332
Income	598	563	502	418	187

The critical size of a viable shareholding is a function of three factors: (1) The size of the household; the minimum size is the number of shares which will provide an average annual income sufficient for the household's requirements. (2) The extent to which the shares are spread throughout the net sequence; the greater the clustering the more shares that are required to meet basic expenses in the least successful seasons.[9] (3) Access to credit; the greater the amount of credit (or other finance) available, the greater degree of clustering that is possible.

Averages are often misleading, but on the basis of the expenditure data in Chapter 5, the viable shareholding for the average middle peasant household is 6.5 shares distributed equidistantly throughout the sequence. One indication of the instability of beachseining is that an average shareholding of this size requires a reduction in the number of shareholders from 159 to 122. In 1971, ninety-five shareholders (58 per cent) held five shares or less.

Maximising or Minimax?

Numerous contingent considerations influence the decision to buy a particular share, including the range of shares available for sale, the opportunity to buy on credit or through a mortgage, and the buyer's relationship with other shareholders. But there is a further consideration, which while taken into account in all sales, is particularly important in 'investment sales' and plays a vital role in middle peasant efforts to retain a foothold in beachseining: the position of the share in the net sequence. Share purchasers have three options with respect to the net sequence: they can seek to distribute their shares throughout the sequence; to cluster them in adjoining nets, or to subordinate the sequence to some other consideration such as price or faction control. I refer to these options as the *sequential*, *cluster* or *random* strategies.

The major advantage of the sequential strategy was discussed in the previous section. Spreading shares throughout the sequence reduces the effects of variation in individual net returns thus minimising the area of uncertainty in annual income and making it possible to plan expenditure accordingly. The results of the individual nets remain uncertain, but they are also interdependent, so that a poor result from one net increases the chances of a good result from another. The distribution of labour demands throughout the year makes it possible for the owner to work his own nets, and the scheduling of income and expenditure reduces dependence upon high cost credit. But while the sequential strategy limits risk, it also limits potential profit: an owner has little chance of improving his economic position by purchasing additional shares with the proceeds of a particularly good year. Spreading shares evenly throughout the sequence ensures that one will benefit from the flush period, but it also limits the benefit to the one share. Further, in comparison with the random strategy, both the sequential and cluster strategy narrow the possible purchases and thus raise prices.

The costs and benefits of the cluster strategy are a function of the size of the shareholding. For men with shareholdings approaching the critical level, the cluster strategy has few advantages. It is true that clustering enables the shareowner to 'gamble against nature' (Davenport 1960). If the nets in which his shares are clustered are used during the flush period, he will make a very high income and can buy additional nets with the profits. The odds, however, are against him: there is a one-quarter chance that adjoining nets will be used in the flush period and a two-thirds chance that they will not meet the production costs. For men with less than ten shares these odds are too risky.[10] Moreover, the cluster strategy makes annual income more difficult to predict, produces high peaks in expenditure, and requires the owner to employ wage labour on some nets.

Similar costs and benefits accrue to men with shareholdings below the critical level, but the cluster strategy appears their best option. While the sequential strategy stabilises their income below their minimum requirements, the cluster strategy gives some chance, albeit a poor one, of improving their position. The cluster strategy, however, has several advantages for the large shareholders. Many of these men have alternative sources of income sufficient to meet recurrent expenditure, and the others have access to savings or credit. Moreover, most do not wish to work the shares they own. For these men the income fluctuations of a clustered holding have positive functions. They have sufficient finance to meet the expenses of a poor season and receiving their profits in a lump is a convenient means of saving. By forgoing the owner's share in all but the most successful seasons, they can pose as the benefactors of their clients at little economic cost. And they need spend only a few consecutive days in each net cycle to supervise their nets and collect the proceeds.

It is important in discussions of this kind, to make clear the extent to which the options are strategies pursued by individuals, as opposed to analyst's constructs designed to account for observed behavioural regularities. The notion of a viable shareholding and its consequences for the outcome of the options was developed after the fieldwork and, as far as I know, is not recognised by the fishermen. But the sequential strategy is a direct, if somewhat more systematic, reflection of views which were often expressed by the Gahavälla beachseiners. They claimed that the sequential strategy was the sensible way to arrange one's shareholding and that establishing an even distribution of shares was always an important criteria in their own purchasing or selling decisions.

If the investment decisions of middle peasants are directed towards this goal, their shares should be distributed throughout the sequence, for while most have been selling rather than buying shares in the past seven years, their holdings should reflect earlier decisions. In fact the sequential strategy is reflected in their holdings. If the sample is limited to men who owned at least two shares before 1964, we find that among men with seven shares, 68 per cent of the shares are more than fifteen nets removed from the preceding share; among men with seven shares 83 per cent are at least ten nets distant from the preceding share; and among men with nine shares, 60 per cent of the shares are separated by at least ten nets. These figures are far greater than would be expected by chance and indicate that, despite the myriad factors influencing share purchases, the sequential strategy was strongly pursued.[11]

Further support comes from a comparison of the 1964 and 1971 shareholdings of men who made investment sales during this period. The holdings of the three most active traders are presented in Table 11.6.

In each case the owner has disposed of shares grouped closely together and purchased shares at other points in the net sequence. I am not aware of the costs of buying and selling shares in this manner, except to note that owner *three* exchanged four shares (89,90,91,104) for three (21,48,69) and shareholders claim losses of up to 50 per cent. A notable point is that only one had as many shares in 1971, as in 1964.

TABLE 11.6. THE SEQUENTIAL STRATEGY, AN ILLUSTRATION

	Shareholders					
	One		Two		Three	
	1966	1971	1966	1971	1966	1971
Nets	-	1	3	-	-	21
	19	19	11	11	-	48
	-	31	13	-	-	69
	-	45	-	37	87	87
	-	69	68	68	89	-
	89	-	72	-	90	-
	90	90	73	-	91	-
	91	-	84	84	102	-
	107	-	-	100	103	-
	108	-			104	
					108	108

Several writers have pointed to a similar emphasis on minimax rather than maximising strategies in peasant economies, and have stressed the survival value of these practices. Scott (1976) pushes the argument even further, suggesting that a subsistence ethic, that is a low risk ethic, may be universal in peasant societies.[12] My Gahavälla informants would no doubt agree with these scholars, but while the sequential strategy was an efficient adaptation to the economic uncertainties and institutional risks of beachseining within a semi-subsistence economy, it has had very different consequences since the emergence of capitalist relations of production. In contemporary Gahavälla, where the average shareholding is insufficient for a subsistence living, the sequential strategy will inexorably dispossess the middle peasants of the means of production. The cluster strategy will, in most cases, have the same result.

A distinction between maximising and minimax strategies has considerable heuristic value in the analysis of these peasant economies which are only partially determined by the logic of the market. It corrects *a priori* assumptions about peasant conservatism and stubbornness, and provides a plausible explanation of why peasants who are in the position to choose often reject technically more efficient innovations. But as capitalist relations of production develop, peasants lose the economic autonomy which effective choices require and at that point the distinction is meaningless. The relevant question in Gahavälla is not whether middle peasants will lose control of beachseining, but when.

CHAPTER 12

CONCLUSION: MARITIME STUDIES IN ANTHROPOLOGY

Raymond Firth's *Malay Fishermen* was an innovative work in a double sense — as an ethnography of an Asian rural community and as a contribution to theoretical developments in peasant studies — but despite Firth's lead, our understanding of both topics remains land-orientated. The diverse maritime adaptations of Southeast Asia ranging from the boat-dwelling sea nomads, through the subsistence exploitation of marine, littoral and terrestrial resources on off-shore archipelagos, to the highly capital-intensive prawn fisheries of Thailand and Sumatra; are represented by a few scattered articles and monographs. South Asia lacks a single comprehensive ethnographic study of a fishing community. The contribution of accounts of maritime societies to theoretical developments in peasant studies is also slight: indeed a widely accepted definition of peasant societies excludes fishing villages from its ambit (Shanin 1973). Nevertheless, the as yet small literature makes it clear that in some respects at least, fishermen are the quintessential peasants. Definitive criteria of peasant societies including dependence on external markets, highly developed risk sharing procedures, multiplex patron-client ties and a factional mode of political competition, are evidently starkly apparent in fishing communities.

The dearth of anthropological studies of maritime communities also has important policy implications. The *Law of the Sea Conference*, especially the declaration of 200 mile jurisdictional limits, has sparked new interests in marine affairs among both governments and international development agencies. Academia has followed suit and there are now specialised marine journals in the fields of law, economics and management. A danger in this flurry of activity is that the equity of traditional fishing communities — which are often disadvantaged sectors of nations which are themselves severely disadvantaged in international terms — will be ignored. While governments may express concern for their traditional fishing communities in international forums, their apparent motive is to use these communities as bargaining counters in negotiations over other issues, for their internal policies show little empathy with the problems of the fishermen. Fisheries are a major protein source for most South and South East Asian nations, but fisheries development has had mixed success. While production has greatly increased, employment has diminished, social inequalities have been exacerbated and peasant fishing households have been further impoverished. Traditional fishing communities have received the short end of the stick: a gift which they are apt to describe rather more graphically.

Fisheries development has also spawned a considerable body of research over the past decade, nearly all of it concerned with economics in the most restrictive sense of the term. Large scale surveys involving a few days in each settlement and interviews with the village elite are standard procedures. Policies based on such 'research' inevitably exhibit a single-minded concern with the technical efficiency of fishing gear and questions of employment and income distribution are ignored. Missing are detailed studies of indigenous concepts of sea tenure and resource conservation; of established practices of marketing and catch distribution; in short of the 'moral economy' of maritime societies. Such research is time-consuming, but it is essential if fisheries development is not to remain synonymous with the impoverishment of traditional fishermen.

My intention in this study has been to analyse Gahavälla's history as a contribution to the understanding of the development of rural capitalism in Sri Lanka. As with most anthropology, the 'conclusions' are imbedded in the analysis and there is no point in restating them. The results of the analysis, however, do have some bearing on the broader question of the role of maritime studies in anthropology.

Fisheries and Agriculture

The professional training of most anthropologists is orientated towards agricultural societies and this poses some initial difficulties for a fieldworker investigating a fishing community. Basic methodological questions, such as adequate sample sizes, as well as established techniques for gathering data, have to be reconsidered. For example, what is an adequate sample of fishermen from whom to collect systematic catch information when vast differences in the fortunes of individuals may be a critical feature of the economy? In view of the substantial seasonal, perhaps daily, fluctuations in catches, does accurate data require every fisherman to be visited every day? And if so, how does the fieldworker find time for anything else? For gathering daily catch data is far more time-consuming (and boring) than investigating an annual or semi-annual harvest. Given such difficulties in using established research techniques, it is not surprising that ethnographers have been impressed by what appear to be unique features of fishing communities and have tended to use these as the framework of subsequent analyses.

Thirty five years ago Firth (1966) listed some of the significant differences between fishing and agricultural production and others have since expanded his list. One obvious difference is that the major resources in agricultural communities have strict spatial boundaries. In a sense the area of a fishery is also bounded — the use of a particular type of gear imposes relatively strict constraints on the sites which may be fished economically — but the fish are not constrained by these limits. This point may appear trivial, but it has the important consequence of giving the fishermen far less control over their annual or daily income. In contrast to agriculture, where seasonal and individual distribution of the crop remains relatively constant, annual and individual catches fluctuate considerably. This makes production planning very difficult. Natural fluctuations make it hard to assess the effects of technological innovations; fishing may extend well past the point of maximum sustainable yield; and the results of over-fishing may first become apparent several years later in an area several hundred miles away.

There are also considerable differences in the consequences of additional labour inputs. Whereas yields in agriculture can often be lifted substantially by higher labour inputs, this is seldom possible in fishing: higher gear utilisation rates seldom result in significant increases in the catch over the long term. Some forms of additional labour in agriculture, intensive weeding for example, may lift yields without requiring additional finance, but greater catches require a concomitant increase in investment in gear, usually in the form of mechanisation which in the long run displaces labour. Moreover, as both men and women usually participate in agriculture, each addition to the household is a potential addition to the household's labour force, whereas offshore fishing is a male pursuit in all societies. Finally, fishing does not require sustained participation so that there is more opportunity for the entrance of marginal workers during the peak seasons with a consequent fall in the incomes of those who depend on fishing alone for their livelihood. These differences in the structure of labour demands are especially important in societies where the population is rapidly increasing.

Investment also has different features in the two types of economy. In agriculture the main investment is the land itself and investments in gear and workstock are normally small (Mellor 1966). Thus there is little risk involved in investment and apart from its production function the land may serve as an avenue of saving. In fishing, however, the entire investment is in gear which has high maintenance costs, depreciates rapidly and is often lost or damaged. Further, in a situation in which per capita output is falling, investments may increase. There are several reasons why this may occur; catch fluctuations make it difficult to establish when marginal productivity is falling; fluctuations in individual catches may result in high profits for some participants; and speculators may be prepared to balance short losses against long term control.

Firth noted several other features of fisheries which affect the political economy of fishing villages. The most important is that fishermen produce fluctuating quantities of a highly perishable product which is not a major item in their diet. This provides scope for the development of specialised middlemen and accounts, in part, for the close relationship between middlemen and fishermen which often have patron-client connotations.

The list of differences can be continued in the areas of social and personality structure. Smith (1977) in a very comprehensive listing of the features of maritime communities includes: greater female autonomy, differentiated child-rearing patterns; and adult male personalities which are compatible with both rapid individual decision-making and close cooperation with others.

The explicit or implicit comparisons with agriculture which underpin most studies of fishing communities, thus reflect not merely anthropologists' training, but also very real empirical differences. Nevertheless, the use of these empirical differences as the framework of analyses has given a misplaced importance to marine ecology in accounts of the social structure of maritime communities: almost unwittingly, ecological functionalism has become the major mode of explanation. The epistemological problems inherent in functional explanations are widely appreciated and need not be reiterated here, but some of the analytical problems stemming from the dominance of this style of explanation can be illustrated by a brief discussion of two topics where the Gahavälla case is especially relevant: Southeast Asian fish marketing and the 'common property' nature of coastal fisheries.

Common Property Resources

Fisheries are often cited as the paradigm of a natural common property resource: no single user has exclusive rights to the resource nor can they prevent others sharing in its exploitation. As the yield is strictly limited, this has the consequence that an increase in the number of participants affects each user's enjoyment of the resource. The individual is in competition with all other participants in an attempt to secure a greater share of the resource and if he restrains his own efforts, he merely increases the share available to others. This notion has become of major importance in neo-classical economics' attempts to explain why the world's deepsea fisheries are susceptible both to 'overfishing' with consequent destruction of the fish breeding stock, and 'overcapitalisation' (i.e. levels of labour and investment in excess of what is required to maximise profits from the fishery as a whole).

In a very influential book Christy and Scott (1965:80) argued that a consequence of the lack of economic restraints upon entry is that:

> there will tend to be an excessive amount of capital and labour applied to the fishery. The fishermen are operating as individuals, each seeking to maximise the differences between his revenues and his costs. But because there are no restrictions on the number of fishermen who can enter the industry, any true profit will attract additional fishermen. This will mean that the total revenue will be shared by more and more producers until no true profit at all remains to be distributed... Eventually the fishery may arrive at an equilibrium of profit and effort, which is likely to be marked by a relatively large amount of effort, a low population and a low sustainable yield.

Overfishing occurs when the point of (short term) profit maximisation is higher than the maximum sustainable yield of the fishery. To avoid overfishing earlier writers (Gordon 1954) had argued for sole ownership of the fishery, but Christy and Scott advocate less drastic restrictions on entry, preferably achieved by selective taxation. The common property nature of ocean fisheries is widely accepted among fisheries administrators and underlies most schemes of fisheries management.

In addition to its unjustified assumption that competitive individualism is an innate mainspring of human behaviour, the common property account of fisheries errs in conflating two analytically distinct types of statements: statements about the ecology of fisheries, and historical statements concerning political and economic arrangements for their exploitation. For example, the statement that 'no single owner has exclusive rights to the resource nor can they prevent others from sharing in its exploitation' is historically true, at least as far as deepsea fisheries are concerned, but it is not inherent in the biological nature of fisheries. Open access to deepsea resources is a political concept which was formulated by Grotius in the seventeenth century, was challenged by his English contemporaries, and is currently being dismantled by the *Law of the Sea Conference*. Moreover, anthropological studies of coastal fisheries have documented various forms of proprietary rights to the sites where fish gather at predictable intervals (Firth 1966; Forman 1970; Cordell 1978). In Sumatara the local landholding groups auction the rights to construct large fixed prawn-fishing platforms in the coastal estuaries, while the forms of ownership of Sri Lankan beachseine sites have been discussed above.

Nor is it obvious that profit maximisation, either for individual participants or the fishery as a whole, should be the goal of fisheries management. The point of profit maximisation is always below the point of maximum (biologically) sustainable yield, and surely a world short of protein requires the maximum yield from its fisheries. Similarly, labour efficiency with its corollary of displacement of individual peasant fishermen seems a singularly inappropriate planning criterion for most Southeast Asian nations with their high rates of unemployment.

Despite its deficiencies as a general model of fisheries, the 'common property myth' (Cordell 1978:2) is not without value in more limited analyses. Comparison of peasant fisheries and agriculture, for example, suggests that the fisheries pose rather different problems of management and control. In an agricultural community each household's portion of the major resource, the land, is geographically delineated, but despite the evolution of various forms of proprietary rights, it is not possible for peasant fishing communities to apportion the resource among members of the community. The inability to geographically delineate each household's share of the resource contains a latent problem. In the agricultural community the interests of the basic economic unit, the household, and the interests of the community as a whole are congruent. Because each household has a stipulated portion of the land, investment or additional labour which does not increase yields rebounds against the household responsible for the increases. In a fishing community, however, a household which increases labour or investment under similar conditions probably profits by annexing a greater share of the resource. The disadvantages of increased effort — a decline in overall profit — is distributed among all members of the community, while the household responsible for the decline lifts its standard of living. In precapitalist societies the potential problems are seldom realised, because the level of effort is well below the point of profit maximisation and there are few incentives to increase it, but the problem becomes acute with the emergence of rural capitalism and subsequent increases in production. Fishing communities are particularly vulnerable to expensive technological innovations, which, although they do not increase the overall catch, concentrate it in fewer hands. One such innovation, the use of nylon nets from non-mechanised or insufficiently mechanised traditional craft as in Gahavälla 'bible' fishing, has decimated the ranks of small-scale fishermen in societies as far apart as Brazil (Cordell 1978) and Java.

Contemporary small-scale fisheries are therefore faced with the potential danger of a competitive spiral of increased effort in which the only possible outcomes are declining welfare or dispossession. To a greater degree than agricultural communities, they depend upon cultural rules to prevent individual greed harming community welfare. The difficulties in developing and maintaining such practices should not be underestimated: they are commonly latent functions of kinship or ritual and are vulnerable to the social changes which destroy the moral authority of these institutions.

Middlemen and Marketing

Fisheries administrators in Sri Lanka, as elsewhere in Asia, regard fish middlemen as 'parasites, living off and exploiting the peasants who are the real source of wealth in the economy' (Stirrat 1973:189-90). Proceeding on this assumption development programmes have looked to the elimination of the middlemen as a major goal, but they have failed miserably. Alternative marketing arrangements such as cooperatives, government-supervised auctions and government purchasing schemes have been rejected by the fishermen they were designed to benefit. These failures can be explained in functional terms. The discussion of 'tied-boat' arrangements in Gahavälla mechanised fishing, for example, stressed the reciprocal benefits of these arrangements. The fishermen gain a guaranteed market at ruling prices as well as interest-free credit for repairs, ceremonies and consumption. Because of the substantial differential between retail prices and accepted producer prices, middlemen maximise their profits by ensuring a regular supply of fish. As the fishermen and middlemen are linked by ties of caste and kinship, this tends to reinforce the patron-client and reciprocal character of their relationship.

Similar arguments have been used to explain common characteristics of beach-level fish marketing throughout Southeast Asia. Fishermen produce varying qualities of a very perishable product which is not a staple food, and the exigencies of their occupation make it difficult for them to market the catch themselves. This leads to the development of specialised middlemen and the peculiar content of fishermen-middlemen relationships should be regarded as an adaptation to the risks associated with fishing enterprises. Long term debts, for example, are not an indication of extreme poverty, but a system which allows fishing families both to balance a variable income against invariant needs for food, clothing and shelter, and to repair damaged boats and gear with a minimal loss of fishing time. The widespread custom of 'cutting the beard' — whereby the middleman pays less than the agreed price if he suffers a loss retailing the fish — spreads the marketing risk between fishermen and middlemen and gives higher incomes to all in the long term. The middleman, so the story goes, is not a parasite, but a vital cog in an efficient and equitable adaptation to the uncertainties inherent in the exploitation of a marine environment.

As with many functionalist accounts this argument has a certain plausibility: it sticks to the observed facts and in the hands of a skilful writer conveys the impression that things could not be otherwise. It is, nevertheless, both theoretically and empirically inadequate. It is theoretically inadequate because it arbitrarily isolates one aspect of an interconnected system and assigns it causal status, and its empirical inadequacies are illustrated by the marketing of the beachseine catch in Gahavälla. Here there is no hint of reciprocity in the relationship between fishermen and middlemen which often involves physical violence. Producer prices are low and the fishermen have a constant struggle to prevent them falling further: middlemen do not provide credit, delay payment as long as possible and renege on payments whenever they can.

This variation in the content of middlemen-fishermen relationships in the two major sectors of the Gahavälla fishery is determined by the political economy, not by marine ecology. Two aspects of the relations of production in Gahavälla fishing are crucial in this regard: the distribution of power and interests, and the potential for direct ownership of the means of production by non-fishermen. Differences in power between middlemen and mechanised boat owners are not significant and each has powerful sanctions if the implicit contract between them is broken. The middlemen's major goal is to maximise the flow of fish and this is congruent with the fishermen's aim of ruling prices and adequate credit. Beachseining on the other hand, pits a powerful and well-organised monopsony against the atomistic and faction-riven fishermen. Because the monopsony ensures the flow of fish the middlemen have no need to offer credit - indeed they forcibly extract credit from the fishermen by delaying payment for three months - and are free to increase profits by various price-cutting tactics.

The possibility of ownership of the means of production by non-producers is a longer term constraint on fishermen-middlemen relationships. The way in which the mechanised boats are operated mean that these craft are not profitable for non-fishing owners who also have problems in obtaining their due share of the catch. This could, of course alter in the future, in other areas of Sri Lanka traditional practices of crew organisation and catch-sharing have been replaced by wage labour with a concomitant growth of non-fishing boat owners, but in the meantime the fishermen have little to fear from the middlemen. Beachseine middlemen, however, already own considerable numbers of beachseine shares and there are numerous incentives for them to increase their holdings: the shares are easy to control, give high profits, provide employment for their political clients and strengthen the monopsony's position in the auctions on the beach. Beachseiners are faced not merely with low prices, but also with the possibility that the middlemen will reduce them to wage labourers.

Gahavälla's experience further suggests that the foundation of the functionalist account of marketing — the claim that specialised middlemen are a response to the problems of marketing variable quantities of a highly perishable product — is untenable. Before 1940 Gahavälla had numerous sources of income and most of the catch was consumed within the immediate area or preserved by members of the fishing households. It was national developments, including such diverse factors as a rising population, better communications and political centralism, which shattered the barriers between localised spheres of production and exchange and amalgamated them into regional and national markets. In other words, it was the emergence of rural capitalism which made Gahavälla dependent upon the sale of a single product marketed in its most perishable form. The post-1940 changes in Gahavälla fishing — the introduction of technically more efficient but socially deleterious technology, the growth of exploitative and monopsonistic fish trading, and the bifurcation of independent smallholders into capitalists and labourers — were not inevitable, they were a product of the market logic of capitalism. Economic dependence on a single highly perishable product is not inherent in maritime economies and it seems probable that villages solely dependent upon specialised petty commodity production, including fishing villages, are a recent development in Asian societies.

NOTES

Chapter 2

1 My use of compound refers solely to the fenced area of land surrounding a house or houses. Leach (1961: 48) introduced the notion of a compound group to refer to the people who owned land in a named area and had the rights to build houses there. Under circumstances similar to those in Pul Eliya the compound group is a group of patrilineal kinsmen and their spouses, with ownership rights to contiguous areas of paddy land. It thus adds an additional dimension to the indigenous notion of the *gedera* and may be a useful analytical concept. But where land sales are more frequent and where there is no direct relationship between residential and kinship propinquity the term has little relevance. Thus Robinson's (1968:403) use of compound group to refer only to a named area of land where the constituent households' members are not close relatives, is of very limited utility. Gahavälla inhabitants do use named areas of land as geographical reference points and most of these areas are congruent with the compounds of men living in the village several generations ago. For example *Liyāna Patabändige watte* is an area of land which the ancestors of the *Liyāna Patabändige pelapata* owned and where they resided. But today men from many *pelapata*, with differing degrees of kin, social, and economic relations live in this area.

2 The number of tea shops fluctuates considerably. Most have a total capital of less than Rs.50 and are run by people, especially elderly widows, lacking other sources of income.

3 The history of the conflict between the priest and the villagers is long and complex, but two incidents were particularly important. In the dispute referred to above, the priest refused a faction leader's request to invite thirty priests, including some from other

nikayas (sects) to the funeral of his sister. The second concerned the priest's refusal to allow some empty buildings in the temple to be used, rentfree, for the overflow classes from the school.

4 Four of the university students are women as are five of the seven teachers in the village school.

5 Exact figures are not available, but on the basis of De Silva's (1964) survey conducted in 1958, less than a tenth of the 7,015 fishing households in the Southern Division live east of Tangalla. The percentage is probably slightly greater today, for more of the fishermen from the heavily populated western coast have taken up new occupations.

6 This is very important for fisheries development because there is some evidence to support the theory that more fish are to be found in inshore waters during the monsoon period (see Bulletin of the Fisheries Research Station, Ceylon, 1962-1966).

7 Even in these areas the sea is sometimes too rough to permit fishing outside the bay, but fishing time lost for this reason amounts to less than ten days per year (see Alexander 1972). In contrast, fishermen at Weligama, a village on the west coast, lose up to 100 days per year because they cannot launch their craft.

8 Three or four decades ago, the supply of drinking water was one of the most important services a patron provided to his clients. Wells for drinking water must be dug to a great depth and need to be lined with brick. The only people who could afford to build them were the large landowners and traders and all drinking wells are situated in the house compounds of the men who were the important leaders in the village thirty years ago.

9 The official figure based on the numbers of ration books registered is 1,053. At the time my census was taken twenty-two people were residing outside the village. These included students (6), *mudalali* and assistants (9), and six others whom I was unable to trace.

10 It is seldom possible for the dowry received by a man to be used for his sister's marriage. Much of the dowry is in kind and even if it could be readily converted into cash such a procedure is unlikely to meet with the wife's approval.

11 The late age of marriage and the stress on premarital

chastity, reduce sexual opportunities for men. There is little prositution, although some married women take lovers while their husbands are at sea, and homosexual relationships, while common among adolescents, are frowned on with respect to older men.

12 I include villages occupied by more than one section of the *Goigama* caste as multi-caste villages.

13 In fact there are occasional inter-caste marriages. Two of the women living in Gahavälla are *Goigama* and a third is *Salāgama*. There is no evidence of prejudice against these women.

14 Stratification is more complex among the *Karāva* near Colombo because many of these people were converted to Christianity.

15 Inshore and lagoon fishing are usually associated because the prawns used for bait in inshore fishing are caught in the lagoons.

16 There are two reasons why the Kottetawa men received more mechanised craft than other fishermen. Firstly, applicants in the ballot were supposed to be experienced deep-sea fishermen and few men outside Kottetawa could meet this condition. Secondly, the Kottetawa people had a long established, if moribund, fisheries cooperative and this society was allocated three craft.

17 See Roberts (1968), Raghavan (1961) and Ryan (1953).

18 Caste conflicts over school admission have been common in the Tangalla region since Independence. One such incident is described in Ryan (1953:292-3).

19 This discussion is concerned with the villages to the west of Tangalla; the villages on the east were all settled comparatively recently, mainly by groups of migrant fishermen, and are all deepsea fishing villages.

20 Beachseining and agriculture tend to be associated. Most of the *Karāva* agricultural villages inland of the coastal belt were settled by families from beachseining villages and the members of the agricultural communities still have close relatives engaged in beachseining.

21 This is particularly true of the coastline between Colombo and Galle, where squalid squatter settlements of mud houses are crushed between the railway lines and the encroaching sea.

22 The Kottetawa people had been engaged in inshore fishing for many years but, as was pointed out above, this hamlet is somewhat of an anomaly in Gahavälla.

23 Not all the *vedda mahataya's* patients are poor. People from all economic levels make use of his services, but the wealthier families use the 'western' medical services as well.

24 The report on each candidate for office was supposed to state 'the social standing, family and position of each candidate, and particulars regarding any landed property he may possess in the district in which a vacancy occurs.' (Sessional Paper 27, 1935).

25 In 1920 R.P. Andrious, Constable *Arrachi* of Gahavälla, received rewards of Rs.10 for 'apprehending a cattle thief' and Rs.5 for 'smart work in a gambling case.' (Administration Report, Government Agent, Hambantota, 1921).

Chapter 3

1 These three levels are intra-village divisions; when discussing Sri Lanka society as a whole men are apt to insist that all Gahavälla inhabitants are poor people.

2 'A world view that uncertainty of resource futures is a basic fact of life' (Smith 1978:8) seems to be common among maritime communities.

3 Fishing is a male task in most societies; but the complete elimination of females from retail activities is unusual. In most societies (Firth 1966) they play some part and in Africa (Hill 1970; Gladwin 1972) retailing is often completely in the hands of the women. In Sri Lanka they play a large part in fish retailing in the Catholic areas near Negombo (Stirrat 1973). The folk explanation for the lack of participation by women in the southern coast, is that fishing is a sinful occupation and that women would be ashamed (*lädjau*).

4 The coconuts from the plantations are sold to non-village traders.

5 Apart from the fact that most money-lenders are women, one of the reasons why women arrange loans is that the usual security is women's jewellery.

6 House-building is the only activity in which cooperative labour groups play a part, and even here the groups are usually limited to five or six close kinsmen or friends spending a couple of hours digging the

foundations or thatching the roof. Wattle and daub houses are normally built by the occupant and close kin without special assistance.

7 An untrained school teacher is, as the name suggests, one who has not attended training college. They are appointed to the less desirable schools and unlike ordinary teachers do not have tenure.

8 According to the most recent figures (1963) 37 per cent of Sri Lanka households earn less than Rs.1,200 from all sources (Central Bank 1964:261). See pp.43 for a higher estimate of the average income calculated on a different basis.

9 I had intended to gather numerical data on savings and indebtedness but this proved impracticable and of doubtful value. Long-term savings are invested in land, non-productive property and fishing gear and thus the extent of long-term savings can be inferred from data presented earlier in the chapter. Short-term savings used for consumption purposes during poor fishing periods or accumulated for purchases such as house-building materials, are retained in cash and householders were reluctant to reveal the amounts because of fear of theft. The question of indebtedness is discussed later.

In this section I am solely concerned with the fishermen and their households. *Mudalali* have far wider sources of finance, including the banking system and the finance houses. At the time of the study the Gahavälla fishermen did not make use of the banking system, but this may change rapidly after the Ceylon Rural Bank establishes a series of pawn shops with low interest rates.

10 This is an approximation, the interest rate is fixed but the repayment period is reasonably flexible. As long as the loan is repaid within two or three months, interest is limited to 10 per cent. Quick repayment is the main condition of this type of loan and because of the importance of short-term credit to many households the borrower usually attempts to meet the obligation. Loans outstanding for more than a year are unlikely to be repaid.

11 This may be contrasted with agriculture where the approximate value of the yield is known in advance and it is comparatively easy for the lender to supervise the harvest and collect his dues. The wide-

spread use of credit to cover off-season consumption expenditure and to finance production which Tilakaratna (1963) has described for agricultural communities in Sri Lanka, is limited to the mechanised craft in the modern fishing communities.

12 *Sittu* have a long history in the Southern Province. Tilakaratna (1963:126) quotes an extract from *Sinhala Samaya* (a Sinhalese newspaper) which describes a *sittuwa* established in 1881.

13 This statement refers only to the present-day situation where the land is usually occupied by house-sites. Foreclosure of mortgaged paddy or coconut land was an important means of acquiring large areas of land in the past (see Chapter 9).

Chapter 4

1 The four exceptions are all married men who have established separate consumption units while continuing to live in the parents' dwelling.

2 Leach (1961:80) has a useful discussion of the problems in defining the Sinhalese household, particularly on the distinction between a cooking unit and a consumption unit. The situation is less complicated in Gahavälla, for Leach's (1961:80) comment that 'every married woman however young, has a separate cooking pot,' does not apply. While the newly married couple are living with a parent, the wife joins with her mother or mother-in-law in preparing food. Gifts of food between households, as in cases of children sending food to an aged parent, seldom involve cooked food other than special festival dishes.

3 The following account is limited to the aspects of marriage which are germane to the topic of the monograph. Descriptions of marriage ceremonies and an analysis of the symbolism can be found in Yalman (1967). His account was based on a fleeting visit however, and in some respects, notably his discussion of the dowry, hypergamy and the *pelapata*, is misleading (see below).

4 The detailed expenses for three weddings are presented in Appendix 1.

5 This remark should be qualified. The interest rates, calculated on a per annum basis, may be as high as 60

per cent, but the loans are usually repaid within a month. These loans are obtained from professional money-lenders in Tangalla and Dikwella. Often the bride's father does not own sufficient land to obtain a loan and a kinsmen or close friend provides the security.

6 For descriptions of these ceremonies see Ames (1964); Obeyesekere (1958); Yalman (1967).

7 There were eleven marriages during my fieldwork; two were similar to the ones discussed above, eight were more modest affairs with dowries ranging from Rs.2,500 to less than Rs.200 and one was an elopement. Several others arranged for the New Year period, were postponed because of the insurrection.

8 In view of the sizeable literature on the topic (e.g. Yalman 1967; Leach 1961; Tambiah 1965) some mention should be made of cross-cousin marriage. Gahavälla people do not recognise rules of prescriptive or preferential cross-cousin marriage and the only endogamous unit is the caste. In as much as they have marriage preferences based on kinship, they feel that it is better to marry a non-relative for this will give a larger dowry and some useful contacts. Among kinsmen, marriage rules are framed negatively; one should not marry across generations or marry parallel cousins. A little less than 8 per cent of *extant* marriages were between first or second cross-cousins and most of these were elopements, or at least against the wishes of the groom's parents. In 82 per cent of *extant* marriages both spouses came from Gahavälla or one of the three neighbouring villages. There is no notion of village exogamy or endogamy. In my opinion much of the controversy concerning cross-cousin marriage in Sri Lanka, especially the assertion by Yalman (1967), Needham (1971) and others, that there is a preferential marriage rule stems from the failure to appreciate that the term *massina* may have two distinct denotata: male cross-cousin and male affine of ego's generation (cf. Stirrat 1977).

9 This is particularly true of the men engaged in beach-seining. Inshore fishermen sell their catch for cash and thus obtain control of their earnings at an earlier stage. But most depend upon their mothers for small sums of money during periods of poor fishing.

10 In a recent paper Stirrat (1977) presents a very

interesting analysis of kinship practices in a fishing village on the north-west coast. In his account, which is far more sophisticated and comprehensive than the paragraphs in this work, Stirrat describes a kinship terminology and marriage practices which are very similar to Gahavälla and this further supports his claim that the variations are related to differences in the mode of production between fishing and agriculture. But he also notes that in a nearby Paravar village where the *madell* is the main fishing method, the standard terminology is used, and suggests that this is because the *madell* is a long term asset like land. As Gahavälla is also a beachseining village this explanation seems unlikely. Sharon Bell informs me that the variant terminology is also used in Goigama villages near Horana and suggests that market-orientated production may be the key factor. The 'ideology' or 'morality' associated with the standard terminology may be incompatible, not with fishing, but with capitalist relations of production.

11 When prompted informants include grandparents and grandchildren, but grandparents seldom long survive the birth of their grandchildren.

12 Generalised kinship terms are terms used without calculation of the exact genealogical relationship. For example distant male relatives of one's own generation are addressed as *aiya/malli* and referred to as *sahodara* (brothers), irrespective of whether they are cross or parallel cousins. Similarly, distant male relatives of the father's generation are addressed as *bappa* (cf. Leach 1961; Yalman 1967; Stirrat 1977).

13 The reasons why the effective domain of kinship is wider in villages such as Pul Eliya than in Gahavälla include: the smaller populations and the restricted area from which spouses are drawn; the importance of kin-based co-operative work groups in agriculture; and the role of kinship in regulating the transmission and utilisation of the main economic resource, land.

14 The following refers to actual FBs and MBs, not all those in the equivalent kinship category. MZH and FZH are terminologically equivalent to FB and MB respectively, but seldom live close by. Where they do the expected behaviour is similar to that discussed below.

15 But this does not prevent close relatives from fishing together on the mechanised craft.

16 I am not arguing that altruism is unknown outside the close kin, this would be a gross distortion of the facts. The richest *mudalali* in the village gives very large sums of money to families in need and most families give alms when they can. There is a considerable difference, however, between the relationships enacted by the constant flow of gifts between close kin and the occasional gift to a poor man or beggar.

17 For a detailed analysis of the sources of *vāsagama* names which also applies to *pelapata* names, see Obeyesekere (1967). Gahavälla people occasionally use *vāsagama* as a synonym for *pelapata*.

18 Wijetunga Liyāna Patabändige, for example, is usually reduced to W.L.P. or Wijetunga.

19 This discussion is very selective and is not intended as a systematic account of village politics. Analysis of post-Independence changes in the rural Sinhalese political structure raises a number of issues of empirical and theoretical interest which I hope to discuss at another time. This account has the limited objective of providing the reader with background information for later discussions of the beachseine economy.

20 It should be stressed that faction membership is not restricted by village boundaries. Six of the seventeen households in the Wijenaike faction core, for example, live outside Gahavälla and most of Danny Wijenaike's followers are from Moraketiara. David Mahattea, the leader with the most widespread political and economic interests, recruits less than half of his supporters from Gahavälla.

21 One was led by Nicholas Ediriweera (see Chapter 10). The other was led by W.A. Peter and W.A. Dawith (see Chapter 8).

22 Members of Sunil's faction have been involved in more than twenty court cases in the past decade, five of which, including two murders, went to the Appeal Court. Sunil claims to have spent more than Rs.20,000 of his own income on these cases, in addition to sums from other members of the family.

23 In what follows client refers to all members of a faction core, including kinsmen of the leader. The term supporters includes both clients and followers. The distinction between faction core and followers was drawn from Bailey (1969:49).

24 Tambiah (1965) presents a very convincing analysis of the role of kinship in faction formation and Leach (1961) also discusses the topic. It appears that kinship and caste play a more significant role in local politics in these smaller and more isolated communities than they do in Gahavälla.

25 This relationship is discussed in detail in Chapter 8 but briefly net owners may allow a substitute to work in their place and take one-third of the catch.

26 This may provide a sizeable income. A.H. Clement who organises the gambling for David's faction cleared more than Rs.400 on New Year's Day in 1971 despite the insurrection.

27 The distribution of hired men positions among the Wijenaike faction is shown in Fig.7.1.

28 Election meetings are highly organised in Sri Lanka. In the national elections of 1970 both the UNP and the SLFP organised two large meetings in Tangalla. For weeks beforehand local party organisers distributed free shirts and hats in the party colours, provided streamers for the park where the meeting was to be held, and built an elaborately decorated stage and sound system. Crowds of more than 10,000, many of them brought in from the villages by free transport, began assembling at midday and did not disperse until after 10 p.m. Village-level meetings (each party had two in Gahavälla) take a similar form, though on a more reduced scale. At the village meetings the clients begin the speeches, followed by the faction leaders and later the candidate. At the town meetings, village-level leaders, each accompanied by as many supporters as he can muster, speak early in the afternoon, followed by the party organisers, the candidate and later the party leader. The presence of village-level leaders at such meetings both indicates the level of grass-roots support for the party and provides additional esteem for the faction leader.

29 Some aspects of the composition of the Wijenaike faction core are discussed in Chapter 7. This account of David's faction core includes only members living in Gahavälla, equal numbers live in other villages and in Tangalla.

30 Danny Wijenaike's faction did some rather half-hearted campaigning for the UNP candidate, but several members of his faction core told me that they themselves had

voted for the SLFP. Votes at local booths are not available; in the electorate as a whole the SLFP received 23,103 votes, with 16,477 for the UNP. Several weeks before the election it was clear that Gahavälla voters were overwhelming supporters of the SLFP and most of the UNP votes appear to have come from interior villages.

31 The extent to which men actually make a decision to join a faction, rather than gradually drift into it over a period is an interesting problem. My own view, which is implicit in much of the discussion, is that with the exception of close kin and childhood friends of the leader, men do consciously weigh the advantages and disadvantages of joining a particular faction.

32 In 1971 Danny Wijenaike hired a bus at a cost of Rs.600 and took three bus-loads of people to the Kataragama festival. His motives for doing so were to reward his supporters who elected him to the Village Council and to take customers away from David Mahattea's bus service. The loss of fares to David's bus was nearly Rs.1,800. In this case, Danny did not charge fares, but it is a common practice for the leader to purchase a commodity, ranging from a bus for a festival trip to cigarettes, at wholesale rates and make it available to his supporters at cost price.

33 The extent and efficacy of bribery is difficult to establish. Accusations of bribery and claims of having offered bribes are rife, but are very difficult to cross-check. In many contexts a reputation for being able to bribe the police is itself sufficient to secure an objective.

Chapter 5

1 The latter is referred to in the report as Suriyagahawella which today is one of the constituent hamlets of Kudawellekele.

2 Either the number of canoes in Gahavälla was greatly overestimated or else some of the canoes belonged to other villages, because there were less than 100 adult males in Gahavälla at that time.

3 Apart from the Sessional Paper concerned with the fish curing scheme, this section is based on the annual

Administrative reports of the Government Agents at Matara and Hambantota.

4 More comprehensive accounts of the *orua* can be found in Raghavan (1961) and Pearson (1923). There is considerable variation in the details of construction, the *oru* on the West Coast, for example, have a triangular sail rigged on two masts.

5 The exceptions are in the villages east of Tangalla, such as Kirinda and Hambantota. Malay and Muslim fishermen in these areas still use *oru* bought from migrant Sinhalese fishermen for deep-sea fishing. A trip in one of these craft travelling at top speed was the most enjoyable experience of my fieldwork.

6 Crews vary from one to four, but a three-man crew is generally regarded as the most efficient and most *oru* have three crew members. In contrast to the mechanised craft, the crews seldom involve close relatives except in the six cases where men are teaching their brothers' sons to fish.

7 There is a considerable difference in the effective range of individual craft, with the craft manned by younger crews often fishing more than two miles further away from the beach than the older men. This is not so much due to the superior fitness of the younger men, but is rather a consequence of the younger men not having other occupations during the day and also fishing on fewer nights. One method of improving 'bible' fishing is by the provision for mechanised craft but the *oru* are not suitable for outboard motors and mechanised craft suitable for inshore fishing are estimated to cost Rs.17,000 (Administration Report, Director of Fisheries, 1969) and would have to be financed by the government.

8 Defined as three or more times per week.

9 Seventeen of the men have no other income except for occasional labouring work for the beachseine fishermen or the traders, eight have regular employment as 'hired men' on the beachseines, and eight own one or two beachseine shares.

10 My data on inshore fishing is unsatisfactory. When I began collecting systematic data I was not aware of the distinction between the two groups of inshore fishermen and thus my sample of seven craft comprises only regular fishermen. When I realised what was happening, I was able to collect data for three of

the additional craft and data were provided by the fish trader (see Chapter 8) who bought the bulk of the catch during the flush season. But my account of inshore fishing rests on a less secure base than that of the beachseines or the mechanised craft.

11 The Administration Reports of the Director of Fisheries indicate that between 1960 and 1969, landings of the main varieties of fish taken by the beachseines and the 'bible' fell by 27 per cent. The main reason for the decrease was undoubtedly the transformation of beachseine sites into mechanised boat anchorages, but it does indicate that the 'bible' did not increase the total landings.

12 See the Administration Report (1960:159), which shows that in most cases the catches were less than double those of traditional craft. In Mirissa 910 landings were recorded for an average catch of 26 lbs.; Negombo, 1,647:44; Tangalla, 658:79. The best catches were Hikkaduwa, 25:282 and Pt.Pedro, 26:332, but in both cases the total number of recorded landings was very low.

13 In 1969 the loan limit was raised to Rs.20,000, but by then the cost of a fully equipped craft was Rs.30,000.

14 In most cases the fisherman had less than five days' instruction before taking over his boat. The school run by the fisheries department to educate fishermen in new methods graduated only thirty fishermen per year.

15 Zoeteweij (Turvey and Wiseman 1957:18-41) argues that the widespread use of the share system of remuneration in the fishing industry throughout the world is related to the small scale of the industry and the high degree of uncertainty involved. If labour costs were fixed, a period of poor catches would put small firms out of business. He also notes that the crew's share is usually high - for example 60 per cent of the net catch in the USA and 36 per cent of the gross catch in Norway - and that the percentage given to the crew appears to remain stable over long periods of time and is not related to the amount of capital invested. For example, the crew's share in the Norwegian fishing industry has remained relatively unaltered since 1895. Zoeteweij suggests that the share system may discourage new investment in technological advances because the

increased income must be shared with the crew. This point may have some relevance in the southern division where the owners are reluctant to buy more than one type of net.

16 Additional data for thirty-three craft operating from three other harbours are given in Alexander (1972). The Gahavälla craft have better operating results than these craft and appear to be among the most successful in the Southern Division. Four had catches exceeding Rs.30,000 for the year; the biggest catch was Rs. 36,000, the lowest Rs.16,000. The performance of the cooperative craft is so bad that they were not included in the table: the catch of the most successful was only Rs.5,000.

17 The system of 'tied' boats is found throughout Indo-Pacific fisheries, (cf.FAO 1960) but studies by economists have tended to misinterpret the system. In describing the advance payment as a loan they have committed themselves to finding some sort of payment that could be described as an interest charge and this has often resulted in assertions that are not confirmed by the empirical data. For example, FAO (1962:68) states, 'In Hong Kong the middleman takes a commission of generally between two and three per cent of the value of the catch sold where no debt is outstanding, but a commission of six to nine per cent where a loan is in existence.' The study on which this statement is based (FAO 1960), however, presents no evidence in support of the view that the size of the commission was increased where the fisherman was indebted. On the basis of the empirical data in the report, it can be inferred that the trader-fisherman relationship in Hong Kong is similar to the one described in this paper and that the size of the commission may decrease when the fisherman has a stable relationship with the trader. As in Sri Lanka, the reason that the trader attempts to keep the fisherman indebted is not to earn money from interest charges, but to ensure a regular supply of fish.

18 The fishermen place a very high value on modern housing and this is invariably the first investment made out of increased earnings. A completed house will cost at least Rs.10,000 and because of the high cost of land (exceeding Rs.5,000 per acre in some cases) and the reluctance of owners to sell in any case, the

house will probably be built on a unit of land in which the owner has inherited a share along with his siblings and often his parents' siblings' children. The houses are built in stages with the materials purchased out of current income and it is unusual for a house to be completed in less than five years. At the end of three years' fishing the mechanised boat owner may have the foundations or part of the walls completed, but will have no money to purchase further materials and will be forced to finish the house with wattle and daub walls and a thatched roof. As houses on undivided land are virtually unsaleable and it is very difficult to raise mortgage money, it is not practicable for the *mudalali* to force the fisherman to sell the house to repay the balance of the loan.

19 De Silva (1964) estimated the number of males engaged in fishing in the southern division for 1958 as 10,517. Of these 47 per cent (4,732) were engaged in deep-sea fishing for at least part of the year. In the 1950 (Administration Reports 1940-50) census of fishing gear, 1,124 sea-going *oru* were listed. Assuming that each had a crew of four this would give 4,496 deep-sea fishermen at that time. However, MacDonald (1954) claims that only 476 of the large deep-sea *orua* were actually engaged in fishing in 1958, giving a total of 1,904-2,856 men employed in deep-sea fishing at that time.

20 In Table 5.5 the figure for the number of men engaged includes both men who work the gear and men whose income is derived solely from gear operated by others. Seven Gahavälla men get the majority of their income from mechanised boats owned by them and operated by others, and approximately seventy men and women from Gahavälla and elsewhere derive income from beachseines which they do not operate themselves. All forty-seven men associated with the mechanised craft are employed full-time but thirty-seven of the 'bible' fishermen also participate in beachseine fishing. Only about 180 of the 274 men employed on the beachseines get the major part of their income from these nets.

Chapter 6

1 The report demonstrates that fishing by Indian immigrants on the Sri Lanka coast was highly organised by 1863. The customs reports show nearly £1,000 worth of gear imported each year, equivalent to 40 *nuldell*. Witnesses claimed that at the height of the season, more than 1,000 Indian fishermen were based on Colombo alone and many more were fishing to the north and south of the capital. Indian traders controlled the main fish market in Colombo and Indian temple committees appointed agents to collect temple levies on fish caught in Sri Lanka waters (see Wright 1868).

2 Larger nets have been reported for other areas of the island (Canagaratnam and Medcof 1956), and this should be kept in mind when labour requirements are discussed.

3 This is not an unusual occurrence. Thirteen nets have been burned over the past five years, including four during the fieldwork period, and only four have been replaced. During a high tide in 1971 five nets were washed out to sea, but all were recovered without serious damage.

4 For a short period in 1971 two other small *madell* were operating on either side of the main fishing stations.

5 An analysis of the species composition of a sample of *madella* catches can be found in Canagaratnam and Medcof (1956).

6 A very poor village east of Tangalla is situated on a turtle spawning ground and the people living there catch turtles for sale to Tamil traders from Jaffna. But although many Gahavälla people relish turtle eggs, they would not sell turtles for slaughter.

7 It is very rare for a crew to miss a shoal once they have set out after it. I witnessed only one occasion and in this case the *marrakalai*, frightened that the net might drift onto the rocks, was less than determined in his attempt.

8 The harness is ten to fifteen strands of coir wrapped around the waist and twisted into the wings of the net. This puts the weight on the hips and legs and considerably increases the effectiveness of the hauling operation. It is the use of the harness that distinguishes the regular net crew from casual helpers.

9 The reason for the disparity is that six of the crew members were also members of the crew of another net used later in the day.

10 Annual catches for each net are given in Appendix 2.

11 Joy (1967:32) makes a similar point when he directs attention to the 'insurance' value of many apparently odd institutional practices.

Chapter 7

1 The view that closer ties between fishing sites and the centralised market often precipitated the demise of shareownership, is supported by Stirrat's account of beachseining in the northwest coast village of Demelagama (1975:159).

2 *Pangu* is the usual term for shares in a wet rice field and supports the view that the beachseine share system was derived from agriculture (cf. Obeyesekere 1967).

3 This procedure cuts both ways, one old man boasted to me that he received more than the ruling rate for all his shares by threatening to sell them to a man whom most villagers regard as a loafer and a drunkard.

4 These lists are deposited in the local District Revenue Office and I was able to copy the complete lists from 1964 and 1971 and the changes in registrations for the same period. The earlier shareholders' lists from Gahavälla are no longer extant, but I had access to the notebooks kept by a man who was *Patabändi Arrachi* between 1933 and 1957 in which are recorded the number of nets for some years, as well as valuable, if unsystematic information on the number of shares owned by particular individuals at various points in the past. As this information was usually recorded in the context of disputes over shares, I have not placed much weight on its veracity and have mainly used it to cross-check data gathered from informants.

5 For an example of this ceremony see Deraniyagala (1959).

6 As with many aspects of culture the procedures are easier to follow than describe. In theory, Gahavälla procedures are codified in a government gazette in

1938 (see Appendix 5) but the anonymous author clearly had difficulty in understanding the system and his account is inoperable.

7 The division between the two fishing stations is marked by a clump of trees. When the nets are launched, the *varaya* craft begins laying its net along the *varaya galaha* boundary, while the *galaha* net begins net-laying along the northern boundary of the *galaha patte*. As both the wind and the tide tend to move the nets from south to north, but the northern drift of the *varaya* net is restricted by a large area of submerged rocks, both nets are usually beached in the centre of the *varaya patte* (see Map 3).

8 'Theoretically, then, the original "owner" of any *gama* is its founding ancestor... At his death his sons would inherit the patrimonial estate equally, but there is no physical partitioning of the estate... The characteristic of *pangu* is that like stock market shares they are not "fixed" or attached to any single area of property or land; the shares are "floating". Thus a descendant who works a share does not work a fixed partitioned area of the estate; rather he works on a rotation basis, so that every year he moves to a new area, till the whole length of the field is covered. This is based on the equalitarian ideology governing the concept of shares or *pangu*: one has shares in the *gama* as a whole hence one must have access through a period of years to the total area of land, ensuring an equitable distribution of both fertile and infertile land among the respective shareholders.' (Obeyesekere 1967:18. cf. Leach 1961; Codrington 1938; Pieris 1956).

9 My data support this view. In cycle two the first turn on the harbour side was the largest on 83 per cent of days.

10 Because the 'helpers' do not use the net harness, their labour contribution is individually much less than the regular net crew over the same period.

11 G.A.P. Charlis sold a share to J.A. Podisingho in 1970 on the condition that he be allowed to work the share, and because of this proviso received only Rs.125. In 1971 a man who was to be married to J.A. Podinsingho's daughter was charged with murder and G.A.P. Charlis' son gave evidence against him. The charge was

dismissed, but when Charlis next attempted to work the share, he was assaulted by members of the J.A. (Sunil Mudalali's) faction and lost the use of the share. This is an unusually clear-cut case, but other men have lost work because of similar disputes.

12 The shortage of Rs.618 was mainly due to the failure of one small fish buyer who had bought six boxes at Rs.100 each. After selling the fish at a loss, he was knocked off his cycle and robbed when he passed through a neighbouring village. Eventually his father, who owned a share in the net, gave the other shareholders Rs.25 each in settlement of the debt. See Appendix 4.

13 The agricultural comparison is with wet rice agriculture. Some forms of agriculture, especially swiddens, are much closer to the fishing situation, while some forms of fishing such as the use of large fishing platforms in tidal estuaries have economic structures identical to agriculture. Moreover some variants of rice production, tank agriculture in the dry zone of Sri Lanka (Brow 1976) for example, also involve high degrees of risk.

14 In this limited sense one aspect of the common property resource problem, the dissipation of economic rent, is more severe in a peasant economy. As Stirrat (1975:157) points out, if there is no differentiation between owners and workers then continued effort will take place at rates of return far lower than needed to attract a capitalist, for the opportunity cost of labour is treated as if it is zero.

Chapter 8

1 This is a simplified description of the relationship between market agents and retail traders. The market agent may sell the fish to the retail trader, fix a price and allow the retailer to keep any profit, or pass the fish to the retail trader to sell on a commission basis.

2 The problems of gathering material on this aspect of marketing are considerable, for short of following the traders around, it is impossible to gather accurate quantitative data. I paid one man, who is generally regarded as the most successful bicycle trader, to

keep a diary for six months (July to December). His total direct purchases during the 187 days amounts to Rs.1,637, and he was able to buy more than Rs.5 worth of fish on 113 days. Profits were Rs.278, an average profit of 17 per cent. In addition, he received Rs. 421 for selling fish on behalf of the *mudalali*. The fish returned a profit of 31 per cent, two-thirds of which went to the *mudalali*.

3 In view of the variation in the size of the boxes, all my data are based on the value of the catch rather than the weight of the fish. Where weights are given they are based on the estimate that the average box holds one hundredweight of fish. The variation in box size has also severely hampered my discussion of prices, especially price fluctuations.

4 The exception occurred when the established *mudalali* pushed up the price in an endeavour to drive a newcomer out of the market. I estimate that the intruder paid Rs.150 per box for four boxes, more than twice the ruling price at the time.

5 For the reasons discussed earlier, it is difficult to give quantitative data on fish prices, but the *hāl mässa* sold between August 1970 and February 1971 averaged Rs.32.50 per box. After the 'insurrection' in April 1971, the average price rose to more than Rs.60 per box.

6 The lower unit price for catches in the 100 to 250 pound range is not solely due to a lack of effective sanctions on the part of the fishermen, for the *mudalali's* marketing costs are also higher for these catches. Two or three catches of this size will glut the section of the local market served by the bicycle traders and the fish will have to be sent in a nearly empty van to the more distant towns. The *mudalali* cannot delay in the hope of filling the van, because the main sale advantage of the beachseine catch is that the fish are landed alive and undamaged. When they are kept for more than six hours, the fish begin to decompose, and the retail price drops accordingly.

7 The figures in this paragraph should be regarded as illustrative, not exact data. The account is based on a statistical analysis of catches, but for reasons mentioned earlier, the figures are subject to considerable margins of error. My observations suggest that the boxes sold at low prices during the flush

period, usually contain more fish, so the fluctuations are greater than the figures indicate.

8 This discussion is based almost solely on informants' statements, for I was not able to record systematically the percentage of the bidding price that was actually received, nor when the proceeds were actually paid. However, all eleven of the distribution meetings I witnessed were held more than three months after the sale and in each case the reason was that the traders had just paid for the fish.

9 It seems likely, however, that several of Sunil's *kattiya* were responsible for burning Danny Wijenaike's nets; an incident that led to the killing of M.A. David's mother-in-law.

Chapter 9

1 The data for this account of nineteenth century settlement is derived from a number of sources of which the most important are: Administration Reports, Government Agents, Hambantota and Matara; Administration Reports, District Judge, Tangalla; Birth, Marriage and Land Records, Tangalla; Final Village Plan and Register of Settlements, Gahavälla, Sinimodera, Kudawellekele, and Nakulagamuwa; Census Reports 1824, 1871, 1891, 1901; Partition Cases Nos.422, 462, 673, 692, 786, 787, Tangalla Court.

2 Population figures for all three villages between 1871 and 1970 are given in Table 9.1. Moraketiara was included in the Gahavälla figures until 1891.

3 My use of *pelapata* here connotes only that the people concerned bear the same patronymic (see Chapter 5).

4 *Chena* is usually defined as shifting cultivation, but in modern parlance it is used for all agriculture other than paddy, tree crops and plantations. It is used in this sense here. Shifting cultivation of dry grain cannot have been possible after the turn of the century, but permanent cultivation of small patches of dry grain was found until 1950.

5 These figures are based on census categories and give a misleadingly high figure for the population growth. The area covered by Gahavälla and Moraketiara in the 1901 census was not identical with the combined Moraketiara-Gahavälla village in the 1891 census. Part of what

was previously Kudawellekele was included in Gahavälla and part of Sinimodera was included in Moraketiara. As it is not possible to establish the precise effect this had on the population figures, I have left the figures as they stand. It is clear that Gahavälla did grow considerably between 1891 and 1901, but the rate was probably closer to that of the 1901-1911 period (25 per cent) than the rate given in the text.

6 As this was her first marriage it suggests that the actual marriage was at least ten years earlier.

7 The actual figures were: 1869-1894 - No. of marriages = 53. Intra-village = 19. Virilocal = 28. Uxorilocal = 2. Unknown = 4. 1895-1905 - No. of marriages = 76. Intra-village = 38. Virilocal = 11. Uxorilocal = 26. Unknown = 1.
The data from the registry is supported by the genealogies I collected. Unlike some other areas of Sri Lanka (Leach 1961) registration of marriages and births has been common in Gahavälla since 1869. It is true that poor families did not register their marriages, but during this period the beachseine fishermen were among the richer peasants.

8 Although there were special circumstances in Garuhamy's case, the planting of tree crops in areas previously used for paddy or *chena* cultivation was common among landlords. Not only did tree crops require considerably less labour and less supervision, but the return per acre appears to have been higher. On the basis of the data in the Government Agent's (Hambantota) Report for 1903 (24 bushels per acre for paddy, 16 bushels per acre for *kurakkan* (millet), 3,000 nuts per acre for coconuts) the value of production per acre of paddy was Rs.35, as opposed to Rs.25 for *kurakkan* and more than Rs.90 per acre for coconut.

9 For example Garuhamy's purchases in 1906 were 4/35, 1/7, 1/3, 1/16, 1/4, 3/28, shares in parcels of land which in no case exceeded a quarter acre.

10 This is a necessarily brief and simplified account of a complicated topic. For a more detailed discussion see Obeyesekere (1967:98 143); Haley (1923); Jayawardene (1925).

11 Obeyesekere (1967:103) suggests that the minimum area which will give a subsistence living from paddy is an acre. The main *chena* crop was millet which gave slightly lower yields than paddy.

12 Eighteen acres of Crown land were sold between 1914 and 1920 and the remaining ten acres were sold as house sites between 1948 and 1964.

13 An important factor influencing population growth later in this period was the control of malaria. I have not been able to establish when malaria ceased to be a danger in Gahavälla, but the informants claim that prior to 1930 many people died from this disease. The lagoon and coir-soaking pits must have been a prolific breeding ground for mosquitoes.

14 Although a full discussion of the topic would be out of place here it is worth noting that the concept of the dual economy, which is of very limited value in any context, is particularly inapplicable to the coastal area. As early as 1910 much of the income of the coastal villages was derived from the production of coconut products for the world market and much of the rice consumed in the village was imported from other colonies. Living conditions in the villages were, even at this early stage, partly a function of world prices. The Report of the Government Agent, Galle, for 1919 gives a full description of the way in which the war diminished living standards of people in his district and remarks that they did not seem highly enthused by the reports of victories!

15 The account of the legislation given here is that which was accepted by the community at the time. In fact, although the legislation limited the number of nets, it did not limit the nets to those in actual use in 1933. If an excessive number of nets were presented for registration in any one year, a ballot was to be held, and the nets eliminated were to be the first registered in the succeeding year. Thus the legislation limited the number of nets to be used in any year, but it did not limit the number of nets that might be constructed. Until 1964, however, the fishermen believed that the legislation provided that only the nets used in 1933 were to be registered in succeeding years (see pp.222).

16 This does not mean 208 Gahavälla households. Many *madell* fishermen lived in Moraketiara and Sinimodera, both men who had married Gahavälla women and descendants of Gahavälla men who had settled in these villages.

17 Assuming that the nets were being used on all occasions

in 1920. There is some evidence from earlier periods (see Chapter 5) that gear was under-employed because of lack of markets, but informants claim that by 1920 the *madella* nets were used whenever possible.

Chapter 10

1 Further support for this argument can be derived from an examination of the registration lists from other beachseines *padu* which were as isolated as Gahavälla prior to 1940. Suriyagahawelle, a small beach which could only be used during the six months of the north-east monsoon, had seventeen nets when it was abandoned in 1965. Nilwelle, a village equal in size and isolation to Gahavälla, had forty-seven nets when the harbour was taken over as a mechanised boat anchorage in 1968. Both these *padu* were only large enough for one net at a time to be used. Tangalla, a much less isolated site, but one which was still cut off from the heavily populated southwest coast market before the Matara ice factory was built in 1940, had 139 *madell* operating in three *padu* when a co-operative was formed in 1937. By 1968, the co-operative had collapsed and the twenty-two nets were owned by sixteen men.

2 The dispute concerned land owned by Rossiappu's father. Rossiappu wanted to build a house and, dissatisfied with the site allocated in the family compound, forced a partition case. As the land had been jointly held by Rossiappu's father and three of Rossiappu's father's siblings, more than forty-five households were involved in the case which lasted for eight years. In the final decree Rossiappu was given 1,440/40,320 of the land (less than 1/32 of an acre) plus 36/50 of a coconut tree (Case No.692, Tangalla Court).

3 W.G. Sammiappu is David Mahattea's father-in-law.

4 Although there were more than thirty eye witnesses, only six men, all of whom were Nicholas' kinsmen, gave evidence against Sunil and it is very doubtful that more than two of them had witnessed the events. Sunil claims that he was acquitted because his father had bribed the local medical officer to give false evidence, but a more likely explanation is that pros-

ecution witnesses giving false evidence broke down under cross-examination. The transcript of the court proceedings was missing from the court records.

5 Informants were asked to list the names of nets in which they had ever owned shares, the details of the acquisition and/or disposal of these shares, including the dates and prices paid, and accounts of any mortgage or hire arrangements. The ability to give detailed accounts of share transactions which Obeyesekere (1967:184) reports with respect to land sales in Madagama, was also clearly apparent here.

6 A comparison of the 1964 and 1971 shareholders' lists indicate at least 148 share transfers between 1964 and 1971, but Table 10.2 gives details of only forty-one. The table, however, lists only sales for which the respondent was willing to give a price. I recorded a further forty-two sales between 1965 and 1971 for which no price could be elicited and the total of eighty-three sales is probably accurate, given the truncated sample.

7 There are differences in the real value of shares; some nets are in poor repair, others do not have their own net-laying craft or have a craft that will soon need to be replaced, and so on. But while the fishermen acknowledge these points when questioned, they do not use them in bargaining over prices. The only factor mentioned in bargaining, is the remaining shareholders. A man will often attempt to have the price lowered on the grounds that the other net crew members are old men who cannot work hard, while men endeavouring to sell shares in a net dominated by a particular faction have a very restricted range of potential buyers.

8 The reason for the increase in the price of *oru* is the introduction of mechanised craft. Today most of the deep-sea *oru* have been replaced by mechanised craft and thus few second-hand *oru* are available for *madella* fishing. In the near future the Gahavälla fishermen will either have to cut the ratio of *oru* to nets still further, or else construct new craft specifically for *madella* fishing. The latter option will increase production costs by at least 25 per cent.

9 David Mahattea told me that the four nets he financed in 1964 cost less than Rs.9,000 in all, including approximately Rs.1,000 for expenses other than con-

struction, such as transport, bribes, liquor, etc.

10 As the new nets were added at the end of the net sequence, the shares of an individual who invested solely in new nets would be grouped closely together, it was thus worthwhile for him to pay a little more so as to spread his shareholdings throughout the sequence.

11 A 'hotel' in Sri Lanka does not usually supply accomodation and corresponds to the English cafe.

12 For a discussion of the Ceylon Fisheries Corporation see Alexander (1972).

13 This is not true of the *Karāva* villages near Colombo such as Negombo, where the elite within the *Karāva* caste are differentiated on hereditary grounds (see Raghavan 1961). But these villages have a much longer period of continuous occupation - more than 400 years.

14 Education is free in the sense that no fees are required even at university level. But ancillary expenses such as books, clothes and transport, as well as keeping the child out of the labour force until he is 20 or older, mean that only the wealthier sections of the rural population can take full advantage of the lack of fees.

Chapter 11

1 The discussion in this section is based on a different set of data from the account of share sales in Chapter 10. Using the shareholders' lists and the changes in registration as a guide, I asked three informants for details of the transactions. In 83 cases the data gained from these informants could be later cross-checked with the property survey and with the exception of the prices, they were in close accord.

2 These are not included in the 148 sales in Table 11.4.

3 Both these cases involved Gahavälla men who married close cross-cousins from interior villages and in effect brought back shares that had left the village through inheritance arrangements in the previous generation. The use of cross-cousin marriage to concolidate shareholdings fragmented by inheritance, is common in agricultural villages (see Tambiah 1965; Leach 1961; Yalman 1967), but these are the only cases

I am aware of in Gahavälla and informants regard them as unusual.

4 'Living outside Gahavälla' must be understood to mean that the individual does not regularly visit Gahavälla Beach, not only that he lives outside the official village boundaries. Many people living in Moraketiara and Sinimodera participate fully in beachseining and own nearly one-fifth of the shares.

5 These men were the fathers of the three faction leaders, and another member of the M.A. *pelapata* (M.A. John) who is a member of David Mahattea's faction. Only one of the 11 largest shareholders in 1971 (David Mahattea's father) is not a member of one of the three factions.

6 My use of the term strategy follows Salisbury (1969: 76)

> a straightforward ethnographic report on a social system of resource allocation (an economy) should contain a number of formal rules about which all informants are agreed, a set of strategy statements (usually of a highly inconsistent nature) often explicitly formulated by numbers of informants as maxims, and enough information about the nature of the game being played to render the different strategies comprehensible.

7 The data in Table 11.5 and 11.6 were derived from Table 6.5 and 6.6. In calculating the estimated revenue, net number one was assigned the average 1970-71 revenue from nets numbers 1-20, net number 21 the average revenue from nets numbers 21-40, etc. This procedure overstates the extent to which incomes can be stabilised in three ways. Firstly, the annual operating results are not solely a function of the position in the net sequence and nets in adjoining positions may differ considerably in revenue (see Appendix 2). Nevertheless, participation in the flush period, which is the major determinant of a successful year, *is* a function of the position in the net sequence. Secondly, because it is based on a single year's sales the table takes no account of annual fluctuations in total beachseine landings; if these fluctuations are substantial and the 1970-71 season was better than average, then the critical size of a viable shareholding is greater than indicated below. As there are no data on fluctuations in

annual landings, I can only repeat informants' claims that 1970-71 was a slightly poorer year than usual. Thirdly, the table understates the extremely skewed distribution of earnings among the most successful nets. For example, although the average revenue per share for the 20 most successful nets in 1970-71 was Rs.463, revenue from shares in individual nets among the top 20 ranged from Rs.970 to Rs.285. The skewing is much less pronounced in other cohorts, but throughout this chapter 'stabilizing incomes' must be understood in a relative rather than an absolute sense.

8 Cf. Lipton's (1968:333) comment

> Small wonder that farmers chose less risky (if ultimately less 'profitable') procedures. MVPE (marginal value-product equalization) maximizes only in the very long run; yet it shortens the probable run over which the would-be maximizer owns, and hence derives benefit from, his factors of production.

9 This point can be illustrated by reference to Table 11.6. If the five shares were clustered in net number 1 his income over five years would be: Year One, Rs.1,899; Year Two, minus Rs.156; Year Three, Rs.19; Year Four, Rs.324; Year Five, Rs.744.

10 Lipton (1968:335) points out that

> risk premium is an increasing function of risk and a decreasing function of assets. A well-off American farmer can safely prefer a 50-50 chance of $5,000 or $10,000 to a certainty of $7,000 per year. An Indian farmer, offered a 50-50 chance of Rs.X or Rs.1,000 as against a certainty of the Rs.700 a year with which he barely feeds his family, cannot set X too far below Rs.700.

11 Informants' claims that the exchange of shares to give a more equidistant distribution, was common in the decade after 1946, should be noted. P.M. Rossiappu (see Chapter 10) for example, used this tactic to good effect. It has been very rare in the past decade, however; I am aware of only four examples involving a total of ten shares. Exchanges of shares between members of opposing factions to facilitate the grouping of faction holdings in particular nets is more common. There have been at least 16 transactions of this type during the past 10 years.

12 Scott's (1976:25) comment 'I am persuaded that

safety-first behaviour characterizes not only the poorest peasants but much of what is known as the middle peasantry as well' has a particular poignancy in Gahavälla. It is only the middle peasants, and not all of them, who are in a position to follow a safety-first policy.

APPENDIX 1

WEDDING EXPENSES

The wedding expenses for three of the 11 weddings in Gahavälla between April 1970 and March 1971 are presented below. The first are the bride's expenses from the biggest wedding, the second the bride's expenses from the fourth biggest wedding, and the third the groom's expenses from a wedding of similar size to the second.

The bride's father was from a poor family but had become a very successful mechanised boat operator. At the time of the marriage he owned three boats with a nett income of around Rs.10,000 per year. The bridegroom was the son of an equally wealthy mechanised boat owner from the next village. When the bride, who was the eldest daughter, became pregnant she returned to her father's house and an elaborate ceremony was held to ensure the health of her child. The total marriage expenses, including this ceremony and the preliminary visits to the bridegroom's house, exceeded Rs.20,000.

Contributions at the wedding feast, which lasted three days, totalled Rs.4,395 of which the largest contributors were brother Rs.350; father's brother Rs.350; father's wife's sister Rs.300, father's sister Rs.200. The bride's father estimated that the other close kin contributed Rs.2,000, with the average contribution of Rs.50 to Rs.75. The 'house cut' from the gambling at the wedding was about Rs.1,500, but the bride's father lost all but Rs.430 gambling himself.

The father is a *madella* fisherman with seven shares and his wife owns two areas of land, totalling about three-quarters of an acre. Their annual income from all sources is about Rs.2,500. The money for the wedding had been saved over a period of several years and was intended for the marriage of their eldest daughter, a

1. WEDDING EXPENSES (BRIDE'S FAMILY)

Preparations	Rs.	
Poruwa	150	
Dhobi	300	
Repairs to House[a]	1,000	
Hire of Sheds	90	
Hire of Lights, Music	250	
Hire of Cars (10)[b]	500	
Printed Invitations	80	
Astrologer	20	
Broker[c]	100	
		Rs.2,490
Food		
Fish[d]	500	
Rice (10 bags)	840	
Curry Stuffs[e]	1,500	
Vegetables	200	
Curd	600	
Kitul Honey	500	
Cigarettes	1,100	
Betel	100	
Arrack	50	
		Rs.5,390
Dowry		
Cash	2,500	
Almirah	900	
Sewing Machine	1,235	
Jewellery[f]	4,500	
		Rs.9,135

Notes:

[a] Whitewashing the house and building a retaining wall.

[b] In addition the father's *mudalali* lent five cars, a van and all the chairs, crockery and eating utensils.

[c] The bridegroom's family also gave a gift of Rs.100

[d] Estimated sale value. The fish came from is own boats.

[e] Includes biscuits, soft drinks, tea, etc.

[f] Necklace, four bangles, chain and sovereign, earrings, ear studs (2), ring, watch.

2. WEDDING EXPENSES (BRIDE'S FAMILY)

	Rs.	
Preparations		
Clothes	150	
Astrologer	20	
Dhobi	175	
		Rs.345
Food		
Fish	125	
Rice (2 bags)	168	
Vegetables and Curry Stuffs	250	
Plaintains	100	
Biscuits	50	
Curd	150	
Kitul Honey	75	
Cigarettes and Cigars	60	
Betel	40	
		Rs.1,018
Dowry		
Half Share in Land	1,500	
Cash	700	
Jewellery	1,600	
Brass-ware	150	
		Rs.3,950

trained graduate school teacher working near Hambantota. About six weeks before the marriage the daughter eloped with an untrained teacher and her parents decided to spend the money on her younger sister's marriage, which was hurriedly arranged. The speed with which the marriage was arranged and a dispute between the bride's father and some of his relatives over the produce of jointly owned land, seriously affected the marriage gifts. Only Rs.400 was collected in contributions (the biggest was Rs.50) and the gambling cut was less than Rs.100. The mother had to sell her remaining area of land to pay off the marriage expenses' loan.

3. WEDDING EXPENSES (GROOM)

	Rs.	
Visits to Bride		
Car Hire	14	
Presents	35	
Wedding Bride's House		
Car Hire	100	
Presents	300	
Suit	65	
Sarees	44	
Ring	35	
Homecoming		
Curry Stuffs	25	
Dhobi	10	
Rice	60	
Fish	35	
Curd and Honey	80	
Vegetables	40	
Car Hire	50	
		Rs.893

This was a similar wedding to the previous one with a dowry of slightly less than Rs.2,500, all of it in jewellery and furniture. The groom's parents were both deceased and only twenty-three guests attended the homecoming at which the contributions were Rs.127. No gambling was held.

APPENDIX 2

ANNUAL CATCH, INDIVIDUAL NETS

Net No.	No. of Turns	Total Catch	Average Per Turn
1	5	505	101
2	4	403	101
3	6	128	21
4	8	2,244	281
6	8	3,129	391
7	9	1,788	199
8	7	898	128
9	9	874	97
10	8	1,698	212
11	12	2,372	198
12	8	2,922	365
13	10	1,908	191
14	9	2,282	254
15	11	2,419	220
16	12	2,746	229
17	13	2,310	178
18	9	3,943	438
19	10	3,868	387
20	13	5,274	406
21	13	5,451	419
22	14	7,762	554
23	12	6,017	501
24	13	4,878	375
25	14	5,159	369
27	14	3,437	246
28	11	2,745	250
29	11	696	63
31	9	779	87
33	4	1,092	273
34	10	1,053	105
35	7	1,549	221

Net No.	No. of Turns	Total Catch	Average Per Turn
36	5	2,351	470
37	5	930	186
38	7	1,700	229
39	8	586	73
40	10	555	56
41	10	631	63
43	11	678	62
45	7	634	91
46	7	453	50
47	6	109	18
48	8	798	100
49	12	1,967	164
50	10	1,535	154
51	10	1,607	161
52	9	1,711	190
53	10	1,982	198
54	7	1,044	149
55	7	1,246	178
56	8	1,993	249
57	7	730	104
58	10	867	86
60	8	373	47
61	8	842	105
62	8	722	90
63	6	480	80
64	8	535	67
65	7	1,177	168
66	11	974	89
68	8	1,267	158
69	10	1,684	168
70	8	520	65
71	7	790	113
72	6	1,806	301
73	6	752	125
74	7	865	124
75	9	1,692	188
76	6	545	91
78	7	1,645	235
79	7	2,040	291
80	9	1,310	146
81	9	2,281	254
82	9	2,083	231

Net No.	No. of Turns	Total Catch	Average Per Turn
83	8	1,280	160
84	6	1,671	279
85	11	1,097	100
86	8	716	90
87	6	531	89
88	9	716	80
89	8	602	75
90	4	565	141
91	9	1,522	172
94	9	2,298	255
95	7	2,611	373
96	7	1,421	203
97	6	400	67
98	8	1,130	141
99	11	1,451	132
100	8	1,557	195
101	13	1,680	129
102	9	635	71
103	6	285	48
104	4	38	9
105	4	687	172
106	7	638	91
107	6	2,139	357
108	4	406	102

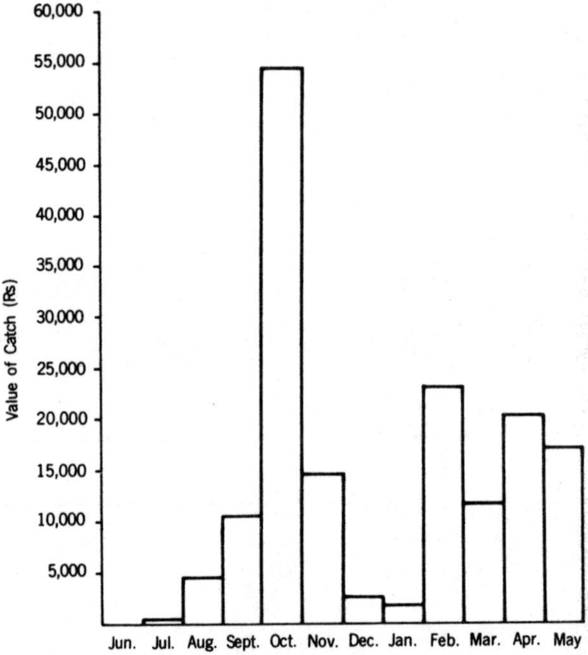

APPENDIX 3: MONTHLY CATCH, MADELL.

APPENDIX 4

DISTRIBUTION OF MADELLA PROCEEDS
FOUR EXAMPLES

	One	Two	Three	Four
	Rs.	Rs.	Rs.	Rs.
Total Proceeds	4,477.0	1,655.0	122.0	390.0
Available for Distribution	4,305.0[a]	1,037.0[c]	83.50[d]	390.0
Expenses Due:				
Debts	39.60[b]	12.30	15.25	2.30[e]
Arrack	12.0			
Wages	15.0	25.0	25.0	15.0
Other				34.25
Expenses Paid	66.60	37.30	Nil	51.55
Amount Paid Per Share	525.0	124.0	10.0	41.0
Secretary's Payment	38.40	7.70	3.50	10.45

[a] The deductions were a 7 per cent cut by one fish trader on the price he bid for the fish (bidding price Rs.77 per hundred, payment received Rs.560 for eight boxes), and Rs.116 due from a bicycle trader who he claimed was unable to pay. When I left eight months later the bicycle trader had still not paid.

[b] This is for two cycles as some of the previous debts had not been paid.

[c] This was the division referred to in the text where the buyer had been robbed of the proceeds. Eventually his father, who was one of the crew members, gave Rs.25 to each of the net crew and Rs.5 to the secretary in

settlement of the debt, because the secretary threatened to deduct the sum due from the father's share of future catches.

[d] This represents five hauls but only one gave enough fish to sell. Two boxes were sold to a fish trader for Rs.80 and the rest were sold in small amounts to people in the village. Of the Rs.42 due from these small sales less than 10 per cent was actually paid. Because of the small sums available for distribution it was decided to carry over the expenses to the next cycle.

[e] Only one haul was made in this cycle. The Rs.2.30 is payment for a meal that the two net stackers had eaten after restacking the net. Some of the shareholders wanted to refuse to pay for the meal, but the net stackers were members of the Wijenaike group who owned three shares in the net and Danny Wijenaike insisted that both the cost of the meal and the wage be paid. The other shareholders had little choice but to acquiesce.

APPENDIX 5

EXTRACT FROM GOVERNMENT GAZETTE NO.8417 (2/12/1938) CONCERNING BEACHSEINE ACCESS RIGHTS AT [GAHAVÄLLA] BEACH

[GAHAVÄLLA] WARAYA Duration of terms (Subject to the Provision of regulation 18).

Morning: 6 a.m. to Noon.

Afternoon: September to January (inclusive) Noon to 6 p.m. February to August (inclusive) Noon on any day to 4 a.m. on the following day.

ORDER OF TURNS: In that position of the Waraya which is known as 'Waraya' the First Madella or Hanadela on the register shall take the first afternoon turn and the morning turn immediately succeeding it, the second net on the register taking the next afternoon turn and the morning turn immediately succeeding it and so on.

In that portion of the Waraya which is known as 'Galaha' the morning turn is taken by the Madella or Hanadela which had the morning turn in 'Galaha' on the previous day.

TABLE REFERRED TO

NET	SUN		MON		TUES		WED		THURS		FRI		SAT	
	am.	pm	am.	pm	am.	pm	am.	pm	am.	pm	am.	pm	am.	pm
1	a	a	a	a		a								
	b	w	w		g			g						
2				w	w		g			g				
3						w	w		g			g		
4									w		g			g
5										w	w		g	
6												w	w	b

W - Denotes 'in Waraya'
G - Denotes 'in Galaha'

(a) & (b), the other nets in Galaha and Waraya respectively are outside the series of nets shown in the table.

Explanation

A Madella or Hanadela gets two turns in succession commencing with the afternoon turn in 'Waraya'. It then misses the other afternoon turn and gets the next morning turn in 'Galaha'. It then misses two turns and gets the next afternoon turn in 'Galaha' after which it waits for its turn in 'Waraya' to come round again.

Example

For the morning turn on the 4th day (the 6th turn of the season) No.3 Net fishes in 'Waraya' (where it had also fished the previous afternoon). No.2 Net which had the morning turn in 'Waraya' preceding No.3 fishes in 'Galaha'; in the afternoon No.4 fishes in 'Waraya' and No.1 which last had the morning turn in 'Galaha' on the preceding day, fishes in 'Galaha'. On the 5th day No.4 fishes in 'Waraya', No.3 in 'Galaha' in the morning; No.5 in 'Waraya' and No.2 in 'Galaha' in the afternoon.

REFERENCES

Abahayaratne, O.E.R. & C.H.S. Jayewardene
1967 *Fertility Trends in Ceylon*, Colombo Apothecaries Ltd., Colombo.

Alavi, H.
1973 'Peasant Classes and Primordial Loyalties' *Journal of Peasant Studies*, 1:22-62.

Alexander, P.
1975a 'Innovation in a Cultural Vacuum', *Human Organization* 34:333-44.
1975b 'Do Fisheries Experts Aid Fisheries Development?', *Maritime Studies and Management* 3:5-11.
1976 'The Modernization of Peasant Fisheries in Sri Lanka' in D. Johnston (ed.) *Marine Policy and the Coastal Community*, Croom Helm Ltd., London.
1977 'Sea Tenure in Southern Sri Lanka', *Ethnology* 16:231-51.
1979 'Malu Mudalali: Monopsonies in Southern Sri Lankan Fish Trading', *Social Analysis* 2:3-17.

Ames, M.
1961 'Ideology and Social Change in Ceylon', *Human Organization* 22:45-53.
1964 'Magical-animism and Buddhism: A Structural Analysis of the Sinhalese Religious System' in E.B. Harper (ed.) *Religion in South Asia*, University of Washington Press, Seattle.

Anon
1922 *Report of the Industries Commission*, Sessional Paper No.1, Appendix C: Fisheries.

Anthonisz
1929 *The Dutch in Ceylon: An Account of their Early Visits to the Island, their Conquests and their Rule over the Maritime Provinces during a Century and a Half*, Colombo Apothecaries Ltd., Colombo.

Arasaratnam, S.
1958 *Dutch Power in Ceylon (1658-1687)*, Djambatan, Amsterdam.

Ariyapala, M.B.
1956 *Society in Mediaeval Ceylon*, Department of Cultural Affairs, Colombo.

Aronoff, J.
1967 *Psychological Needs and Cultural Systems*, Van Nostrand, New Jersey.

Arunachalam, P.
1902 *Census of Ceylon 1901*, Government Printer, Colombo.

Bailey, F.G.
1969 *Stratagems and Spoils: A Social Anthropology of Politics*, Blackwell, Oxford.

Barth, F. (ed.)
1963 *The Role of the Entrepreneur in Social Change in Northern Norway*, Norwegian University Press, Oslo.

Bergman, N.
1827 *Census of Ceylon*, Government Press, Colombo.

Beverton, R.J.H. & S.J. Holt
1956 'The Theory of Fishing' in M. Graham (ed.) *Sea Fisheries*, Edward Arnold, London.
1957 *On the Dynamics of Exploited Fish Populations*, H.M.S.O., London.

Blake, B.
1970 'Technological Change among the Coastal Marine Fishermen of Madras State', Ph.D. Dissertation, University of Wisconsin.

Bottemanne, C.J.
1959 *Principles of Fisheries Development*, North Holland Publishing Co., Amsterdam.

Brohier, R.L.
1929 'Vestiges of Dutch Occupation in the Hambantota District', *Journal of Dutch Burgher Union of Ceylon*, 18:164-72;

Brow, J.
1976 'The Impact of Population Growth on the Agricultural Practices and Settlement Patterns of the Anuradhapura Veddahs'. *Contributions to Asian Studies* 9:80-96.

Canagaratnam, P.
1965 'Coastal Fisheries', *Bulletin of the Fisheries Research Station, Ceylon* 18:53-58.

Canagaratnam, P. & J.C. Medcof
1956 'Ceylon's Beachseine Fishing', *Bulletin of the Fisheries Research Station, Ceylon* 4.

Cancian, F.
1965 *Economics and Prestige in a Maya Community: The Religious Cargo System in Zinacantan*, Stanford University Press, Stanford.
1972 *Change and Uncertainty in a Peasant Community*, Stanford University Press, Stanford.

Carter, C.
1965 *Sinhalese-English, English-Sinhalese Dictionary*, 2 vols., 2 edition, Gunasena and Co., Colombo.

Central Bank
1964 *Survey of Ceylon's Consumer Finances, 1963*, Central Bank of Ceylon, Colombo.

Ceylon Fisheries Corporation
1965 *Draft Ten Year Plan for the Development of the Fishing Industry*, Ceylon Government Press, Colombo.

Christy, F.T. & A. Scott
1965 *The Common Wealth in Ocean Fisheries: Some Problems of Growth and Economic Allocation*, Johns Hopkins Press, Baltimore.

Codrington, H.W.
1938 *Ancient Land Tenure and Revenue in Ceylon*, Ceylon Government Press, Colombo.

Cordell, J.C.
1978 'Carrying Capacity Analysis of Fixed-Territorial Fishing'. *Ethnology* 17:1-24.

Crutchfield, J.A. (ed.)
1959 *Biological and Economic Aspects of Fisheries Management*, University of Washington, Seattle.

Davenport, W.
1960 'Jamaican Fishing: A Game Theory Analysis', *Yale University Publications in Anthropology* 59:3-11.

David, K.
1973 'Spatial Organization and Normative Schemes in Jaffna, Northern Sri Lanka', *Modern Ceylon Studies* 4:21-52.

1974 'Hierarchy and Equivalence in Ceylon' in K. David (ed.) *The New Wind: Changing Identities in South Asia,* Mouton, The Hague.

Denham, E.B.
1912 *Ceylon at the Census of 1911,* Government Printer, Colombo.

Deraniyagala, P.E.P.
1932 'The Fisheries of Ceylon', *Journal of the Ceylon Economic Society* 4:35-44.
1959 *Some Sinhala Combative, Field and Aquatic Sports and Games,* National Museum of Ceylon, Colombo.

Devereux, G.
1967 *From Anxiety to Method in the Behavioural Sciences,* Mouton, The Hague.

Dixon, R.B.
1971 'Explaining Cross-Cultural Variations in Age at Marriage and Proportions Never Marrying', *Population Studies* 25:215-233.

Driver, H.E. & K.F. Schuessler
1967 'Correlation Analysis of Murdock's 1956 Ethnographic Sample', *American Anthropologist* 69:332-52.

Epstein, T.S.
1962 *Economic Development and Social Change in South India,* Manchester University Press, Manchester.
1967 'Productive Efficiency and Customary Systems of Rewards in Rural South India' in Raymond Firth (ed.) *Themes in Economic Anthropology,* Tavistock Press, London. pp.229-52.

Fairbanks, G.H., J.W. Gair & M.W.S. De Silva
1968 *Colloquial Sinhalese,* South Asia Programme, Cornell University Press, Ithaca, New York.

Food & Agriculture Organization
1960 *The Economic Role of Middlemen and Cooperatives in Indo-Pacific Fisheries,* FAO, Rome.
1962 *Financial Assistance Policies and Administration for Fisheries Industries,* FAO, Rome.

Food & Agriculture Organization and International Bank for Reconstruction & Development

1967 *Draft Report of the Fisheries Project Preparation Mission to Ceylon*, Ministry of Planning and Economic Affairs, Colombo.

Faris, J.C.

1966 'Cat Habour: A Newfoundland Fishing Settlement', *Newfoundland Social and Economic Studies*, No.3, St.John.

Farmer, B.

1957 *Pioneer Peasant Cultivation in Ceylon*, Cambridge University Press, London.

Firth, R.

1966 *Malay Fishermen*, (2nd edition) Routledge and Kegan Paul, London.

1969 'Social Structure and Peasant Economy: The Influence of Social Structure upon Peasant Economies' in C.R. Wharton (ed.) *Subsistence Agriculture and Economic Development*, Aldine, Chicago, pp.23-37.

1972 'Methodological Issues in Economic Anthropology', *Man* 7:467-75.

Firth, R. & B.S. Yamey (eds)

1964 *Capital, Savings and Credit in Peasant Societies*, George Allen and Unwin, London.

Fish Sales Union

1942-63 *Annual Reports*, Colombo (Mimeo).

Forman, S.

1971 *The Raft Fishermen*, Indiana University Press, Indiana.

Fraser, T.M.

1962 *Rusembilan, a Malay Fishing Village in South Thailand*, Cornell Studies in Anthropology, Cornell University Press, Ithaca, New York.

Geertz, C.

1963 *Agricultural Involution: The Process of Ecological Change in Indonesia*, University of California Press, Berkeley.

Gladwin, H.

1970 'Decision Making in the Cape Coast Fishing and Fish System', Ph.D. Dissertation, Stanford University, Stanford.

Glanville, A.
1954 'A Report to the Government of Ceylon on the Mechanization of Fishing Operations', *FAO Report No.284:*1-24, Rome.

Goonetilike, H.A.I.
1970 *A Bibliography of Ceylon,* vol.1-2.3, Inter-documentation Company, Switzerland.

Gordon, H.S.
1954 'The Economic Theory of a Common-Property Resource: The Fishery', *Journal of Political Economy* 62:124-42.

Gunasinghe, N.
1975 'Production Relations and Classes in a Kandyan Village', *Modern Ceylon Studies* 6:116-39.

Haley, F.A.
1923 *A Treatise on the Laws and Customs of the Sinhalese,* H.W. Cave, Colombo.

Hardin, G.
1968 'The Tragedy of the Commons', *Science* 162: 1243-8.

Hickling, C.F, *et al.*
1951 *Ceylon Fisheries: Recommendations of Experts on Fisheries Development, Research, Socio-Economic and Industrial Problems,* Sessional Paper No.6, 1951, Government Press, Ceylon.

Hill, P.
1970 *Rural Capitalism in West Africa,* Cambridge University Press, London.

International Bank for Reconstruction and Development
1952 *The Economic Development of Ceylon,* Government Press, Colombo.
1960 (?) *Reprint of a Report Prepared by the Mission of International Engineering Consultants Association, Japan,* Government Press, Colombo.

International Labor Organization
1972 *Matching Employment Opportunities and Expectations: A Programme for Ceylon,* ILO, Geneva.

Jayawardene, A. St.V.
1925 *The Law of Partition in Ceylon,* Ceylon Daily News Press, Colombo.

Joachim, A.W.R.
1937 'The Soils of Ceylon', *Tropical Agriculturist* 79:89-92.

Jones, G.W. & S. Selvaratnam
n.d. 'An Analysis of Unemployment Problems in Ceylon, Central Bank, Colombo (Mimeo).

Johnston, D. (ed.)
1976 *Marine Policy and the Coastal Community*, Croom Helm, London.

Joy, L.
1967 'One Economist's View of the Relationship between Economics and Anthropology', in R. Firth (ed.) *Themes in Economic Anthropology*, ASA Monograph No.6, Tavistock, London, pp.29-46.

Kahn, J.S.
1975 'Economic Scale and the Cycle of Petty Commodity Production', in M. Bloch (ed.) *Marxist Analyses and Social Anthropology*, Malaby Press, London.

Kaplinsky, R.
1971 'Myths about the "Revolutionary Proletariat" in Developing Country', *Bulletin, Institute of Development Studies* 3:15-21.

Karunatilike, H.N.S.
1971 *Economic Development in Ceylon*, Praeger, New York.

Kenny, M.
1962 *A Spanish Tapestry: Town and Country in Castile*, University of Indiana Press, Bloomington.

Kirby, E.S. & E.F. Szczepanik
1957 'Special Problems of Fisheries in Poor Countries' in R. Turvey and W. Wiseman, (eds) *The Economics of Fisheries*, FAO, Rome, pp.83-119.

Klausen, A.M.
1961 *Kerala Fishermen and the Indo-Norwegian Pilot Project*, Prior Monographs from the International Peace Research Institute Oslo, Norway: Universitetsforlaget.

Knight, F.
1921 *Risk, Uncertainty and Profits*, Houghton Mifflin, Boston.

Leach, E.R.

1960 'The Sinhalese of the Dry Zone of Northern Ceylon' in G.R. Murdock (ed.) *Social Structure in South East Asia*, Viking Publications in Anthropology, No.29, New York pp.116-26.

1961 *Pul Eliya: A Village in Ceylon*, Cambridge University Press, London.

1967 'An Anthropologist's Reflections on a Social Survey' in D.G. Jongmans & P.W. Gutkind (eds) *Anthropologists in the Field*, Van Gorcum, Assen,pp.75-88.

Lee, L.

1892 *Census of Ceylon 1891*, Government Printer, Colombo.

Le Clair, E.E.

1962 'Economic Theory and Economic Anthropology', *American Anthropologist* 64:1179-1203.

Lipton, M.

1968 'The Theory of the Optimizing Peasant', *Journal of Development Studies* 4:327-51.

1977 *Why Poor People Stay Poor: Urban Bias in World Development*, The Australian National University Press, Canberra.

Macdonald, A.H.

1954 'A Survey of Ceylon Fisheries with Special Emphasis on Co-operatives and Coop. Development', unpublished report to the Department of Fisheries, Ceylon.

Mayer, A.C.

1966 'The Significance of Quasi-Groups in the Study of Complex Societies', in M. Banton (ed.) *The Social Anthropology of Complex Societies*, ASA Monograph 4, Tavistock, London.

Mellor, J.W.

1966 *The Economics of Agricultural Development*, Cornell University Press, Ithaca, New York.

Ministry of Planning and Economic Affairs

1967 *Economic Development 1966-68*, Government Press, Colombo.

Ministry of Planning and Employment

1970 'Employment Programme: Draft Outline', Ministry of Planning and Employment, Colombo.

Moerman, M.
1968 *Agricultural Change and Peasant Choice in a Thai Village*, University of California Press, Berkeley.

Munro, J.S.R.
1955 *The Marine and Fresh Water Fishes of Ceylon*, Department of External Affairs, Canberra.

Needham, R.
1971 'Introduction', in R. Needham (ed.) *Rethinking Kinship and Marriage*, ASA Monograph No.11, Tavistock Press, London.

Newman, P.
1965 *Malaria Eradication and Population Growth: with Special Reference to Ceylon and British Guyana*, University of Michigan Press, Ann Arbor.

Obeyesekere, G.
1958 'The Structure of a Sinhalese Ritual', *Ceylon Journal of Historical and Social Studies*, 1:2-10.
1967 *Land Tenure in Village Ceylon*, Cambridge University Press, London.
1968 Review of Yalman (1967), *American Anthropologist*, 70:790-3.
1974 'Some Comments on the Social Backgrounds of the April 1971 Insurgents in Sri Lanka', *Journal of Asian Studies*, 33:367-84.

Oliver, H.M.
1957 *Economic Development and Public Opinion in Ceylon*, Duke University Press, Durham.

Parsons, T. & N.T. Smelser
1956 *Economy and Society*, Free Press, Glencoe.

Paulusz, J.H.D. (ed. & trans.)
1954 *Secret Minutes of the Dutch Political Council, 1762.* Government Press, Colombo.

Pearson, J.
1923 'Fishing Appliances of Ceylon', *Ceylon Journal of Science Bulletin*, 3:65-134.

Peebles, P.
1976 'Land Use and Population Growth in Colonial Ceylon', *Contributions to Asian Studies*, 9:64-71.

Pieris, R.
1956 *Sinhalese Social Organization*, Ceylon University Press Board, Colombo.

Pitt-Rivers, J.
1954 *The People of the Sierra,* Criterion Books, New York.

Raghavan, M.D.
1961 *The Karava of Ceylon,* K.V.G. De Silva and Sons, Colombo.

Rajapurohit, A.R.
1963 'Business Organization, Caste and Technological Change in a Fishing Community', *Artha Vijnana,* 5:112-32.

Reimers, E.
1925 'Old Matara and the Rebellion of 1760-61', *Journal of the Dutch Burgher Union of Ceylon,* 15:7-14, 59-64, 88-95.

Reimers, E. (trans.)
1950 *The Dutch Parish Registers (School Thombos) of Ceylon. Ambalangoda, Patabendimulla, Welitara and Kosgoda,* Times of Ceylon, Colombo.

Richards, P.J.
1971 *Employment and Unemployment in Ceylon,* Organization for Economic and Cultural Development, Paris.

Roberts, M.
1974 'Problems of Social Stratification and the Demarcation of National and Local Elites in British Ceylon', *Journal of Asian Studies* 23:549-77.
n.d. *Caste Conflict and Elite Formation: The Rise of a Karāva Elite in Sri Lanka 1500-1931.* Cambridge University Press. forthcoming.

Robinson, M.S.
1968 'Some Observations on the Kandyan Sinhalese Kinship System', *Man* 3:402-21.
1975 *Political Structure in a Changing Sinhalese Village,* Cambridge University Press, Cambridge.

Ryan, D.
1953 *Caste in Modern Ceylon,* Rutgers University Press, New Brunswick.
1956 *The Sinhalese Village,* University of Miami Press, Coral Gables.

Salisbury, R.F.
1969 'Formal Analysis in Anthropological Economics: The Rossel Island Case', in Buchler, I.R. and Nutini, H.G. (eds) *Game Theory in the Behavioural Sciences*, University of Pittsburg Press, Pittsburg.

Samarakkody, S.
1941 *Report of a Sub-Committee of the Executive Commissioner of Local Administration of the Fishing Industry*, Sessional Paper No.11 of 1941, Government Press, Ceylon.

Sawyer, J. & R.A. Levine
1966 'Cultural Dimensions: A Factor Analysis of the World Ethnographic Sample', *American Anthropologist*, 68:708-31.

Schultz, T.
1964 *Transforming Tropical Agriculture*, Yale University Press, New Haven.

Scott, A.
1955 'The Fishery: The Objective of Sole Ownership', *Journal of Political Economy*, 63:116-24.

Scott, J.C.
1976 *The Moral Economy of the Peasant: Rebellion and Subsistence in South East Asia*, Yale University Press, New Haven.

Scott, J.S.
1969 'The Analysis of Corruption in Developing Nations', *Comparative Studies in Society and History*, 11:315-41.

Seers, Dudley
1970 *The Meaning of Development*, Agricultural Development Council Reprint, New York.
1972 'New Light on Structural Unemployment: Lessons on a Mission to Ceylon', *International Labor Review* 105:99-108.

Selvadurai, A.J.
1976 'Kinship and Land Rights in the Context of Demographic Change', *Contributions to Asian Studies*, 9:97-112.

Sclvaratnam, S. *et al.*
1970 'Population Projects for Ceylon, 1968-1998', unpublished monograph, Ministry of Planning and Employment, Colombo.

Selvaratnam, S. & L.S. Fernando
1970 'Measurement of the Employed and Unemployed in Ceylon', Ministry of Planning and Employment, Colombo, (Mimeo).

Shanin, T.
1973 'The Nature and Logic of the Peasant Economy' *Journal of Peasant Studies*, 1:63-80, 186-206.

Silva, A.H. De
1919 *The Dutch in Ceylon*, Pearl Press, Dehiwela.

Silva, C.R. De
1953 *Ceylon Under the British Occupation, 1795-1833*, 2 vols., Colombo Apothecaries, Colombo.

Silva, G.N. De
1964 'Socio-economic Survey of Fisher Families 1958-59', *Bulletin of the Fisheries Research Station, Ceylon*, 17:1-44.

Silva, K. De
1977 *Sri Lanka: A Survey*, C. Hurst, London.

Silva, N.N. De
1964 'The Role of Technology in Fisheries Development in Ceylon', *Bulletin of the Fisheries Research Station, Ceylon*, 17:257-65.

Sivasubramaniam, K.
1965 'Exploitation of Tuna in Ceylon's Coastal Waters', *Bulletin of the Fisheries Research Station, Ceylon*, 18:59-74.

Smith, M.E.
1977 'Comments on the Heuristic Utility of Maritime Anthropology', *The Maritime Anthropologist* 1:2-5,8.

Smith, M.E. (ed.)
1977 *Those Who Live from the Sea*, West Publishing Co., New York.

Snodgrass, D.R.
1966 *Ceylon: An Export Economy in Transition*, R.D. Irwin, Homewood.

Stirrat, R.
1973 'Fish to Market: Traders in Rural Sri Lanka', *South Asian Review*, 7:189-207.
1975 (1978) 'The Social Organization of Fishing in a Sinhalese Village', *Modern Ceylon Studies*, 6:140-162.

Stirrat, R.
1977 'Dravidian and Non-Dravidian Kinship Terminologies in Sri Lanka', *Contributions to Indian Sociology*, 11:22-37.

Szanton, D.L.
1971 *Estancia in Transition: Economic Growth in a Rural Philippine Community*, Atenco de Manila University Press, Manila.

Tambiah, H.W.
1968 *Sinhala Laws and Customs*, Lake House Press, Colombo.

Tambiah, S.J.
1958 'The Structure of Kinship and its Relationship to Land Possession and Residence in Pata Dumbara', *Journal of the Royal Anthropological Institute*, 88:21-44.
1965 'Kinship Fact and Fiction in Relation to the Kandyan Sinhalese', *Journal of the Royal Anthropological Institute*, 95:131-73.
1966 'Polyandry in Ceylon', in C.O. Furer-Haimendorf, (ed.) *Caste and Kin in Nepal, India and Ceylon*, Asia Publishing House, London.

Tambiah, S.J. & N.K. Sakar
1957 *The Disintegrating Village*, Ceylon University Press, Colombo.

Tiews, K. & K. Minnemann
1963 *Report on the Fishery of Ceylon and the Possibility of Development under Special Consideration of Fishing Ports in Galle and Trincomalee*, Sessional Paper No.20 of 1963, Government Press, Ceylon.

Tilakaratna, W.M.
1963 *Agricultural Credit in a Developing Economy-Ceylon*, Central Bank of Ceylon, Colombo.

Turner, L.
1923 *Census of Ceylon, 1921*. Government Printer, Colombo.
1931 *Census of Ceylon, 1931*. Government Press, Colombo.

Turvey, R. & W. Wiseman, (eds)
1957 *The Economics of Fisheries*, FAO, Rome.

Weingrod, A.
1968 'Patrons, Patronage and Political Parties', *Comparative Studies in Society and History*, 10:377-400.

Wharton, C.R.
1969 *Subsistence Agriculture and Economic Development*, Aldine, Chicago.

Whitehead, A.N.
1948 *Science and the Modern World.* Menton, New York.

Wijesekera, N.D.
1949 *The People of Ceylon*, Daily News Press, Colombo.

Wijeyewardene, G.
1966 'A Note on Ecology and Social Structure', *Man*, 1:95-102.

Wikkramatilike, R.
1963 *South East Ceylon: Trends and Problems in Agricultural Settlement*, The University of Chicago, Illinois.

William, G.S.
1873 *Census of Ceylon, 1871*, Registrar General's Office, Colombo.

Worsley, P.M. (ed.)
1971 *Two Blades of Grass*, Manchester University Press, Manchester.

Wright, W.D. et al
1868 *Report of the Commissioners Appointed to Inquire into the Sea Fisheries of Ceylon*, Sessional Paper No.4 of 1868, Government Press, Ceylon.

Yalman, N.
1960 'The Flexibility of Caste Principles in a Kandyan Community', in E.R. Leach (ed.) *Aspects of Caste in South Ceylon and N.W. Pakistan*, Cambridge University Press, London.
1962 'The Structure of the Sinhalese Kindred', *American Anthropologist*, 64:548-75.
1967 *Under the Bo Tree*, University of California Press, Berkeley.

Zoeteweij, H.
1957 'Fishermen's Remuneration', in R. Turvey and W. Wiseman (eds), *The Economics of Fisheries*, FAO, Rome, 18-41.

MAIN INDEX

INDEX OF SINHALESE WORDS

INDEX OF PERSONS